U0508086

西华师范大学学术著作出版资助

文学与艺术

文学研读
（英汉对照）

［美］阿尔洛·贝茨　著

杜　平　译

吉林大学出版社

·长春·

图书在版编目（CIP）数据

文学研读：英汉对照 ／（美）阿尔洛·贝茨著；杜平译 . —长春：吉林大学出版社，2022.7
ISBN 978 - 7 - 5768 - 0167 - 5

Ⅰ.①文… Ⅱ.①阿… ②杜… Ⅲ.①英语—汉语—对照读物②文学研究 Ⅳ.①H319.4：I

中国版本图书馆 CIP 数据核字（2022）第 146805 号

书　　名　文学研读：英汉对照
　　　　　WENXUE YANDU：YINGHAN DUIZHAO
作　　者　[美] 阿尔洛·贝茨　著　杜平　译
策划编辑　李潇潇
责任编辑　闫竞文
责任校对　邹燕妮
装帧设计　中联华文
出版发行　吉林大学出版社
社　　址　长春市人民大街 4059 号
邮政编码　130021
发行电话　0431-89580028/29/21
网　　址　http：//www.jlup.com.cn
电子邮箱　jdcbs@ jlu.edu.cn
印　　刷　三河市华东印刷有限公司
开　　本　710mm×1000mm　1/16
印　　张　20
字　　数　350 千字
版　　次　2023 年 1 月第 1 版
印　　次　2023 年 1 月第 1 次
书　　号　ISBN 978 - 7 - 5768 - 0167 - 5
定　　价　95.00 元

版权所有　　翻印必究

目 录
CONTENTS

I
WHAT LITERATURE IS

Just as the birth of new life begins with a fertilized egg, all discussions must proceed from a definition. Indeed, it is generally necessary to follow definition by definition, fixing the meaning of the terms used in the original explanation, and again explaining the words employed in this exposition.

I once heard a learned but somewhat pedantic man begin to answer the question of a child by saying that a lynx is a wild quadruped. He was allowed to get no further, but was at once asked what a quadruped is. He responded that it is a mammal with four feet. This of course provoked the inquiry about what a mammal is; and so on from one question to another, until the original subject was entirely lost sight of, and the lynx disappeared in a maze of verbal distinctions as completely as it might have vanished in the tangles of the forest primeval. I feel that I am not wholly safe from danger of repeating the experience of this well-meaning pedant if I attempt to give a definition of literature. The temptation is strong to content myself with saying, "Of course we all know what literature is." The difficulty which I have had in the endeavor to frame a satisfactory explanation of the term has convinced me, however, that it is necessary to assume that few of us do know, and has impressed upon me the need of trying to make clear what the word means to me. If my statement seems insufficient for general application, it will at least show the sense which I shall give to "literature" in these talks.

In its most extended signification literature of course might be taken to include whatever is written or printed; but our concern is with that portion only which is indicated by the name "polite literature," or by the imported term "belles-lettres," —both antiquated though respectable phrases. In

1

other words, I wish to confine my examination to those written works which can properly be brought within the scope of literature as one of the fine arts.

第一讲 什么是文学

正如新生命的孕育始于受精卵，所有的讨论都必须从一个定义开始。实际上，通常有必要逐个界定，确定最初释义中使用术语的含义，并再次解释在本论述里使用该词语的意义。

我曾经听到一个博学但有点迂腐的人在回答一个孩子的问题。他说猞猁是一种野生的四足动物。然后，他不再进一步解释，但小孩立即问道，四足动物是什么？他又回答说，它是一种四只脚的哺乳动物。这样的回答当然引发了对哺乳动物是什么的探究。以此类推，直到最初的主题完全消失了，猞猁也消失在语言特质的迷宫中了，正如它会完全消失在枝蔓缠绕的原始森林中一样。如果我尝试给文学下一个定义，我觉得我也无法完全避免重蹈这个好心的"书呆子"经历过的风险。但我也受到了一种很强烈的诱惑，那就是自鸣得意地说，"我们当然都知道文学是什么"。然而，在努力对该术语做出令人满意的解释时遇到的困难使我确信，有必要假设我们中很少有人知道文学是什么，并使我意识到有必要弄清楚这个词对我来说意味着什么。如果我的陈述对于一般应用来说似乎不够，但它至少表明我在谈话中将赋予"文学"的意义。

就其最广泛的意义而言，文学当然可以包括任何书写或印刷的物品，但我们只关心用"雅文学"这个名称，或用一个外来词"美文学"（belles-lettres）表示的那部分文学——尽管这两个词都有些过时了，但仍值得推崇。换句话说，我希望将我的考察限制在那些书面作品上，因为它们可以作为艺术品之一恰如其分地纳入文学范畴。

Undoubtedly, we all have a general idea of the limitations which are implied by these various terms, and we are not without a more or less vague notion of what is indicated by the word literature in its most restricted and highest sense. The important point is whether our idea is clear and well realized. We have no difficulty in saying that one book belongs to art and that another does not; but we often find ourselves perplexed when it comes to telling why. We should all agree that "*The Scarlet Letter*" is literature and that the latest sensational novel is not, —but are we sure what makes the difference? We know that Shakespeare wrote poetry and Tupper doggerel, but it by no means follows that we can always distinguish doggerel from poetry; and while it is not perhaps of consequence whether we are able to inform others why we respect the work of one or another, it is of much importance that we be in a position to justify our tastes to ourselves. It is not hard to discover whether we enjoy a book, and it is generally possible to tell why we like it; but this is not the whole of the matter. It is necessary that we be able to estimate the justice of our preferences. We must remember that our liking or disliking is not only a test of the book, —but is a test of us as well. There is no more accurate gauge of the moral character of a man than the nature of the books which he really cares for. He who would progress by the aid of literature must have reliable standards by which to judge his literary feelings and opinions; he must be able to say, "My antipathy to such a work is justified by this or by that principle; my pleasure in that other is fine because for these reasons the book itself is noble."

It is hardly possible to arrive at any clear understanding of what is meant by literature as an art, without some conception of what constitutes art in general. Broadly speaking, art exists as a consequence of the universal human desire for sympathy. Man is forever endeavoring to break down the wall which separates him from his fellows. Whether we call it egotism or simply humanity, we all know the wish to make others appreciate our feelings; to show them how we suffer, how we enjoy ourselves. We batter our fellow-men with our opinions sufficiently often, but this is as nothing to the insistence with which we pour out to them our feelings. A friend is the most valued of earthly possessions largely because he is willing to receive without appearance of impatience the unending story of our mental sensations. We are all of us more or less conscious of the constant impulse which urges us on to expression; of the inner necessity which moves us to continual endeavors to make others share our thoughts, our experiences, but most of all our emotions. It seems to me that if we trace this instinctive desire back far enough, we reach the beginnings of art.

　　毫无疑问，我们都对这些不同术语所隐含的局限性有一个大致的了解，对文学一词在其最严格和最崇高的意义上所表示的内容，或多或少有几分模糊的认识。重点在于我们的想法是否清晰，是否能很好地得以实现。我们可以毫不费力地说，一本书属于艺术而另一本书不属于艺术，然而谈及原因时，常常发现自己非常困惑。我们应该都同意《红字》是文学，而最新的哗众取宠的小说就不是文学，但我们这样确定有什么不同吗？我们知道莎士比亚是写诗的，塔珀是写顺口溜的，但绝不是说我们总能把顺口溜和诗区分开来。尽管能否告知他人我们为什么尊重一个人或另一个人的作品也许并不重要，但站在自己的立场上证明自己的品位却非常重要。发现我们是否喜欢一本书并不困难，且一般情况下还能说出喜欢它的原因，但这并不是事情的全部。我们必须能够评价我们偏爱一本书的正当理由。我们必须记住，我们喜欢或不喜欢一本书不仅是对这本书的检验，也是对我们自己的检验。一个人真正关心的书籍的本质最能准确地衡量一个人的道德品质。靠文学进步的人，必须有可靠的标准来判断自己的文学感受和见解。他必须能够说："我反感这样一部作品是由这个或那个原则证明的；我满意另一部作品是因为它很优秀，因为由于这些原因，这本书本身是高贵的。"

　　如果不了解一般艺术构成的概念，就很难明白无误地理解文学作为艺术的含义。从广义上讲，艺术的存在是人类普遍渴望同情的结果。人类永远都在致力于推倒将他与他的同类隔开的那堵围墙。无论我们称之为自我主义还是单纯的人性，我们都有一种愿望：让别人理解我们的感受，向他们展示我们如何历尽苦难，如何深怀喜悦。我们常常坚持己见而抨击我们的同胞，但这与持续不断倾注我们的情感相比毫无意义。朋友是世人拥有的最大一笔财富，大部分是因为，他愿意接受我们精神感受的无休止的故事，并且不会表露出不耐烦。我们每个人或多或少地意识到了促使我们表达的持续冲动，内在的必要性促使我们不断努力让他人分享我们的想法和经历，但最重要的是分享我们的情感。在我看来，如果将这种本能的欲望追溯到足够远的地方，我们就会来到艺术的原点。

It may seem that the splendidly immeasurable achievements of poetry and painting, of architecture, of music and sculpture, are far enough from this primal impulse; but I believe that it is to be found their germ. Art began with the first embodiment of human feelings by permanent means. Let us suppose, by way of illustration, some prehistoric man, thrilled with awe and terror at the sight of a mastodon, and scratching upon a bone rude line in the shape of the animal, —not only to give information, not only to show what the beast was like, but also to convey to his fellows his feelings when confronted with the monster. It is as if he said, "See! I cannot put into words what I felt; but look! the creature was like this. Think how you would feel if you came face to face with it. Then you will know how I felt." Something of this sort may the beginnings of art be conceived to have been.

I do not mean, of course, that the prehistoric man who made such a picture—and such a picture exists—analyzed his motives. He felt a thing which he could not say in words; he instinctively turned to pictorial representation, —and graphic art was born.

The birth of poetry was probably not entirely dissimilar. Barbaric men, exulting in the wild delight of victory, may seem unlikely sponsors for the infant muse, and yet it is with them that song began. The savage joy of the conquerors, too great for word, found vent at first in excitement, bounding leaps and uncouthly ferocious gestures, by repetition growing into rhythm; then broke into inarticulate sounds which timed the movements, until these in turn gave place to words, gradually moulded into rude verse by the measures of the dance. The need of expressing the feelings which swell inwardly, the desire of sharing with others, of putting into tangible form, the emotions that thrill the soul is common to all human beings; and it is from this that arises the thing which we call art.

The essence of art, then, is the expression of emotion; and it follows that any book to be a work of art must embody sincere emotion. Not all works which spring from genuine feeling succeed in embodying or conveying it. The writer must be sufficiently master of technique to be able to make words impart what he would express. The emotion phrased must moreover be general and in some degree typical. Man is interested and concerned in the emotions of men only in so far as these throw light on the nature and possibilities of life. Art must therefore deal with what is typical in the sense that it touches the possibilities of all human nature. If it concerns itself with much that only the few can or may experience objectively, it has to do with that only which all human beings may be conceived of as sharing subjectively. Literature may be broadly defined as the adequate expression of genuine and typical emotion. The definition may seem clumsy, and hardly exact enough to be allowed in theoretical asthetics; but it seems to me sufficiently accurate to serve our present purpose. Certainly, the essentials of literature are the adequate embodiment of sincere and general feeling.

诗歌、绘画、建筑、音乐及雕塑创造出的辉煌成就不可估量，似乎与这种原始冲动相去甚远。但我相信从中可以找到艺术的胚芽。艺术始于通过永恒的方法体现人类情感。举例为证，我们假设某个史前时期的人看到一个庞然大物时感到惊恐万分，然后在动物形状的骨头上画上一道道粗线条——不仅是为了提供信息，不仅是为了说明野兽长得像什么样子，也是为了向同伴传达他在面对怪物时的感受。就好像他在说："看啊！我无法用语言表达我的感受，但是看看！这个动物是这样的。想想如果你与它面对面时，你会有什么感受。然后你就会知道我的感受了。"艺术的开端可能就是这样的。

当然，我的意思并不是说史前时期的人绘制了这样一幅画——存在这样一幅画——而且分析了他的动机。他感觉到了一种他无法用语言表达的东西，本能地转向了用绘画来表现，于是绘画艺术应运而生。

诗歌的诞生可能并无多大差异。野蛮人在胜利的狂喜中欢欣鼓舞，他们似乎不太可能是早期诗歌灵感的激发者，但诗歌正是从他们那里孕育而生。征服者狂暴的欢乐过于猛烈，以至无法用言语表达，一开始他们只能在兴奋地跳跃、粗鲁而疯狂的手势以及重复且逐渐发展而来的节奏中寻找宣泄，进而迸发出能使动作合拍的含糊不清的声音，直到这些声音又被文字取代，最终逐渐被舞蹈的节奏塑造成粗糙的诗句。需要表达内心澎湃的感觉，与他人分享愿望，将激动人心的情感转化为具体的形式，这一切愿望为人类所共有，也正是由此产生了我们称之为艺术的东西。

因此，艺术的本质是情感的表达，由此可知，任何一本书要成为艺术品，都必须体现真实的情感。并非所有来自真实情感的作品都能成功地体现或传达真实情感。作家必须充分掌握一定技巧才能使文字传达出他要表达的内容。进一步而言，用言辞抒发情感必须是普遍的，并且在某种程度上是典型的。只有在这些情感能够揭示生命的本质和可能性的范围内，人类才会对情感产生兴趣并给予关注。因此，艺术必须针对典型的事物，因为它触及所有人性的可能性。如果艺术关注的仅仅是少数人能够或可能客观体验的很多东西，那么它只是与所有人都可以被认为是主观分享的东西有关。从广泛意义上讲，文学可以定义为真实和独特情感的充分表达。这个定义似乎很笨拙且不太准确，难以得到美学理论的认可，但在我看来，它足以满足我们当前的意图。当然，文学的本质是充分体现真实和普遍的感情。

By sincerity here we mean that which is not conventional, which is not theoretical, not artificial; that which springs from a desire honestly to impart to others exactly the emotion that has been actually felt. By the term "emotion" or "feeling" we mean those inner sensations of pleasure, excitement, pain, or passion, which are distinguished from the merely intellectual processes of the mind, —from thought, perception, and reason.

It is not necessary to trespass just now on the domain of the psychologist by an endeavor to establish scientific distinctions. We are all able to appreciate the difference between what we think and what we feel, between those things which touch the intellect and those which affect the emotional nature. We see a sentence written on paper, and are intellectually aware of it; but unless it has for us some special message, unless it concerns us personally, we are not moved by it. Most impressions which we receive touch our understanding without arousing our feelings. This is all so evident that there is not likely to arise in your minds any confusion in regard to the meaning of the phrase "genuine emotion."

Whatever be the origin of this emotion it must be essentially impersonal, and it is generally so in form. There are comparatively few works of art which are confessedly the record of simple, direct, personal experience; and perhaps none of these stand in the front rank of literature. Of course, I am not speaking of literature which takes a personal form, like any book written in the first person; but of those that are avowedly a record of actual life. We must certainly include in literature works like the "*Meditations*" of Marcus Aurelius, the "*Les Confessions*" of Augustine, and—though the cry is far—Rousseau, and the "*Journal Intime of Henri-Frdric Amiel*" of Amiel, but there is no one of these which is to be ranked high in the scale of the world's greatest books. Even in poetry the same thing is true. However, we may admire "*In Memoriam*" and that much greater poem, Mrs. Browning's "*Sonnets from the Portuguese*," we are little likely to regard them as standing supremely high among the masterpieces. The "*Sonnets*" of Shakespeare which we suppose to be personal are yet with supreme art made so impersonal that as far as the reader is concerned the experiences which they record might be entirely imaginary. It is in proportion as a poet is able to give this quality which might be called generalization to his work that it becomes art.

这里所说的真实是指非传统的、非理论的、非人为的真实，它源自将实际感受到的情感准确地传达给他人的真诚愿望。借助术语"情感"或"感觉"，我们是指那些内在的愉悦、兴奋、痛苦或充满激情的感受，它们不同于大脑的单纯精神过程——与思想、知觉和理性不同。没有必要为了确立科学的区别而刻意僭越心理学家的领域。我们都能够体会到所想和所感之间的差异，那些触及精神的事物与那些影响情感本质的事物之间的差异。我们看到写在纸上的一个句子，并在理智上意识到它，但除非它对我们有什么特别的寓意，或除非它与我们个人有关，否则它很难打动我们的心。我们获得的大多数印象能够影响我们的理解，但不一定会唤起我们的情感。这一切都如此明确，以至你的内心对"真实的情感"一词的含义不会产生任何混淆。

无论这种情感的起源是什么，它本质上都必须是非个人的，而且在形式上通常也应如此。只有相对较少的艺术作品自称是对个人经验简单明了的叙述，也许这样的作品还没一部位于文学的前列。当然，我不是在谈论采用个人形式的文学，如任何以第一人称叙事角度写成的书，我谈的是那些公然宣称记录现实生活的作品。当然，我们必须将马可·奥勒留的《沉思录》、奥古斯丁的《忏悔录》，以及尽管相差悬殊的卢梭的《忏悔录》和阿米尔的《亨利·弗雷德里克·阿米尔的私人日记》包括在文学作品中，尽管这些作品中尚无一部能位列最伟大书籍的前茅。即使在诗歌中也是如此。然而，我们可能会欣赏《悼念》和那些更伟大的诗——勃朗宁夫人的《葡萄牙十四行诗》，但我们仍不太可能把它们置于名著的前茅。莎士比亚的《十四行诗》，我们认为是个人的，但它以至高无上的非个人化的艺术造就而成，在读者看来，诗歌记载的经历可能完全是想象性的，因为诗人能够恰如其分地将这种可以称为普遍化的品质赋予作品使之成为艺术。

The reason for this is not far to seek. If the emotion is professedly personal it appeals less strongly to mankind, and it is moreover likely to interfere with its own effective embodiment. All emotion in literature must be purely imaginative as far as its expression in words is concerned. Of course, poetical form may be so thoroughly mastered as to become almost instinctive, but nevertheless acute personal feeling must trammel utterance. It is not that the author does not live through what he sets forth. It is that the artistic moment is not the moment of experience, but that of imaginative remembrance. The "*Sonnets from the Portuguese*" afford admirable examples of what I mean. It is well known that these relate a most completely personal and individual story. Not only the sentiments but the circumstances set forth were those of the poet's intimate actual life. It was the passion of love and of self-renunciation in her own heart which broke forth in the fine sonnet：—

> Go from me. Yet I feel that I shall stand
> Henceforward in thy shadow. Nevermore
> Alone upon the threshold of the door
> Of individual life, I shall command
> The uses of my soul, or lift my hand
> Serenely in the sunshine as before
> Without the sense of that which I forbore, —
> Thy touch upon the palm. The widest land
> Doom takes to part us, leaves thy heart in mine
> With pulses that beat double. What I do
> And what I dream include thee, as the wine
> Must taste of its own grapes. And when I sue
> God for myself, he hears that name of thine,
> And sees within my eyes the tears of two.

　　究其原因，并非遥不可及。如果自称这种情感是个人的，它对人类的吸引力就会减弱，而且很可能会干扰其自身的表达效果。文学中的一切情感，就其文字表达而言，都必须是纯想象的。当然，有些诗的形式可能已是炉火纯青，几乎达到浑然天成的程度，但敏锐的个人情感必定束缚诗歌的言说方式。这并不是因为作者没有经历过他所描述的情感，而是因为艺术的时刻不是体验的时刻，反而是想象的回忆时刻。《葡萄牙十四行诗》为我说的这层意思提供了一个绝佳的例证。众所周知，这些诗讲述了一个完全个性化的、独特的故事，表达的不仅是情感，也包括诗人私密的现实生活。在优美的十四行诗中爆发出的是她内心深处的爱和自我克制的激情：

舍下我，走吧。可是我觉得，从此
我就一直徘徊在你的身影里。
在那孤独的生命的边缘，从今再不能
掌握自己的心灵，或是坦然地
把这手伸向日光，像从前那样，
而能约束自己不感到你的指尖
碰上我的掌心。劫运天悬地殊
隔离了我们，却留下了你那颗心，
在我的心房里搏动着双重声响。
正像是酒，总尝得出原来的葡萄，
我的起居和梦寐里，都有你的份。
当我向上帝祈祷，为着我自个儿
他却听到了一个名字、那是你的，
又在我眼里，看见有两个人的眼泪。

（方平　译）

There came to Mrs. Browning a poignant moment when she realized with a thrill of anguish what it would mean to her to live out her life alone, separated forever from the lover who had won her back from the very grasp of death. It was not in the pang of that throe that she made of it a sonnet; but afterward, while it was still felt, it is true, but felt rather as a memory vividly reproduced by the imagination. In so far both he who writes impersonally and he who writes personally are dealing with that which at the instant exists in the imagination. In the latter, however, there is still the remembrance of the actuality, the vibration of the joy or sorrow of which that imagining is born. Human self-consciousness intrudes itself whenever one is avowedly writing of self; sometimes even vanity plays an important part. From these and other causes it results that, whatever may be the exceptions, the highest work is that which phrases the general and the impersonal with no direct reference to self. Personal feelings lie behind all art, and no work can be great which does not rest on a basis of experience, more or less remotely;

yet the greatest artist is he who embodies emotion, not in terms of his own life, but in those which make it equally the property of all mankind. It is feeling no longer egotistic, but broadly human. If the simile does not seem too homely, we might say that the difference is that between arithmetic and algebra. In the one case it is the working out of a particular problem; in the other of an equation which is universal.

Mankind tests art by universal experience. If an author has really felt what he has written, if what he sets down has been actual to him in imagination, whether actual in experience or not, readers recognize this, and receive his work, so that it lives. If he has affected a feeling, if he has shammed emotion, the whole is sure to ring false, and the world soon tires of his writings. Immediate popular judgment of a book is pretty generally wrong; ultimate general estimate is invariably correct. Humanity knows the truth of human feeling; and while it may be fooled for a time, it comes to the truth at last, in act if not in theory. The general public is guided by the wise few, and it does not reason out the difference between the genuine and the imitation; but it will in the end save the real, while the sham is forgotten through utter neglect.

　　勃朗宁夫人经历了一个令人痛苦的时刻，与曾经把她从死亡怀抱中夺回来的爱人永久分离，她痛苦地意识到独自生活对她来说意味着什么。诗人并不是在剧痛中把这一刻写成了十四行诗，而是在后来，仍然能真切地感受到这种痛苦时，诗人通过想象生动地再现了那段记忆。到目前为止，无论是非个人写作还是个人写作，作者都是在处理当下存在于想象中的东西。然而，在后者中，现实的回忆依旧存在，无论是快乐或悲伤的共鸣都是想象产生的源头。每当有人公开宣称书写自我时，人类的自我意识就会侵扰自己，有时甚至虚荣也起着重要的作用。由于这些和那些原因产生的结果表明，无一例外，最崇高的作品都是用言语表达一般性和非个人化的东西，而不是直接涉及自我。所有艺术的背后都隐藏着个人情感，任何作品均或多或少以比较遥远的经验为基础。但最伟大的艺术家不是根据他个人的生活来表现情感，而是使情感平等地成为全人类共同的财富。情感不再是自负的感觉，而是广义上的人性。如果这个比喻看起来不太亲切，我们不妨说，这种区别就如同算术和代数的区别一样。在一种情况下，它可能解决特定问题，而在另一个情形下，这一方程式针对的是普遍问题。

  人类往往通过普遍经验来检验艺术的真伪。如果一个作家真的感受到了他所写的东西，如果他所写的东西在想象中对他来说是真实的，无论他所经历的真实与否，读者都会认同这一点，并接受他的作品，因此它就具有了生命力。如果他假定了一种感情，如果他欺骗了情感，那么这一切肯定是虚假的，世人也很快会对他的作品感到厌倦。直接采用流行的观点去判断一本书一般都是不正确的，最终的普遍评价总是正确的。人类会知道情感的真相，如果不是理论上，而是在行动中，虽然人们可能会被欺骗一段时间，但最终还是会真相大白。一般公众为极少数有见识的人所操纵，无法推断出真假，但公众最终会挽救真相，虚假的东西终因完全忽视而被遗忘。

Even where an author has seemingly persuaded himself that his pretended emotions are real, he cannot permanently deceive the world. You may remember the chapter in Thomas Bailey Aldrich's delightful "*The Story of a Bad Boy*" which relates how Tom Bailey, being crossed in love at the mature age of fourteen, deliberately became a "blighted being;" how he neglected his hair, avoided his playmates, made a point of having a poor appetite, and went mooning about forsaken graveyards, endeavoring to fix his thoughts upon death and self-destruction; how entirely the whole matter was a humbug, and yet how sincere the boy was in supposing himself to be unutter-ably melancholy. "It was a great comfort," he says, "to be so perfectly miserable and yet not to suffer any. I used to look in the glass and gloat over the amount and variety of mournful expressions I could throw into my features. If I caught myself smiling at anything, I cut the smile short with a sigh. The oddest thing about all this is, I never once suspected that I was not unhappy. No one ... was more deceived than I." We have all of us had experiences of this kind, and I fancy that there are few writers who cannot look back to a stage in their career when they thought that it was a prime essential of authorship to believe themselves to feel things which they did not feel in the least. This sort of self-deception is characteristic of a whole school of writers, of whom Byron was in his day a typical example. There is no doubt that Byron, greatly gifted as he was, took his mooning melancholy with monstrous seriousness when he began to write it, and the public received it with equal gravity. Yet Byron's mysterious misery, his immeasurable wickedness, his misanthropy too great for words, were mere affectations, —stage tricks which appealed to the gallery. Nobody is moved by them now. The fact that the poet himself thought that he believed in them could not save them. Byron had other and nobler qualities which made his best work endure, but it is in spite of his Bad-Boy-ish pose as a "blighted being." The fact is that sooner or later time tries all art by the tests of truth and common sense, and nothing which is not genuine is able to endure this proving.

To be literature a work must express sincere emotion; but how is feeling which is genuine to be distinguished from that which is affected? All that has been said must be regarded as simply theoretical and of very little practical interest unless there is some criterion by which this question may be settled. Manifestly we cannot so far enter into the consciousness of the writer as to tell whether he does or does not feel what he expresses; it can be only from outward signs that we judge whether his imagination has first made real to him what he undertakes to make real for others.

即使作者似乎能说服自己相信他伪装的情感是真实的，他也不可能永远欺骗世人。你可能还记得托马斯·贝里·奥尔德里奇令人愉快的《坏男孩的故事》中的那一章。该章节讲述了汤姆·贝利在十四岁成熟时，如何坠入爱河，如何刻意变成了一个"受摧残的人"，如何不在乎自己的头发，如何躲避他的玩伴，如何特意说自己胃口不好，如何在废弃的墓地里闲逛，如何一门心思去考虑死亡和自我毁灭，整件事情完全是一个骗局，然而男孩故作无比忧郁，伪装的何其真实！"这是一种极大的安慰，"他说，"如此苦不堪言，却没有遭受任何痛苦。

我曾常常对着镜子，幸灾乐祸地看着自己脸上流露出各种各样的悲伤表情。如果我发现自己对任何事情都在微笑，我会叹息着停止微笑。这一切最奇怪的是，我从来不怀疑我的快乐。没有人……比我受骗更多。"我们都有过这样类似的经历，我猜想很少有作家不去回顾他们职业生涯的某一个阶段。他们会想，创作的精髓就是说服自己相信，他们自己能感受到他们丝毫没有感受到的东西。这种自欺欺人是整个作家流派的特征。拜伦在他那个时代就是一个典型的例子。毫无疑问，拜伦尽管才华出众，在他刚开始写作时，他极其严肃的态度始终流露出难以排遣的忧郁。公众也同样以严肃的态度认可了这种忧郁。然而，拜伦带有几份神秘感的苦难、无法估量的邪恶和厌世情绪，一切强烈的表现难以言表，纯粹是装模作样——吸引观众的舞台戏法。现在没有人为此感动了。诗人自认他相信这些舞台戏法，但这一事实无法拯救它们。拜伦还有其他及更高尚的品质，使其最好的作品能够经久不衰，但这与他的"受摧残的人"的坏男孩式的伪装无关。事实是，时间迟早会用真理与常识的考验来检验所有艺术，任何不真实的东西都经不起这种考验。

　　文学作品必须表达真挚的情感，但是如何区分真实的感受和伪装的感受呢？除非有某种标准可以用于解决这个问题，否则一切所谈到的都必定被视为纯理论性的，没有什么实际意义。显然，我们目前还无法进入作者的意识，去判断他是否感受到了他所表达的东西，我们只能从外在表象来判断他的想象是否真实，可以先看他对其他人承诺的真实的东西是否变成了现实。

Something may be judged by the amount of seriousness with which a thing is written. The air of sincerity which is inevitable in the genuine is most difficult to counterfeit. What a man really feels he writes with a certain earnestness which may seem indefinite, but which is sufficiently tangible in its effects upon the reader. More than by any other single influence mankind has in all its history been more affected by the contagion of belief; and it is not easy to exaggerate the susceptibility of humanity to this force. Vague and elusive as this test of the genuineness of emotion might seem, it is in reality capable of much practical application. We have no trouble in deciding that the conventional rhymes which fill the corners of the newspapers are not the product of genuine inner stress. We are too well acquainted with these time-draggled rhymes of "love" and "dove," of "darts" and "hearts," of "woe" and "throe;" we have encountered too often these pretty, petty fancies, these twilight musings and midnight moans, this mild melancholy and maudlin sentimentality. We have only to read these trig little bunches of verse, tied up, as it were, with sad-colored ribbons, to feel their artificiality. On the other hand, it is impossible to read "*Helen of Kirconnel*," or Browning's "*Prospice*," or Wordsworth's poems to Lucy, without being sure that the poet meant that which he said in his song with all the fervor of heart and imagination. A reader need not be very critical to feel that the novels of the "*Duchess*" and her tribe are made by a process as mechanical as that of making paper flowers; he will not be able to advance far in literary judgment without coming to suspect that fiction like the pleasant pot-boilers of William Black and W. Clark Russell, if hand-made, is yet manufactured according to an arbitrary pattern; but what reader can fail to feel that to Hawthorne "*The Scarlet Letter*" was utterly true, that to Thackeray Colonel Newcome was a creature warm with human blood and alive with a vigorous humanity? Theoretically we may doubt our power to judge of the sincerity of an author, but we do not find this so impossible practically.

Critics sometimes say of a book that it is or is not "convincing." What they mean is that the author has or has not been able to make what he has written seem true to the imagination of the reader. The man who in daily life attempts to act a part is pretty sure sooner or later to betray himself to the observant eye. His real self will shape the disguise under which he has hidden it; he may hold out the hands and say the words of Esau, but the voice with which he speaks will perforce be the voice of Jacob. It is so in literature, and especially in literature which arouses the perceptions by an appeal to the imagination. The writer must be in earnest himself or he cannot convince the reader. To the man who invents a fiction, for instance, the story which he has devised must in his imagination be profoundly true or it will not be true to the audience which he addresses. To the novelist who is "convincing," his characters are as real as the men he meets in his walks or sits beside at table. It is for this reason that every novelist with imagination is likely to find that the fictitious personages of his story seem to act independently of the will of the author. They are so real that they must follow out the laws of their character, although that character exists only in imagination. For the author to feel this verity in what he writes is of course not all that is needed to enable him to convince his public; but it is certain that he is helpless without it, and that he cannot make real to others what is not real to himself.

　　可以通过书写一件事的严肃程度来判断某一件事是否真实。真实的东西中透露出的那种逼真的气氛最难伪造。一个人的真实感受是他以某一种认真的态度写就的，这种认真的态度看似不确定，但对读者的影响却切实可见。与人类历史上任何其他唯一的影响相比，信仰的蔓延对人类的影响最大；并且要夸大人类对这种力量的敏感性并不容易。尽管这种对情感真实性的检验看似模糊且难以捉摸，但现实中却可广泛应用。我们可以毫不费力地确定，充斥在报纸角落的陈旧押韵诗并不是真正的内心压力的产物。我们太熟悉这些拖延时间的韵脚了，如："爱"（love）和"鸽子"（dove）、"飞镖"（darts）和"心"（hearts）、"悲哀"（woe）和"痛苦"（throe）。我们经常遇到这些漂亮的、琐碎的幻想之物，如黄昏的沉思和午夜的呻吟、温和的忧郁和淡淡的伤感。我们只需阅读这些古板的、仿佛用悲伤彩色丝带连接起来的小诗串，就能感受到它们的矫揉造作。另一方面，如果阅读《基尔康奈尔的海伦》、勃朗宁的《期待》或华兹华斯的露西组诗，一定会感受到诗人饱含热诚之心，富有想象地表达了真实感受。如读者不是太过挑剔，就会觉得《公爵夫人》和她的部落的小说是通过像制作纸花一样机械的过程创作而成的；如果阅读威廉·布莱克和 W. 克拉克·罗素搞笑的粗制滥造的小说时，一个读者不怀疑它们是按照样板随意编造出来的，那么他的文学判断力不可能取得长足的进步。但是，什么样的读者才会不认为霍桑的《红字》是完全真实的呢？什么样的读者才不会觉得萨克雷笔下的纽康姆上校是一个血气方刚、充满活力的人呢？从理论上讲，我们可能会怀疑我们判断作者真实性的能力，但实际上，我们认为这是不可能的。

评论家有时会谈论一本书是否"令人信服"。他们的意思是，作者是否能使他书写内容在读者的想象中看起来是真实的。在日常生活中试图装腔作势的人迟早会在敏锐的眼光中暴露自己。他真实的自我将塑造一个伪装隐藏起来。他可以伸出手说以扫的话，但他说话的声音必定是雅各的声音。在文学中，尤其是通过诉诸想象力来唤起感知的文学中更是如此。作者必须自己真诚严肃，否则他无法说服读者。例如，对于虚构小说的人来说，他所构思的故事在他的想象中必须是非常真实的，否则对于他所面对的观众来说就不会是真实的。对于"令人信服的小说家"，他塑造的人物角色就像他在散步时遇到或坐在桌子旁边的人一样真实。正因如此，每一个有想象力的小说家都会发现，他在故事中虚构的人物似乎独立于作者意愿而行动。尽管这种性格只存在于想象中，但人物非常真实，完全按照他们的性格规律塑造而成。对于作者来说，感受到这种真实性并不代表他能够使公众心悦诚服相信所需要的全部内容，但可以肯定的是，离开它，作家将陷于无助，他无法使自己都认为是不真实的东西却让别人相信是真实的。

In emotion we express the difference between the genuine and the counterfeit by the words "sentiment" and "sentimentality." Sentiment is what a man really feels; sentimentality is what he persuades himself that he feels. The Bad Boy as a "blighted being" is the type of sentimentalists for all time. There is about the same relationship between sentimentality and sentiment that there is between a paper doll and the lovely girl that it represents. There are fashions in emotions as there are fashions in bonnets; and foolish mortals are as prone to follow one as another. It is no more difficult for persons of a certain quality of mind to persuade themselves that they thrill with what they conceive to be the proper emotion than it is for a woman to convince herself of the special fitness to her face of the latest device in utterly unbecoming headgear. Our grandmothers felt that proper maidenly sensibility required them to be so deeply moved by tales of broken hearts and unrequited affection that they must escape from the too poignant anguish by fainting into the arms of the nearest man. Their grandchildren today are neither more nor less sincere, neither more nor less sensible in following to extremes other emotional modes which it might be invidious to specify. Sentimentality will not cease while the power of self-deception remains to human beings.

With sentimentality genuine literature has no more to do than it has with other human weaknesses and vices, which it may picture but must not share. With sentiment it is concerned in every line. Of sentiment no composition can have too much; of sentimentality it has more than enough if there be but the trace shown in a single affectation of phrase, in one unmeaning syllable or unnecessary accent.

　　在情感上，我们用"情感"和"多愁善感"这两个词来表达真假的区别。情感是一个人真实的感受，多愁善感是指说服自己相信他感觉到的东西。那个坏男孩作为一个"受摧残的人"一直是一个多愁善感的人。多愁善感和情感之间的关系，就像纸做的玩偶和它所代表的可爱小女孩之间的关系一样。情感有时尚，就像软帽也有时尚一样，愚蠢的人很容易向其他人一样去追逐时尚。具有某种精神品质的人要说服自己相信他们自己认为是正确的情感，并因此而感到兴奋并不是一件容易的事情，其困难程度不亚于女人要说服自己相信，戴上根本不适合的头饰特别符合她最新设计的脸型。我们的祖母认为，少女要适度善感，对伤心的和单相思的故事不能无动于衷，她们要昏倒在离自己身边最近的男人怀里，这样才能从极度悲伤中解脱出来。今天，他们的孙儿们真诚不足，也缺乏理性，追求的极端情感模式令人反感，难以细说。对人类而言，当自欺欺人的权力仍然存在时，多愁善感就不会消失。

　　与多愁善感相比，真正的文学与人类的弱点和其他恶习并无多大关系，它可以描绘但绝不能分享。情感却与每一行诗句每一行台词有关。感情的成分再多也不为过，但对多愁善感来说，只要在一个短语中，在一个毫无意义的音节或不必要的重音中，表现出一丝矫揉造作的痕迹就成了冗词赘句。

There are other tests of the genuineness of the emotion expressed in literature which are more tangible than those just given; and being more tangible they are more easily applied. I have said that sham sentiment is sure to ring false. This is largely due to the fact that it is inevitably inconsistent. Just as a man has no difficulty in acting out his own character, whereas in any part that is assumed there are sure sooner or later to be lapses and incongruities, so genuine emotion will be consistent because it is real, while that which is feigned will almost surely jar upon itself. The fictitious personage that the novelist actually shapes in his imagination, that is more real to him than if it stood by his side in solid flesh, must be consistent with itself because it is in the mind of its creator a living entity. It may not to the reader seem winning or even human, but it will be a unit in its conception and its expression, a complete and consistent whole. The poem which comes molten from the furnace of the imagination will be a single thing, not a collection of verses more or less ingeniously dovetailed together. The work which has been felt as a whole, which has been grasped as a whole, which has as a whole been lived by that inner self which is the only true producer of art, will be so consistent, so unified, so closely knit, that the reader cannot conceive of it as being built up of fortuitous parts, or as existing at all except in the beautiful completeness which genius has given it.

What I mean may perhaps be more clear to you if you take any of the little tinkling rhymes which abound, and examine them critically. Even some of more merits easily afford examples. Take that pleasant rhyme so popular in the youth of our fathers, "*The Old Oaken Bucket*," and see how one stanza or another might be lost without being missed, how one thought or another has obviously been put in for the rhyme or to fill out the verse, and how the author seems throughout always to have been obliged to consider what he might say next, putting his work together as a joiner matches boards for a table-top. Contrast this with the absolute unity of Wordsworth's *Daffodils*, Keats' *Ode on a Grecian Urn*, Shelley's *Stanzas Written in Dejection*, or any really great lyric. You will perceive the difference better than anyone can say it. It is true that the quality of which we are speaking is sufficiently subtle to make examples unsatisfactory and perhaps even dangerous; but it seems to me that it is not too much to say that any careful and intelligent reader will find little difficulty in feeling the unity of the masterpieces of literature.

　　对于文学中情感表达的真实性，除刚才提到的方法，还有一些更切实、更具体且更易应用的检验方法。我说过，虚假的情感听起来肯定就是假的，这是因为它不可避免地会表现出前后不一致。正如要把自己的性格表现出来并不困难一样，但在他承担的任何角色里，迟早都会有失误和不协调，所以真正的情感将是一致的，因为它是真实的，而伪装的情感肯定会彼此不协调。虚构人物实际上是小说家在想象中塑造出来的，对作者来说这个人物比活生生的人站在他身边更真实，因此它必须与自身保持一致，因为它在创作者的脑海中是一个有生命的实体。对读者来说，虚构的人物可能看起来不那么迷人，甚至没有人情味，但它在其构思和表达中将是一个整体，一个完整而协调的个体。从想象的熔炉中打造出来的诗歌将是一个唯一的东西，而不是勉强巧妙地吻合在一起的一部诗歌集。如果能够从整体去感知和把握一部作品，甚至由唯一真正艺术创造者的内在自我去表现这部作品，那么这部作品应该是完整一致的，也是统一及紧密联系的，以至读者无法设想它是由各个偶然的部分组合而成，或者只能认为这部作品完全是以天才创造的十全十美之物而存在的。

　　如果你选择比比皆是的、任何悦耳的韵文，并以批判性的眼光去审视它们，对你而言，我的意思可能就会更清晰了。这里甚至可以拿一些更有价值的小诗作为例证。就拿我们父辈青年时代流行的脍炙人口的诗歌《老橡木桶》为例，看看一节诗或另一节诗如何消失了，但不会给人被遗漏的感觉，一个或另一个意思很明显地被插入韵律中或用来填充诗句，以及从头到尾作者似乎始终都在急迫考虑他接下来可能会说什么，就像木匠把木板拼配在一起作为桌面一样。将此与华兹华斯的《水仙花》、济慈的《希腊古瓮颂》、雪莱的《那不勒斯的悲色诗节》或任何真正伟大的抒情诗的绝对统一进行对照，你可能会更清楚地感受到差异。诚然，我们提到的作品质量非常微妙，那些给出的例证并不令人满意，甚至可能有些冒险。但在我看来，毋庸赘言，任何细心而聪明的读者都不难觉察到文学杰作的统一性。

This lack of consistency is most easily appreciated, perhaps, in the drawing of character. Those modern writers who look upon literature as having two functions, first, to advance extravagant theories, and second, —and more important, —to advertise the author, are constantly putting forward personages that are so inconsistent that it is impossible not to see that they are mere embodied arguments or sensationalism incarnate, and not in the least creatures of a strong and wholesome imagination. When in "*The Doll's House*" Ibsen makes Nora Helma an inconsequent, frivolous, childish puppet, destitute alike of moral and of common sense, and then in the twinkling of an eye transforms her into an indignant woman, full of moral purpose, furnished not only with a complete set of advanced views but with an entire battery of modern arguments with which to support them, —when, in a word, the author, for the sake of his theory, works a visible miracle, we cease to believe in his imaginative sincerity. We know that he is dogmatizing, not creating; that this is artifice, not art.

Another test of the genuineness of what is expressed in literature is its truth to life. Here again we tread upon ground somewhat uncertain, since truth is as elusive as a sunbeam, and to no two human beings the same. Yet while the meaning of life is not the same to any two who walk under the heavens, there are certain broad principles which all men recognize. The eternal facts of life and of death, of love and of hate, the instinct of self-preservation, the fear of pain, the respect for courage, and the enthrallment of passion, —these are laws of humanity so universal that we assume them to be known to all mankind. We cannot believe that any mortal can find that true to his imagination which ignores these unvarying conditions of human existence. He who writes what is untrue to humanity cannot persuade us that he writes what is true to himself. We are sure that those impossible heroes of Ouida, with their superhuman accomplishments, those heroines of beauty transcendently incompatible with their corrupt hearts, base lives, and entire defiance of all sanitary laws, were no more real to their author than they are to us. Conviction springs from the imagination, and imagination is above all else the realizing faculty. It is idle to say that a writer imagines every extravagant and impossible whimsy which comes into his head. He imagines those things, and those things only, which are real to his inner being; so that in judging literature the question to be settled is: Does this thing which the author tells, this emotion which he expresses, impress us as having been to him when he wrote actual, true, and absolutely real? To unimaginative persons it might seem that I am uttering nonsense. It is not possible for a man without imagination to see how things which are invented by the mind should by that same mind, in all sanity, be received as real. Yet that is precisely what happens. No one, I believe, produces real or permanent literature who is not capable of performing this miracle; who does not feel to be true that which has no other being, no other place, no other significance save that which it derives from the creative power of his own inner sense, working upon the material furnished by his perception of the world around him. This is the daily miracle of genius; but it is a miracle shared to some extent by every mortal who has the faintest glimmer of genuine imagination.

　　也许，这种一致性的缺乏最容易体现在人物描绘中。那些把文学看成有两个功能的现代作家，一是提出了华丽的理论，二是——更重要的是——为作者自己做宣传。他们不断推出前后矛盾的人物，人们不可能看不出来那些人物不过是具体化的论点或煽情的化身，一点都算不上是强大而健全的想象力的人物。在《玩偶之家》中，易卜生刚开始把娜拉·海尔茂塑造成了一个无足轻重的、轻浮的、幼稚的玩偶和缺乏道德及常识的人物。但转眼间作者又把她变成了一个愤世嫉俗的女人，充满道德目的，不仅给她装备了一套完整的先进的观点，而且背后还有一整套现代论据来支撑她。总之，当作者为了他的理论，创造了一个看得见的奇迹时，我们便不再相信他的想象力的真实性了，我们知道他在宣扬其教条，而不是在创造，这是欺骗，而非艺术。

　　另一个检验文学表达真实性的标准是看它是否忠实于生活。在这里，我们会再次踏入一个有些不确定的地域。因为真理像阳光一样难以捉摸，对任何两个人来说没有什么不一样。然而，生活的意义对于行走在大地上的任何两个人来说不尽一致，但有一些法则却为所有人广泛认可。如生与死、爱与恨的永恒事实，自我保护的本能，对痛苦的恐惧，对勇气的尊重，以及对激情的迷恋，——这些皆为人类的法则，它们如此普遍，我们认为它们为全人类所共知。我们无法相信任何凡人都可以发现他的想象力是真实的，而忽略了人类生存的这些不变条件。如果一个人书写的东西对人类不真实，那么他无法说服我们相信他写的真实对他自己也是真实的。我们确信，韦达的那些拥有超人成就的主人公完全不可思议；那些惊艳之美的女主角与堕落的灵魂、卑鄙的生活和公然蔑视健康法律完全不相匹配。这些人物无论是对我们还是对读者而言，都不是真实的。说服力源于想象力，而想象力是最重要的实现能力。假定一个作家想象的都是浮现在脑海中夸张而不真实的异想天开是徒劳无益的。他想象那些事物，而那些事物仅对他的内在存在是真实的，所以在评判文学时要回答的问题是：作者讲述的事，他表达的情感，是否就像他在写作时曾亲眼见过那样具体、真实、绝对真实，而让我们印象深刻？对于缺乏想象力的人来说，我似乎在信口雌黄。一个没有想象力的人是不可能明白，头脑虚构的东西如何被同一个完全清醒的头脑接受为真实的。然而，这正是千真万确发生的事情。我不相信，一个无法创造这一奇迹的人能创造出真实或永恒的文学作品。我也不相信，一个认为除了源于他自己的内在感觉的创造力中获得的东西，并依靠对周围世界感知来获取素材创作的人，能够创造出真实或永恒的文学作品，因为他不认为没有其他存在、没有其他地方、没有其他意义的东西是真实的。这是天才人物司空见惯的奇迹，但在某种程度上，这也是每一个拥有哪怕一丝真实想象力的凡人共同享有的奇迹。

To be convincing literature must express emotion which is genuine; to commend itself to the best sense of mankind, and thus to take its place in the front rank, it must deal with emotion which is wholesome and normal. A work phrasing morbid emotion may be art, and it may be lasting; but it is not the highest art, and it does not approve itself to the best and sanest taste. Mankind looks to literature for the expression of genuine, strong, healthy human emotion; emotion passionate, tragic, painful, the exhilaration of joy or the frenzy of grief, as it may be; but always the emotion which under the given conditions would be felt by the healthy heart and soul, by the virile man and the womanly woman. No amount of insane power flashing here and there amid the foulness of Tolstoi's *Kreutzer Sonata* can reconcile the world to the fact that the book embodies the broodings of a mind morbid and diseased. Even to concede that the author of such a work had genius could not avail to conceal the fact that his muse was smitten from head to feet with the unspeakable corruption of leprosy. Morbid literature may produce a profound sensation, but it is incapable of creating a permanent impression.

The principles of which we are speaking are strikingly illustrated in the tales of Edgar Allan Poe. He was possessed of an imagination narrow, but keen; uncertain and wayward, but alert and swift; individual and original, though unhappily lacking any ethical stability. In his best work he is sincere and convincing, so that stories like *The Cask of Amontillado*, *The Gold Bug*, or *The Purloined Letter* are permanently effective, each in its way and degree. Poe's masterpiece, *The Fall of the House of Usher* is a study of morbid character, but it is saved by the fact that this is viewed in its effect upon a healthy nature. The reader looks at everything through the mind of the imaginary narrator, so that the ultimate effect is that of an exhibition of the feelings of a wholesome nature brought into contact with madness; although even so the ordinary reader is still repelled by the abnormal elements of the theme. There is in all the work of Poe a good deal that is fantastic and not a little that is affected. He is rarely entirely sincere and sane. He shared with Byron an instinctive fondness for the rôle of a "blighted being," and a halo of inebriety too often encircles his head; yet at his best he moves us by the mysterious and incommunicable power of genius. Many of his tales, on the other hand, are mere mechanical tasks, and as such neither convincing nor permanent. There is a great deal of Poe which is not worth anybody's reading because he did not believe it, did not imagine it as real, when he wrote it. Other stories of his illustrate the futility of self-deception on the part of the author. *Lygeia*, Poe always announced as his masterpiece. He apparently persuaded himself that he felt its turgid sentimentality, that he was thrilled at its elaborately theatrical setting, and he flattered himself that he could cheat the world as he had cheated himself. Yet the reader is not fooled. Every man of judgment realizes that, however, the author was able to deceive himself, *Lygeia* is rubbish, and sophomoric rubbish at that.

　　具有说服力的文学必须表达真实的情感。为了称颂人类最美好的情感，并因此占据领先地位，文学必须表达健康和正常的情感。一部表达病态情感的作品可以是艺术，也可能是恒久的，但它不是最崇高的艺术，因为它没有赞许最美好、最健全的品位。人类期待文学表达真实、强烈、健康的人类情感，激昂的情感、悲惨的情感、痛苦的情感、喜悦的兴奋或悲伤的狂乱，可能就是这些吧！但在特定条件下，情感应该是那些健康的心灵和灵魂、阳刚的男人和阴柔的女人永远能感受到的情感。托尔斯泰的《克罗采奏鸣曲》在残酷中到处闪露出疯狂的力量，无法使世界接受这样一个事实，即这本书体现了病态和不健康的大脑的郁郁沉思。即使承认这样一部作品的作者才华横溢，也无法掩饰他的灵感女神从头到脚都患上了麻风病。病态文学可能会产生一种深刻的感觉，但无法给人留下永久的印象。

　　我们所说的原则在埃德加·爱伦·坡的故事中得到了惊人的说明。坡的想象力狭隘且不确定和任性，但另一方面，他的想象力也表现出了敏锐、警觉、敏捷、独特且别出心裁的特点，但很不幸的是他的想象力缺乏任何道德稳定性。在他最优秀的作品中，他真诚而令人信服，因此像《阿蒙蒂拉多木桶》《金甲虫》《失窃的信件》这样的故事每一个都以独特的方式给人留下了永恒不灭的印象。坡的杰作《厄舍府的倒塌》是对病态性格的探讨，但因其描述的内容基于对健康本性的影响而得以存世。读者通过一位想象的叙述者的记忆观察一切，因此最终的效果展示了健康本性与疯癫接触后的感受，即便如此，普通读者仍然会因这一主题的变态元素感到反感。在坡的所有作品中，有很多怪诞之作，而且不乏伤感的情绪。他很少表现出全然的真诚和理智的清醒。与拜伦一样，坡本能地喜欢扮演"受摧残的人"的角色，嗜酒癖的光环一直笼罩在他的头上。然而，在他状态最佳的时期，他也能够用一种神秘和无法传达的力量令我们感动。另一方面，他的许多故事只是机械呆板的任务，既无法令人信服，也不具有永久意义。坡有大量的作品不值得任何人去阅读，因为作者在创作时，就不相信它们，没有想象它们是真实的。他的其他故事说明了作者自欺欺人的徒劳。坡一直宣称《丽姬娅》是他的杰作，显然，他是想要说服自己相信，他感受到了那种浮夸的多愁善感，他为精心设计的戏剧背景欣喜若狂，并且自以为可以像欺骗自己一样欺骗世界。然而，读者并没有被愚弄。每一个有判断力的人都意识到了，无论作者如何欺骗自己，《丽姬娅》都是垃圾，而且是肤浅无知且自命不凡的垃圾。

There has probably never before been a time which afforded so abundant illustrations of morbid work as today. And here it is enough to note that the diseased and the morbid are by definition excluded from literature in the best sense of the word. Good art is not only sincere; it is human, and wholesome, and sound.

可能以往从未像今天一样，提供如此丰富的示例说明文学中的病态作品。在此，我们足以注意到，从定义上来看，不健康的、病态的作品应被排除在最优秀文学的范围之外。好的艺术不仅是真诚的，也是人性的、健康的和健全的。

第二讲　文学表达

那么，文学必须表达的东西就这么多了，现在可以稍微考察一下文学表达方式。感受真实的情感并不代表作家所需要的全部，但在艺术家中这一点的重要性不可估量。

> 在悲伤的日里，一个天生就有诗心的人
>
> 因为与诗人的语言无法匹配；
>
> 他激昂的诗在唇边挣扎，
>
> 还是死了，唉！无人称颂。

他必须会唱这首歌，让读者分享他内心的悸动。人人都有情感，艺术家能够通过使用惯例把他的情感传达给世人。音乐家使用声音的惯例，画家使用色彩的惯例，雕塑家则使用形式的惯例，而作家必须使用最不自然的手段——语言惯例。

如果有空间，在这里可以考虑整个艺术技巧的主题，但就我们的目的而言，能够意识到检验艺术技巧精湛与否应是与追求目标适应的手段的完整性就足够了。关于艺术技艺至为关键的问题就在于，"艺术技巧是否忠实而完整地传达作为作品本质的情感？"一件艺术作品不仅须使人在智力上能够理解，而且能够使人有所感觉，它必须触及内心和大脑。如果一幅画、一尊雕像、一件音乐作品或一首诗能引发你的赞赏，却没能触动你的情感，那要么是这件作品，要么是你存在根本性的问题。

首先，文学表达必须是充分的。如果表达漫不经心、支离破碎、技不如人，这种表达就不能传递作为它目的的情感。我们都曾心潮涌动地坐下来，努力把我们的感受付诸笔端，结果却发现我们对自己及表达手段的把控远远不足，无法充分表达我们最真实的感受。的确，风格在某种意义上是次要的，但它依然是不可或缺的。如果一个人不能说的话，他必须说的话对世界来说显然没有什么意义。如果哑巴有声音的话，他唱出的歌不会不令我们激动。

但要记住，表达虽然要充分，但也必须是从属的。它是一种手段而不是目的，如果把充分表达放在首位，毫无疑义，它会破坏我们对它所包含的情感的真实感。如果发现一位女演员一边慷慨激昂的朗诵，一边在整理她的衣饰，她的表演艺术就不再具有说服力了。例如，没有人在感受到凯瑟琳王后令人心潮澎湃的话语时，会不加遮掩地关心王后整理衬裙的效果。阅读过于复杂和精细的诗句，如法国的八行诗、十行诗、十四行诗等形式，读者会本能地感觉到，一个诗人的注意力如过于集中在复杂而巧妙的诗句上，无论他如何强烈地为他的诗申辩，他也不会有任何深刻的情感体验。过于明显巧妙的表达会立即引起人们的怀疑，认为这种表达只是为了自己的缘故精心制作出来的。

Technical excellence which displays the cleverness of the artist rather than imparts the emotion which is its object, defeats its own end. A book so elaborated that we feel that the author was absorbed in perfection of expression rather than in what he had to express leaves us cold and unmoved, if it does not tire us. The messenger has usurped the attention which belonged to the message. It is not impossible that I shall offend some of you when I say that Walter Pater's "*Marius the Epicurean*" seems to me a typical example of this sort of book. The author has expended his energies in exquisite excesses of language; he has refined his style until it has become artfully inanimate. It is like one of the beautiful glass flowers in the Harvard Museum. It is not a living rose. It is no longer a message spoken to the heart of mankind; it is a brilliant exercise in technique.

Literature, then, is genuine emotion, adequately expressed. To be genuine it must come from the imagination; and adequate expression is that which in turn reaches the imagination. If it were not that the phrase seems forbiddingly cumbersome, we might, indeed, define literature as being such writings as are able to arouse emotion by an appeal to the imagination.

A sensational story, what the English call a "penny dreadful" or a

human, informed every page with genuine feeling, and produced a romance permanently vital. The plot of those superb masterpieces of adventure, the "*D'Artagnan Romances*" is as wild, perhaps as extravagant, as that of the marrow-curdling tales which make the fortunes of sensational papers; but to the excitement of adventure is added that unification, that humanization, that perfection of imaginative realism which mark Dumas as a genius.

The difference of effect between books which are not literature and those which are is that while these amuse, entertain, glance over the surface of the mind, those touch the deepest springs of being. They touch us asthetically, it is true. The emotion aroused is impersonal, and thus removed from the keen thrill which is born of actual experiences; but it depends upon the same passions, the same characteristics, the same humanity, that underlie the joys and sorrows of real life. It is because we are capable of passion and of disappointment that we are moved by the love and anguish of Romeo and Juliet, of Francesca and Paolo. Our emotion is not identical with that with which the heart throbs in personal love and grief; yet art which is genuine awakes emotion thoroughly genuine. Books of sensationalism and sentimentality may excite curiosity, or wonder, or amusement, or sham feeling; but they must have at least some spark of sacred fire before they can arouse in the intelligent reader this inner throb of real feeling.

The personal equation must be considered here. The same book must affect different readers differently. From the sentimental maid who weeps in the kitchen over "*The Seventy Sorrows of Madelaine the Broken-hearted*", to her master in his library, touched by the grief of King Lear, is indeed a far cry; and yet both may be deeply moved. It may be asked whether we have arrived at a standard which will enable us to judge between them.

The matter is perhaps to be cleared up somewhat by a little common sense. It is not hard to decide whether the kitchen-maid in question has an imagination sufficiently well developed to bring her within the legitimate grounds of inquiry; and the fiction which delights her rudimentary understanding is easily ruled out. It is not so easy, however, to dispose of this point entirely. There is always a border-land concerning which doubts and disagreements must continue to exist. In all matters connected with the feelings it is necessary to recognize the fact that the practical is not likely to accord fully with the theoretical. We define literature only to be brought face to face with the difficulty which is universal in art, the difficulty of degree. No book will answer, it may be, to a theoretical definition, no work conforms completely to required conditions. The composition which is a masterpiece stands at one end of the list, and comes so near to the ideal that there is no doubt of its place. At the other end there is the rubbish, equally unquestioned in its worthlessness. The troublesome thing is to decide where between comes the dividing line above which is literature. We call a ring or a coin gold, knowing that it contains a mixture of alloy. The goldsmith may have a standard, and refuse the name gold to any mixture into which enters a given per cent of baser metal; but in art this is impossible.

　　不同的是，斯托克顿在《豪恩船长历险记》中用巧妙的手法来娱乐读者，而在《金银岛》中，史蒂文森则把他所写的想象得淋漓尽致，使人物变得人性化，让小说每一页都渗透了真情实感，创造了一部具有永恒活力的罗曼史。冒险小说的巅峰之作《达尔大尼央浪漫三部曲》的情节狂暴，也许有些过度夸张，就像是在那些轰动一时的报纸上刊登的令人毛骨悚然的发财故事的情节一样。但除了冒险的刺激，小说还增添了统一、人性化、完美的想象现实主义这些元素，这些特征均可称得上是大仲马小说天赋的标志。

　　非文学书籍与文学书籍之间的效果差异就在于，非文学书籍旨在娱乐、消遣，浮光掠影式地掠过心灵的表面，而文学书籍则要触及存在最深处的源头。它们在审美上触动我们，它们所唤起的情感是非个人化的，因此脱离了由实际经验产生的强烈刺激，但它取决于相同的激情、相同的特征、相同的人性，这些都是构成现实生活中欢乐和悲伤的基础。正是因为我们有表达激情和失望的能力，我们才被罗密欧与朱丽叶、弗朗西斯卡和保罗的爱与痛苦所感动。我们从书中体验的情感与在个人的爱和悲伤中令人内心悸动的情感完全不一样，然而，

be considered literature; and, did space warrant, we might go on to examine the principles which determine the rank of work. They are of course largely to be inferred from what has been said already. The merit of literature will be chiefly dependent upon the closeness with which it conforms to the rules which mark the nature of literature. The more fully genuine its emotion, the more adequate its expression, the higher the scale in which a book is to be placed.

　　在这里，每个读者必须自己做出决定。位于分界线附近的作品是否被视为是文学，是一个需要单独决定的问题。每个读者都有理由做出自己的决定，前提是他依据明确的原则做出决定。这个问题主要观察一个人自己对文学的反应是什么。有些人认为托尔斯泰的《战争与和平》是一部伟大的作品，而其他人却在书中找不到任何东西，认为这部小说只能是一个不负责任的天才混乱无序的笔记。《约翰·英格里沙》作为一部永恒之美的小说吸引了许多有品位的人，而对一些人来说，它似乎充满多愁善感和矫揉造作。洛厄尔先生等人将西尔维斯特·贾德的《玛格丽特》视为美国小说的经典之一，但这部小说从来没有吸引过大众的关注，不久前一位著名的文人还告诉我，他觉得这本书很乏味。对于这些和所有其他不同的意见，只有一件事要说，如果建立在确定原则的逻辑应用基础上，任何人都有权做出自己的判断。无论是否定还是赞同的意见，任何真诚的、基于标准的意见都必须受到尊重。

　　另一方面，很难认为出于个人心血来潮而不是故意判断的偏见存在任何道德借口。意见不应该是无意中被衣服挂住的芒刺，而应是从树上精心挑选出来的最好的水果。事实是，除非绝对被迫，否则形成合理判断的努力比大多数人愿意承担的后果更为严重。直到需要人们学习如何集中精神去面对被忽视的危险之前，现代生活给人的感觉似乎是整个都在朝着培养头脑灵活性的方向发展。人们接受各种训练以应对精神上的紧急情况，但人们如何承受后续不断的精神压力却并没有得到训练。人们能够通过短暂的努力克服需要战胜的困难，但当需要他们从容以待并持之以恒时，这种训练的弱点就会暴露无遗。今天，不仅是男人也许还包括更多的女性，更乐意用一眨眼的工夫便决定了一本书的价值，并且应该承认，这些仓促间做出判断的合理性居然比预期的还要高得多。然而，当谈到他们如此有信心的理由时，令人遗憾的是，有不少有才智的人也完全无法公正且逻辑清晰地考察文学。必须承认，判断一本书是否应该纳入文学尊贵的名下，还应有其他检验的方法，而不应抱定教条主义的断言，"好吧，我不在乎任何人反对它，我喜欢它！"

我们已经讨论了决定什么是文学的区别，而且如果空间允许的话，我们可以继续考察决定作品等级的原则。当然，它们主要是依据已经说过的内容来推断。文学的价值将主要取决于它与标志着文学基本特点的标准的密切程度。一部作品表达的情感越真实，表达就越充分，它被置于的等级就越高。

The more sane and healthful, the more entirely in accord with the needs and springs of general human life, the greater the work. Indeed, beyond this there is little to say save that the nobility of intention, the ethical significance of the emotion embodied, mark the worth and the rank of a composition.

I have tried to define literature, and yet in the end my strongest feeling is that of the inadequacy of my definition. He would be but a lukewarm lover who was capable of framing a description which would appear to him to embody fully the perfections of his mistress; and art is a mistress so beautiful, so high, so noble, that no phrases can fitly characterize her, no service can be wholly worthy of her. Life is full of disappointment, and pain, and bitterness, and that sense of futility in which all these evils are summed up; and yet even were there no other alleviation, he who knows and truly loves literature finds here a sufficient reason to be glad that he lives. Science may show man how to live; art makes living worth his while. Existence today without literature would be a failure and a despair; and if we cannot satisfactorily define our art, we at least are aware how it enriches and ennobles the life of every human being who comes within the sphere of its wide and gracious influence.

childhood. It is apt to bring to mind bitter hours when some examples in long division stood like an impassable wall between us and all happiness; when complex fractions deprived life of all joy, or the future was hopelessly blurred by being seen through a mist of tears and irregular French verbs. The word "study" is therefore likely to seem to indicate a mechanical process, full of weariness and vexation of spirit. This is actually true of no study which is worthy of the name; and least of all is it true in connection with art. The word as applied to literature is not far from meaning intelligent enjoyment; it signifies not only apprehension but comprehension; it denotes not so much accumulation as assimilation; it is not so much acquirement as appreciation.

By the study of literature can be meant nothing pedantic, nothing formal, nothing artificial. I should like to call the subject of these talks "experiencing literature", if the verb could be received in the same sense as in the old-fashioned phrase "experiencing religion". That is what I mean. The study of literature is neither less nor more than experiencing literature, —the taking it to heart and the getting to its heart.

第三讲　文学研读

　　清楚地了解什么是文学后，对它的研读仍然可能存在很大的模糊性。人们在传统意义上对此类研读的普遍看法是模糊的，所以它对智力发展而言远远不够。文学研读为什么值得热心的人们认真关注？对这一问题应该有一个清晰而明确的理解。

　　乍一想，这个问题似乎不需要讨论。一般认为，整个问题都已一清二楚，这就是它的全部内容。然而，显而易见的事物往往是最后被察觉的。这就是人性中难以琢磨的东西，把一件事情说得过于简单而不需要证明，这通常只是一种掩饰无法证明的方法。人们时常无法察觉到离他们最近的东西，同时为了掩饰他们的盲目和无知，他们乐意不加推论地接受其他人推荐的几乎任何假设。与对现成意见的需求相比，对专利药物的需求虽然广泛，但微不足道。大多数人接受普遍的信念，并且不会花功夫去考察这种信念所依据的理由，以便使它真正成为他们自己的。我们都认可研读文学有很多益处，这是可能的，但恐怕能确切说出研读文学为什么好的人不会占多数。

顺便说一句，"研读"这个词就此而论并不是一个完全愉快的词。确实，它有许多令人愉快的联想，特别是对于那些真正学会了如何研读的人，但它也有某种令人沮丧的暗示性，会唤起人们童年的痛苦回忆。一些长期分割的例子就如同横亘在我们与所有幸福之间无法逾越的一堵墙，很容易令人想起痛苦的时光，复杂的分式夺去了生活的所有乐趣，或者透过不规则的法语动词和模糊的泪水，未来也变得模糊和绝望。因此，"研读"二字似乎表示一个机械刻板的过程，充满了精神疲倦和烦恼。事实上，没有任何一项名副其实的研读不是如此，最重要的是，它与艺术有关。用于文学的这个词与所指的理智的享受之意相去不远，然而它不仅意味着了解（apprehension），而且意味着理解（comprehension）；它表示的意思与其说是积累，不如说是同化，与其说是获得，不如说是欣赏。

文学研读可能意味着没有学究，没有拘谨，没有做作。我想把这些谈论的主题称为"体验文学"，如果这个动词可以被重新理解为与老式短语"体验宗教"相同的意义，那就是我的意思。对文学的研读不亚于体验文学，即把它放在心上，进入它的心脏。

To most persons to study literature means nothing more than to read. There is, it is true, a vague general notion that it is the reading of some particular class of books, not always over clearly defined. It is not popularly supposed that the reading of an ordinary newspaper is part of the study of literature; while on the other hand there are few persons who can imagine that the perusal of Shakespeare, however casual, can be anything else. Since literary art is in the form of written works, reading is of course essential; but by study we mean something more grave and more fruitful than the mere

有任何手段可以实现其目的，这不是享受。歌德曾说过："总是把人指向终点而不是顺便让他快乐，这是文化的悲哀。"任何研读本身不是一种乐趣，就不会有任何更高的价值，同样，仅仅为了自己而进行的研读也是没有价值的。每个老师都知道，学生不感兴趣的功课是多么徒劳无益。换句话说，这对他来说不是乐趣。心灵在所有真正的活动和收获中才能找到快乐。他当然可以积累一些正式或肤浅的知识，但学生必须对他的功课感到高兴，否则他能学到的东西很少。不能因为乘法表的学习很少伴随激情享受的刺激，就认为它无用而搁置一旁。教育必须有一些苦差事，但至少我所说的肯定适用于所有与更深入、更高阶段心智的培养相关的事情。

因此，文学研读既是一种责任，也是一种乐趣。研读文学本身就是一种乐趣，是对更美好事物的一大助益。通过它，人们可以理解那些被列为艺术作品的书籍。通过它，人们可以努力使自己有资格与人类伟大的思想和伟大的想象力进行交流。

What we gain in this may be broadly classified as pleasure, social culture, and a knowledge of life. Any one of these terms might almost be made to include the other two, but the division here is convenient in discussion.

Pleasure in its more obvious meaning is the most superficial, although the most evident, gain from art. In its simplest form this is mere amusement and recreation. We read, we say, "to pass the time." There are in life hours which need to be beguiled; times when we are unequal to the fatigue or the worry of original thought, or when some present reality is too painful to be faced. In these seasons we desire to be delivered from self, and the self-forgetfulness and the entertainment that we find in books are of unspeakable relief and value. This is of course a truism; but it was never before so insistently true as it is today. Life has become so busy, it is in a key so high, so nervously exhaustive, that the need of amusement, of recreation which shall be a relief from the severe nervous and mental strain, has become most pressing. The advance of science and civilization has involved mankind in a turmoil of multitudinous and absorbing interests from the pressure of which there seems to us no escape except in self-oblivion; and the most obvious use of reading is to minister to this end.

At the risk of being tedious it is necessary to remark in passing that herein lies a danger not to be passed over lightly. There is steadily increasing the tendency to treat literature as if it had no other function than to amuse. There is too much reading which is like opium-eating or dram-drinking. It is one thing to amuse one's self to live, and quite another to live to amuse one's self. It is universally conceded, I believe, that the intellect is higher than the body; and I cannot see why it does not follow that intellectual debauchery is more vicious than physical. Certainly, it is difficult to see why the man who neglects his intellect while caring scrupulously for his body is on a higher moral plane than the man who, though he neglects or drugs his body, does cultivate his mind.

In an entirely legitimate fashion, however, books may be read simply for amusement; and greatly is he to be pitied who is not able to lose himself in the enchantments of books. A physical cripple is hardly so sorrowful an object. Everybody knows the remark attributed to Talleyrand, who is said to have answered a man who boasted that he had never learned whist, "What a miserable old age you are preparing for yourself." A hundredfold is it true that he who does not early cultivate the habit of reading is neglecting to prepare a resource for the days when he shall be past active life. While one is in the strength of youth or manhood it is possible to fill the mind with interests of activity. As long as one is engaged in affairs directly the need of the solace of books is less evident and less pressing. It is difficult to think without profound pity of the aged man or woman shut off from all important participation in the work or the pleasure of the world, if the vicarious enjoyment of human interests through literature be also lacking. It is amazing how little this fact is realized or insisted upon.

我们从研读中获得的可以大致分为快乐、社会文化和生活知识。

wares.

Real talk about books, however, the expression of genuine opinions about real literature, is one of the most delightful of social pleasures. It is at once an enjoyment and a stimulus. From it one gets mental poise, clearness and readiness of ideas, and mental breadth. It is so important an element in human intercourse that it is difficult to conceive of an ideal friendship into which it does not enter. There have been happy marriages between men and women lacking in cultivation, but no marriage relation can be so harmonious that it may not be enriched by a community of literary tastes. A wise old gentleman whom I once knew had what he called an infallible receipt for happy marriages, "Mutual love, a sense of humor, and a liking for the same books." Certainly, with these a good deal else might be overlooked. Personally, I have much sympathy with the man who is said to have claimed a divorce on the ground that his wife did not like Shakespeare and would read Ouida. It is a serious trial to find the person with whom one must live intimately incapable of intellectual talk.

建议年轻人为他们的晚年做物质安慰的准备，这是很常见的，但值得怀疑的是，建议他们为精神安慰做好准备是否就不那么重要了？阅读是年轻人欢乐的花园，但对于老年人而言，它是避难所。

阅读的第二个目标是提高社会修养。几乎没有必要评论书籍在现代交谈中的作用有多大，或者通过明智的阅读可以增加多少对话应变能力。诚然，不少关于书籍的谈论有某种特质，不至于让真正的文学爱好者啼笑皆非。谈论书籍不是阅读文学的结果，而是关于文学的阅读结果。据说波士顿文化只不过是《利特尔的生活时代》稀释过的摘录，并且本着同样的精神，可以断言，许多现代关于书籍的讨论都是报纸上对序言的简缩。这里有一个故事，讲的是一家苏格兰救济院非常节俭的一些贫民，其中有贵族让朋友送了一些茶叶给他们，接着把珍贵的药草反复浸泡，然后把叶子晒干再卖给下一级的救济人员。使用完后，反过来再次将煮沸的叶子晒干，并将它们卖给一些老人。晒干的叶子被研磨成某种假鼻烟，可怜的老人们用它来设法欺骗他们枯萎的鼻孔，还装出几份孱弱的快乐。在我那个时代，我听过不少所谓的文学谈话，在我看来，这些谈论已经走到了最后该收场的地步了，其质量低劣，就像用反复浸泡过的茶叶做成的鼻烟！的确，必须承认，在一般社会中，谈论书籍最好仅限于闲聊一些未曾读过的书，以及在此方面贩卖一些二手意见。大多数人喜欢获得想法的方法，就如同他们喜欢在廉价货柜上购置家用物品一样。这样做可能比没有想法更好，但要记住，在廉价货柜上肯定只能找到便宜或破损的商品。

然而，真正的书谈表达了对真实文学的真实看法，是最令人愉快的社交乐趣之一。它既是一种享受，也是一种刺激，从中可以获取精神上的宁静、清晰而敏锐的观点以及思想广度。在人际交往中，它是如此重要的一个元素，理想的朋友之间不谈书论道几乎难以想象。缺乏修养的男女婚姻也有过得美满的，但没有哪一种婚姻关系能比得上有共同文学品位滋养的婚姻关系更和谐。我曾经认识的一位聪明的老绅士便拥有他所谓的幸福婚姻绝对可靠的秘诀："互爱，幽默感，喜欢相同的书籍。"当然，有了这些，其他很多东西可能会被忽视。据说有一个男人因妻子不喜欢莎士比亚且只会读作家韦达的书，提出与妻子离婚。对这个男人，我倒是非常同情。找一个必须与之亲密生活的人却无法进行思想交谈是一个严峻的考验。

He who goes into general society at all is expected to be able to keep up at least the appearance of talking about literature with some degree of intelligence. This is an age in which the opportunities for what may be called cosmopolitan knowledge are so general that it has come to be the tacit claim of any society worth the name that such knowledge shall be possessed by all. I do not, of course, mean simply that acquaintance with foreign affairs which is to be obtained from the newspapers, even all wisdom as set forth in their vexingly voluminous Sunday editions. I mean that it is necessary to have with the thought of other countries, with their customs, and their habits of thought, that familiarity which is by most to be gained only by general reading. The multiplication of books and the modern habit of travel have made an acquaintance with the temper of different peoples a social necessity almost

　　一个人出入社会，总是被期望至少能以某种程度的睿智谈论文学，并以此来撑撑门面。在这个时代，可以接触那些所谓的世界性知识的机会非常普遍，因此所有人都应拥有这些知识，这是任何名实相符的社交圈子已默认的一种主张。当然，我指的不是仅从报纸上了解外交事务，甚至也不是了解刊登在周日版上恼人心烦的学问。我的意思是，有必要对其他国家的思想、风俗及思维习惯有所熟悉，而这种熟悉程度通常只能通过一般阅读才能获得。书籍大量增加，现代旅行习惯越来越普及，因此了解不同民族的性情特征已成为一种几乎绝对的社会需求。

　　在很大程度上，现代社会也期望对以往社会的状况和审美情况有所了解。从形式上讲，这与其说是历史，不如说是某种程度上熟悉过去人们的生活方式、思维习惯和举止的结果。巴雷特·温德尔教授有一句令人钦佩的话，"只有在书本中才能穿越时间。"在目前的社会状态下，期望功成名就的男人或女人应该去穿越时间。就心智而言，他应该回到过去，不应仅从枯燥的历史学家的观点，而应从最广泛意义上的人类研究学者的观点去观察欧洲。我们最感兴趣的是远方或其他时代居民的性情特征，而这正是那些有意在社交场合大放异彩的人必须熟悉的一点。

　　一个人只有在受过教育的人的陪伴下才能找到自己的位置。通过一个讲述卡莱尔的故事就可说明，一个人可能对以往的重要事情多么无知。萨克雷和卡莱尔曾一道做客伦敦皇家学院的一次晚宴，在餐桌上，他们周围的艺术家之间的谈话转向谈起了提香。"关于提香的一个事实，"一位画家说，"就是他灿烂的色彩。""而他辉煌的绘画艺术是关于提香的另一个事实，"另一个人马上说道。然后一个人又加了一句赞美的话，于是一个接着一个都在谈起提香，直到卡莱尔打断了他们，以一种自负和深思熟虑的腔调说："坐在这里，我是一个按照上帝的样子制造的人，对提香一无所知，并且对他一点不感兴趣；——这是关于提香的另一个事实。"但是，萨克雷一边啜饮红葡萄酒，一边听别人谈论，这时停了下来，向客人庄严地鞠了一躬。"请原谅，"他说，"这不是关于提香的事实。这是关于托马斯·卡莱尔的事实——也是一个非常可悲的事实。"以冷漠或优越感为幌子来掩饰无知的做法很常见，但最终没有任何一个值得欺骗的人会被他们误导。

将好书的陪伴比作与聪明为伴有点像陈词滥调，但不断重复一个真理并不会使真理变成谬误。认识人类，认识自我，是塑造品格的伟大力量。人们经常说，无论如何言甚详明，都需要坚持这一主张——文学可能在很大程度上代表了经验，但这里还可以恰当地补充一点，在阅读中，人们可以选择他将接触到的经验。

在生活中，我们经常被卑鄙无耻的东西所包围，但这不一定会发生在图书馆里，除非我们故意选择。艾默生曾贴切地说过：

> 和卑鄙的人在一起，你会认为生活很卑鄙。那么就去阅读普鲁塔克的作品，你便会发现，这个世界是一个值得骄傲的地方，到处都有积极品质的人，英雄和半神站在我们身边，他们不会让我们沉睡。

我们经常在日常生活中被迫遇到与卑鄙的人打交道，如果不是因为有伟大思想家的幸福陪伴，并与他们的作品至诚交流，我们的整个生活都将陷于变得无可救药的肮脏和卑鄙的巨大危险中。

关于阅读的社会影响，还有一点值得一提。社交的从容自信当然只能靠实际体验才能获得，但除此之外，熟悉最优秀的书籍更是行之有效。带着同感去理解文学即是对生活的间接体验。这是穿越其他人的意识，穿越亘古至今最富有聪明才智、影响最深远的人的意识。单纯只知道读书的人接触现实世界会感到迷惘无助，但是当天性的羞怯和困惑渐渐消失后，他就能够回忆和使用他在研读文学中获得的知识，并能迅速适应他可能发现的任何领域。我不是说一个人可以独自解读社会的优雅和安逸，但可以肯定的是，任何特定的人在从书本中了解到社会是什么后，便会在社会上处于非常明显的有利地位。

家正潜心研究人的行为和思想。在这两个极端之间的长长距离中，有各个层次的智力和修为。在每一件事情中，最能引起人们感兴趣的是人类的行为、思想，尤其是人类所有的感情。拉丁剧作家的座右铭实际上也是人类的座右铭："没有人对我冷眼旁观。"

我们都非常渴望知道人类的潜能是什么。我们试图了解这一答案，如同一个继承人试探性地询问他能到手的继承物有多少。文学是人类遗产的存货清单，人生不过是一连串的情感。至诚的心热切渴望了解其可能性范围内的情感。发现一种出人意料的接受快乐的能力，意识到一种未知的感觉，哪怕是痛苦的感觉，这些情感都将使赋予人的财富范围大大增加。正如在一个新国家，探险者总会相互告知他们偶然发现的泉水、肥沃的草地、贫瘠的岩石或茂密的丛林一样，人们会互相讲述他们在情感中的新发现。生命的知识——这是全人类最热切的追求。

All that most deeply concerns man, all that reaches most penetratingly to the roots of being, is recorded, so far as humanity has been able to give to it expression, in art. Of all art, literature is perhaps the most universally intelligible; or, if not that, it is at least the most positively intelligible. Our interest in life shows itself in a burning curiosity to know what goes on in the minds of our friends; to discover what others make out of existence, what they find in its possibilities, its limitations, its sorrows, and its delights. In varying degrees, according to individual temperament, we pass life in an endeavor to discover and to share the feelings of other human beings. We explain our feelings, our motives; we wonder whether they look to others as they do to us; we speculate whether others have found a way to get from life more than we get; and above all are we consciously or unconsciously eager to learn whether any other has contrived means of finding in life more vivid sensations, more vibrant emotions, more far-reaching feelings than those which we experience. It is in this insatiable curiosity that our deepest interest in literature lies.

Books explain us to ourselves. They reveal to us capabilities in our nature before unsuspected. They make intelligible the meaning and significance of mental experiences. There are books the constant rereading of which presents itself to an imaginative man as a sort of moral duty, so great is the illumination which they throw upon the inner being. I could name works which I personally cannot leave long neglected without a feeling of conscious guilt. It is of books of this nature that Emerson says that they—

> Take rank in our life with parents and lovers and passionate experiences, so medicinal, so stringent, so revolutionary, so authoritative, —books which are the work and the proof of faculties so comprehensive, so nearly equal to the world which they paint, that though one shuts them with meaner ones, he feels the exclusion from them to accuse his way of living. —*Books*.

就人类能够在艺术中给予的表达而言，所有最深切涉及人类的事物和所有最深入地触及存在根源的事物都会被一一记录下来。在所有艺术中，文学也许是最容易理解的，或者，如果不是这样，至少也是最易于明确理解的。我们对生活的兴趣自然而然会表现出强烈的好奇心，如打探挚友的心思，发现他人的生活创造，探寻他们从可能性、局限性、悲伤和快乐中获得了什么。在不同程度上，根据个人的气质，我们度过一生是为了发现和分享其他人的感受。我们向世人吐露我们的情感，为我们的目的辩解；我们好奇地打探他们是否如指望我们一样也指望别人；我们绞尽脑汁猜想其任何他人是否已别开生路，硕果累累。尤其是，我们有意无意渴望知道，其他人是否千方百计在生活中觅得了远比我们能体验的更强烈的感觉，更富活力的情感、更为深远的感情。正是在这种永不满足的好奇心中，我们对文学最浓厚的兴趣才找到了所在。

书籍把我们昭示给自己。人们在未被察觉前，书籍揭示了我们本性中的能力，使心理体验的意义和价值变得浅显易懂。有些书不断为世人重读，对富有想象力的人来说，书籍呈现的是一种道德责任，它们发人深省，照亮着人们的内心世界。若有的书长久遭遇冷落，会让我感到内疚，这些书的名字我都能一一道出。艾默生谈到的书正是这种性质的书籍：

　　它们在我们的生活中占有一席之地，与我们父母和恋人同在，充满激情的经历，如良药，如此严谨，如此富有革命性，如此权威，——这些书是努力和能力的证明，包罗万象，与所描绘的世界几乎相差无几。尽管一个人用更低廉的书把好书拒之门外，但他感到，把这些书排斥在外就是对生活方式的责难。

——《书籍》

There are probably none of us who have lived in vital relations to literature who cannot remember some book which has been an epoch in our lives. The times and the places when and where we read them stand out in memory as those of great mental crises. We recall the unforgettable night in which we sat until the cold gray dawn looked in at the window reading Lessing's "*Nathan the Wise*", the sunny slope where we experienced Madame de Gasparin's "*Near and Heavenly Horizons*", the winter twilight in the library when that most strenuous trumpet blast of all modern ethical poetry, "*Childe Roland to the Dark Tower Came*", first rang in the ears of the inner self. We all have these memories. There are books which must to us always be alive. They have spoken to us; we have heard their very voices; we know them in our heart of hearts.

That desire for sympathy which is universal is another strong incentive to acquaintance with literature. The savage who is less miserable in fear or in suffering if he finds a fellow whose living presence saves him from the awful sense of being alone is unconsciously moved by this desire. The more fully the race is developed the more is this craving for human companionship and human appreciation conscious. We know how impossible it is ever completely to blend our consciousness for the smallest instant with that of any other human being. The nearest approach to this is the sharing with another some common feeling. There are blissful moments when some other is absorbed in the same emotion as that which we feel; when we seem to be one with the heart and the mind of another creature because the same strong passion sways us both. These are the mountain-tops of existence. These are the times which stand out in our remembrance as those in which life has touched in seeming the divine impossible.

It is of the greatest rarity, however, that we find, even in our closest friends, that comprehension and delicate sympathy for which we long. Indeed, such is human egotism that it is all but impossible for anyone so far to abandon his own personality as to enter fully into the more delicate and intangible feelings of his fellow. A friend is another self, according to the proverb, but it is apt to be himself and not yourself. To find sympathy which comes from a knowledge that our inmost emotions are shared we turn to books. Especially is this true in bereavement and in sorrow. The touch of a human hand, the wistful look in the eye of the friend who longs to help, or the mere presence of some beautiful and responsive spirit, is the best solace where comfort is impossible; but even the tenderest human presence may jar, while in books there is a consolation and a tenderness unhampered by the baffling sense of a consciousness still outside of our own no matter how strenuously it longs to be in perfect unity. I knew once a mother who had lost her only child, and who used to sit for hours pressing to her heart Plutarch's divinely tender letter to his wife on the death of his own little one. It was almost as if she felt her baby again in her arms, and the leather covers of the book were stained with tears consecrated and saving. Who could count the number to whom " *In Memoriam* " has carried comfort when living friends had no message? The critical defects of that poem are not far to seek; but it would ill become us to forget how many grief-laden hearts it has reached and touched. The book which lessens the pain of humanity is in so far higher than criticism.

我们的生活与文学有着至关紧要的联系，没有人不记得某一本书曾是我们生活中的一个时代。当初阅读这些书的时间和地点犹如经历过的重大精神危机，在我们记忆深处至今记忆犹新。我们回忆起那个难忘的夜晚，坐在那里读埃夫莱姆·莱辛的《智者纳旦》，直到寒冷的灰色黎明溜进窗户；我们想起了，在阳光明媚的斜坡上体验德·加斯帕林夫人的《近处和天堂地平线》；曾记得图书馆的冬暮里，现代伦理诗歌《去黑暗塔的罗兰公子》中最激烈的喇叭声，第一次在内心自我的耳边响起。我们都有这些曾经的回忆。有些书对我们来说必须永远活着。它们曾对我们娓娓而谈；我们聆听它们的声音；我们在内心深处认识它们。

获取同情是普遍的愿望，也是我们与文学为伴的强大刺激。一个原始人如果找到一个活生生的存在使他从可怕的孤独感中解脱出来，他就会在恐惧或痛苦中变得不那么痛苦。人类发展得越充分，与人为伴，被人欣赏的愿望就会越强烈。我们知道，在最小的瞬间将我们的意识与任何其他人的意识融为一体是完全不可能的。对此，最接近的方法是与另一个人分享一些共同的感受。当其他人沉浸在与我们所感受到的相同的情绪中时，是一个非常幸福的时刻；当我们似乎与另一个人的心和思想合二为一时，同样强烈的激情便会支配着我们。这些就是存在的巅峰。这些都是我们的记忆历久弥新的时刻，因在此刻的记忆中，生活似乎触动了完美的不可能。

然而，最为稀有的是，即使在我们最亲密的朋友身上，我们也能找到我们渴望已久的理解和微妙的相同感受。的确，人类如此自负，以至任何人都几乎不可能放弃自己的个性，而完全进入同胞更微妙和无形的感情中。谚语说，朋友是另一个自我，但它很容易成为他自己，而不是你自己。为了找到来自内心深处的同情之心并与他人共享，我们只能求助于书籍，这种情形在丧亲之痛和悲伤之中尤其如此。亲切的抚摸，渴望伸出援助之手的朋友伤感的眼神，甚或只是一些美好热情的情绪的表现，都是无法安慰的最佳安慰。但有时即使是最温柔的人出现，也可能会带来烦躁不安的感觉，然而在书籍中，无论它多么努力亟盼完美的统一，有一种安慰和温柔却不受自己意识之外莫名其妙的感觉所阻碍。我曾经认识一位失去了唯一孩子的母亲，她习惯坐上几个小时，把普鲁塔克写给妻子的关于他自己的小孩子去世的无比温柔的信贴在心间。她仿佛感觉自己的孩子又回到了她怀里，皮子做的封面上沾满了奉献和拯救的泪水。当活着的朋友杳无音信时，谁能数得清丁尼生的《悼念》给多少人带来了抚慰？那首诗的关键缺陷并不难觅，但我们很难忘记它曾经感染和触动了多少悲伤的心。在这个程度上，能减轻人类痛苦的诗歌遑论苛责。

Josiah Quincy used in his old age to relate how his mother, left a young widow by the death of her husband within sight of the shores of America when on his return from a mission to England, found comfort in the soothing ministration of books: —

> She cultivated the memory of my father, even in my earliest childhood, by reading me passages from the poets, and obliging me to learn by heart and repeat such as were best adapted to her own circumstances and feelings. Among others the whole leave-taking of Hector and Andromache, in the sixth book of Pope's *Homer*, was one of her favorite lessons.... Her imagination, probably, found consolation in the repetition of lines which brought to mind and seemed to typify her own great bereavement.
> And think'st thou not how wretched we shall be, —
> A widow I, a helpless orphan he?

These lines, and the whole tenor of Andromache's address and circumstances, she identified with her own sufferings, which seemed relieved by the tears my repetition of them drew from her.

This comforting power of literature is one which need not perhaps have been enlarged upon so fully, but it is one which has to do with the most intimate and poignant relations of life.

It is largely in virtue of the sympathy which it is possible to feel for books that from them we not only receive a knowledge of the capacities of human emotion, but we are given actual emotional experience as well. For literature has a twofold office. It not only shows the possibilities of life, but it may make these possibilities realities. If art simply showed us what might be without aiding us further, it would be but a banquet of Tantalus. We must have the substance as well as the shadow. We are born not only with a craving to know what emotions are the birthright of man, but with an instinctive desire to enter into that inheritance. We wish to be all that it is possible for men to be. The small boy who burns to be a pirate or a policeman when he grows up, is moved by the idea that to men of these somewhat analogous callings come a richness of adventure and a fullness of sensation which are not to be found in ordinary lives. The lad does not reason this out, of course; but the instinctive desire for emotion speaks in him. We are born with the craving to know to the full the emotions of the race. It is to few of us in modern civilized life that circumstances permit a widely extended experience in actual mental sensations. The commonplace actualities of every-day life show plain and dull beside the almost infinite possibilities of existence. The realization of the contrast makes not a few mortals unhappy and dissatisfied; but those who are wiser accept life as it is, and turn to art for the gratification of the instinctive craving which is unsatisfied by outward reality.

乔赛亚·昆西年老时常常讲起他母亲的一则故事。从英国执行任务返回美国海岸时父亲去世了，母亲年轻守寡，一直从阅读那些帮助人慰藉的书中寻找安慰：

> 即使在我最早的童年时代，她也通过给我朗读诗人的段落，并强迫我背诵最适合她自己情况和感受的内容，以此来培养我对父亲的记忆。其中，亚历山大·蒲伯的《荷马史诗》第六卷中，描写赫克托尔和安德洛马赫告别的内容是她最喜欢的课文之一……她的想象力可能在重复台词中找到了安慰，这些台词让人想起并似乎象征了她自己的伟大的丧亲之痛。
> 你难道不认为我们将多么悲惨，——
> 我，一个寡妇，他，一个无助的孤儿？

在这些台词里，安德洛玛赫的讲话主调及环境中，母亲认为找到了与自己一样的痛苦，我背诵的那些台词使她凄然泪下，似乎也减轻了她的痛苦。

文学的这种安慰力量也许不需要如此渲染，但它与生活中最亲密和最凄美的情感有关。

主要凭借对书中内容的感同身受，我们不仅在书籍中获得了关于情感能力的知识，而且还获得了切身的情感体验。文学拥有双重作用，它不仅展示生活的可能性，还可以使这些可能性转变为现实。如果艺术只是向我们展示了可能是什么，而无法进一步帮助我们，那将只是一场坦塔罗斯的盛宴——可望而不可即。我们不仅要有影子，而且必须有实体。我们生来不仅渴望知道人类与生俱来的权利是什么，而且本能地希望拥有那个继承物。我们希望成为男人所能成为的一切。一个小男孩的愿望是长大后当一名海盗或警察，那么这种愿望会一直激励着他。对于怀有这些相似使命感的人来说，说不定他们便会有很多奇异的经历和满满的刺激感，而这些在平凡的生活中却再难寻觅。当然，这一点并不是少年通过推理得出来的，情感的本能渴望在他身上不言自明。我们生来就渴望彻底了解人类情感。仅对现代文明生活中的少数人而言，境遇允许他们在真实心理感觉中去进行广泛的延伸体验。除了几乎无限的生存可能性之外，每一天日常生活的平凡现实展现出的是平淡和沉闷。意识到这一悬殊使不少凡夫俗子感到不悦与不满，但更明智的人则会接受生活的本来面目，转而从艺术中寻求外在现实无法满足的本能欲求。

It may be that fate has condemned us to the most humdrum of existences. We trade or we teach or are lawyers or housekeepers, doctors or nurses, or the curse of the gods has fallen upon us and we are condemned to the dreariness of a life of pleasure-seeking. We cannot of ourselves know the delights of the free outlaw's life under "the greene shaw" —the chase of the deer, the twang of the bowstring, the song of the minstrel, the relish of venison pasty and humming nut-brown ale, are not for us in the flesh. If we go into the library, however, take down that volume with the cover of worn brown leather, and give up the imagination to the guidance of the author, all these things become possible to the inner sense. We become aware of the reek of the woodland fire, the smell of the venison roasting on spits of ash-wood, the chatter of deep manly voices, the cheery sound of the bugle-horn afar, the misty green light of the forest, the soft sinking feel of the moss upon which in imagination we have flung ourselves down, while Will Scarlet teases Friar Tuck yonder, and Allan-a-Dale touches light wandering chords on his harp. —Ah, where are the four walls of the library, where is the dull round of cares and trifles which involve us day by day? We are in merry Sherwood with bold Robin Hood, and we know what there was felt and lived.

We cannot in outward experience know how a great and generous heart must feel, broken by ingratitude and unfaith, deceived and tortured through its noblest qualities, outraged in its highest love. The poet says to us, "Come with me; and through the power of the imagination, talisman more potent than the ring of Solomon, we will enter the heart of Othello, and with him suffer this agony. We will endure the torture, since behind it is the exquisite delight of appeasing that insatiable thirst for a share in human emotions. Or would you taste the passion of young and ardent hearts, their woe at parting, and their resolved devotion which death itself cannot abate? We will be one with Romeo and one with Juliet." Thus, if we will, we may go with him through the entire range of mortal joys and sorrows. We live with a fullness of living beside which, it may be, our ordinary existence is flat and pale. We find the real life, the life of the imagination; and we recognize that this is after all more vital than our concern over the price of stocks, our petty bother about the invitation to the Hightops' ball on the twenty-fourth, or the silly pang of brief jealousy which we experienced when we heard that Jack Scribbler's sonnet was to appear in the next number of the magazine which had just returned our own poem "with thanks". The littlenesses of the daily round slip out of sight before the nobility of the life possible in the imagination.

也许，命运注定了我们是最平凡的存在。我们从事经商或教书，或成为律师或管家、或医生或护士，或者众神的诅咒降临在我们身上，我们注定不得不过一种追求享乐的沉闷生活。我们自己无法知道，自由自在的亡命之徒啸聚山林，有着怎样快活的生活——猎鹿、弓弦的声音、吟游诗人的歌声、鹿肉馅饼和嗡嗡作响的栗色啤酒的美味。对我们本人来说，这些都不是现实。然而，如果我们走进图书馆，把那卷用破旧的棕色皮革作封面的书取下来，任由作者带领我们的想象驰骋，所有这些对我们的内在感知而言都会成为可能。我们开始意识到林地大火的恶臭，在白蜡木上烤鹿肉的气味，男人低沉的声音的喋喋不休，远处号角的欢快声，森林里朦胧的绿光，苔藓柔软的下沉感，我们在想象中把自己扔在了上面，而这时威尔斯·卡雷特在那边取笑塔克修士，阿拉纳·戴尔则在他的竖琴上抚摸着轻飘飘的和弦。——啊，四壁图书馆，日复一日牵扯到我们那些无聊琐事到哪里去了？我们与勇敢无畏的罗宾汉在欢乐的舍伍德森林，我们知道那里的感受和那里的生活。

我们无法从外在的经验中得知，一颗伟大而慷慨的心有何感受，忘恩负义和不忠不义令他伤心欲碎，高尚的品格反使他遭受蒙蔽和磋磨，至高无上的爱令他激怒。诗人对我们说："跟我来，透过想象的力量，戴着比所罗门的魔戒更强大的护身符，我们将进入奥赛罗的心脏，与他一起承受那些痛苦。我们愿意去忍受痛苦，因为在痛苦后面，要去安抚共享人类情感无法满足的渴求，那将给我们带来无比的喜悦。或者你是否会体验年轻的心炽热的激情，离别的悲哀，至死不渝的坚定信仰？我们将与罗密欧和朱丽叶同在。"因此，如果我们愿意，我们可以与他一起经历整个尘世的悲欢离合。除了我们的生活颇为殷实，而我们平凡的人生可能苍白无华。我们找到了真实的生活，想象的生活。我们或担心股票价格，或为二十四日受邀参加高鼎舞会的琐碎之事而烦恼，或当听说杰克·斯克伯勒的十四行诗即将刊登在下一期杂志上，而方才我们的诗却被该杂志"带着感谢"退稿了，那一时刻我们心里泛出了一阵可笑的嫉妒。毕竟比起这些日常生活中的担心和烦恼，想象的生活更加生气勃勃，更为紧要。在可想象的高贵生活面前，日常生活的琐碎之事将从视线中消失得无影无踪。

It is not necessary to multiply examples of the pleasures possible through the imagination. Every reader knows how varied and how enchanting they are. To enter into them is in so far to fulfill the possibilities of life. The knowledge which is obtained through books is not the same, it is true, as that which comes from actual doing and enduring. Perhaps if the imagination were sufficiently developed there would be little difference. There have been men who have been hardly able to distinguish between what they experienced in outward life and what belonged solely to the inner existence. Coleridge and Wordsworth and Keats made no great or sharply defined distinction between the things which were true in fact and those that were true in imagination. To Blake the events of life were those which he knew through imagination, while what happened in ordinary, every-day existence he regarded as the accidental and the non-essential.

It will probably be thought, however, that those who live most abundantly are not likely to feel the need of testing existence and tasting emotions through the medium of letters. The pirate, when decks are red and smoke of powder is in the air, is not likely to retire to his cabin for a session of quiet and delightful reading; the lover may peruse sentimental ballads or make them, but on the whole everything else is subordinate to the romance he is living. It is when his lady-love keeps him at a distance that he has time for verse; not when she graciously allows him near. It is told of Darwin that his absorption in science destroyed not only his love of Shakespeare but even his power of enjoying music. The actual interests of life were so vivid that the artistic sense was numbed. The imagination exhausted itself in exploring the unknown world of scientific knowledge. It is to be noted that boys who go deeply into college sports, especially if they are on the "teams", are likely to become so absorbed in the sporting excitement that literature appears to them flat and tame. The general rule is that he who lives in stimulating and absorbing realities is thereby likely to be inclined to care less for literature.

It is to be remembered, however, that individual experience is apt to be narrow, and that it may be positively trivial and still engross the mind. That one is completely given up to affairs does not necessarily prove these affairs to be noble. It is generally agreed, too, that the mind is more elastic which is reached and developed by literature; and that even the scientist is likely to do better work for having ennobled his perceptions by contact with the thoughts of master spirits. Before Darwin was able to advance so far in science as to have no room left for art, he had trained his faculties by the best literature. At least it is time enough to give up books when life has become so full of action as to leave no room for them. This happens to few, and even those of whom it is true cannot afford to do without literature as an agent in the development and shaping of character.

没有必要通过想象来添加更多可以令人愉快的例证了。每个读者都知道这样的例子不胜枚举，令人入迷。讨论这些例子是为了实现人生的各种潜能。从书本上获得的知识与从实际发生的事和体验得来的知识是不一样的，这是一个事实。也许如果想象力已经获得足够充分的发展，可能就不会有多大的差别了。有些人几乎无法区分外在生活中的经历和只属于内在存在的东西。柯尔律治、华兹华斯和济慈在实际真实的事物和想象中真实的事物之间就没有进行很大或明确的区分。对布莱克来说，生活中的事件正是他通过想象知道的那些，而在平凡的日常生活中发生的事情，他认为是偶然的和非本质的。

然而，人们可能会认为，那些生活最充实的人会觉得有必要通过文字这一媒介，去检验生活并体验情感。当甲板烧红了，空气中已弥漫着火药的烟雾时，海盗不可能退避船舱进行一次安静而愉快的阅读；相爱的人可能会细读，甚至自己创作感伤的民谣。但总的来说，其他一切都从属于他快乐的浪漫生活。只有当他的爱人与他保持一段距离，毫无热情地允许他靠近时，他才有时间写诗。据说，达尔文对科学的痴迷不仅毁掉了他对莎士比亚的热爱，而且还毁掉了他欣赏音乐的能力。生活中的实际利益真真切切，艺术的感觉也为之变得麻木。在探索未知科学知识世界中，想象力也会耗尽。需要注意的是，迷恋大学体育运动的男生，特别是如果他们在那个"队伍"里很可能会沉湎于体育运动的刺激中，而文学在他们看来，单调而乏味。通常情况下，生活在刺激和吸引人的现实中的人据此可能不太喜欢文学。

然而，需要记住的是，个人经验往往是狭隘的，它可能无足轻重，但依然能令人全神贯注。一个人沉溺于事务中并不一定就能证明这些事务是高尚的。人们也普遍认同，受文学影响和熏陶的心智更豁达大度，并且即便是科学家也可能做得更好，因为他通过接触伟大人物的思想可以使认知能力变得崇高。达尔文在科学上取得了如此大的进步，却没有给艺术剩下空间，但在之前，他受到过最优秀文学的熏陶。至少现在是放下书籍的时候了，因为生活已经变得如此充满活力，没有给书籍留下任何空间。这种现象仅发生在少数人身上，即使对那些确实如此的人，也无法承担放弃文学作为性格发展和塑造媒介所带来的后果。

The good which we gain from the experiences of life we call insight. No man or woman ever loved without thereby gaining insight into what life really is. No man has stood smoke-stained and blood-spattered in the midst of battle, caught away out of self in an ecstasy of daring, without thereby learning hitherto undreamed-of possibilities in existence. Indeed, this is true of the smallest incident. Character is the result of experience upon temperament, as ripple-marks are the result of the coming together of sand and wave. In life, however, we are generally more slow to learn the lessons from events than from books. The author of genius has the art so to arrange and present his truths as to impress them upon the reader. The impressions of events remain with us, but it is not easy for ordinary mortals so to realize their meaning and so to phrase it that it shall remain permanent and clear in the mind. The mental vision is clouded, moreover, by the personal element. We are seldom able to be perfectly frank with ourselves. Self is ever the apologist for self. Knowledge without self-honesty is as a torch without flame; yet of all the moral graces self-honesty is perhaps the most difficult to acquire. In its acquirement is literature of the highest value. A man can become acquainted with his spiritual face as with his bodily countenance only by its reflection. Literature is the mirror in which the soul learns to recognize its own lineaments.

Above all these personal reasons which make literature worthy of the serious attention of earnest men and women is the great fact that upon the proper development and the proper understanding of it depend largely the advancement and the wise ordering of civilization. Stevenson spoke words of wisdom when he said: —

>One thing you can never make Philistine natures understand; one thing, which yet lies on the surface, remains as unseizable to their wits as a high flight of metaphysics, —namely, that the business of life is mainly carried on by the difficult art of literature, and according to a man's proficiency in that art shall be the freedom and fullness of his intercourse with other men.

　　我们把从生活经验中获得的好处称之为洞察力。男人或女人爱过才会因此洞察生活的真正含义。只有经历过硝烟弥漫与血迹斑斑战斗的人，才会在大胆的狂喜中摆脱自我，才会由此懂得迄今为止人生中做梦都没有想过的前景。事实上，最小的事件也是如此。好比波纹是沙与浪交汇的结果，性格是经验加性情产生的结果。然而，在生活中，我们从事件中吸取教训的速度通常比从书本中吸取教训更缓慢。天才的作家拥有这样的技巧，即改编和呈现各种真相，以便给读者留下深刻的印象。事件的印象会留在我们身边，但一般人却很难理解它们的意义，用语言表达出来，并让它永远清晰地留在我们脑海中。此外，个人因素也模糊了我们的心理视野。我们很少能够对自己完全坦诚，自我永远是自我的辩护者。离开自我诚实的知识就像没有火焰的火炬。然而，在所有的道德美德中，自我诚实也许是最难获得的，拥有最高的文学价值。就像了解他身体的面容一样，一个人只有通过镜子的反光，才能熟悉他的精神面貌。文学是一面镜子，只有在其中的人才能学会识别自己的面部轮廓。

　　文学值得真挚的男男女女严肃关注的一切个人原因，首先是基于一个重要的事实，即对文学的适当发展和正确理解在很大程度上取决于文明的进步和开明的秩序。史蒂文森说：

>你永远无法让非利士人的本性明白一件事。这件事，尽管存在于表面上，仍然像高高飞翔的形而上学令人难以捉摸，即生活的责任主要是由文学这一高难度的艺术来承担，与其他人交往的自由和充实将根据一个人在这艺术方面的熟练程度来确定。

In a fine passage in a little-known pamphlet, James Hannay touches upon the relation of literature to life and to the practical issues of society:——

A notion is abroad that that only is "practical" which can be measured or eaten. Show us its net result in marketable form, the people say, and we will recognize it! But what if there be something prior to all such "net results," something higher than it? For example, the writing of an old Hebrew Prophet was by no manner of means "practical" in his own times! The supply of figs to the Judean markets, the price of oil in the synagogue-lamps, did not fluctuate with the breath of those inspired songs! But in due time the prophet dies, stoned, perhaps,... and in the course of ages, his words do have a "practical" result by acting on the minds of nations... A dozen or two of earnest men two centuries ago were stirred to the depths of their souls by the visions of earnest men many centuries before that; do you not see that the circumstance has its practical influence in the cotton-markets of America at this hour? —Quoted in Espinasse's *Literary Recollections* .

It is impossible to separate the influences of literature from the growth of society and of civilization. It is because of the reaching of the imagination into the unknown vast which incloses man that life is what it is. "The world of imagination," Blake wrote, "is the world of eternity." Whatever of permanent interest and value man has achieved he has reached through this divine faculty, and it is only when man learns to know and to enter the world of imagination that he comes into actual contact with the vital and the fundamental in human life. Easily abused, like all the best gifts of the gods, art remains the noblest and the most enduring power at work in civilization; and literature is its most direct embodiment. To it we go when we would leave behind the sordid, the mean, and the belittling. When we would enter into our birthright, when we remember that instead of being mere creatures of the dust we are the heirs of the ages, then it is through books that we find and possess the treasures of the race.

在一本鲜为人知的小册子的精彩段落中，詹姆斯·汉奈谈到了文学与生活及社会实际问题的关系：

> 国外有一种观点认为，只有可以测量或食用的才算"实用"。人们说，以适销对路的形式向我们展示它的最终结果，我们会认可这一观点！但是，如果在所有这些"最终结果"之前，有一些东西，比它更高尚的东西呢？例如，一位古老的希伯来先知的著作在他自己的时代绝不是"实用的"！犹太市场供应的无花果，犹太教堂灯油的价格，并没有随着那些富有灵感的歌曲的声息而波动！但在适当的时候，先知死了，也许被石头打死了，……而且在岁月的流逝过程中，他的话确实具有通过影响各国的思想而产生的"实际"结果……两个世纪前，许多或两个老实人因他们看到了几个世纪前的老实人的幻象，灵魂深处受到了震动，难道你没有看到这种情况在这个时刻对美国的棉花市场有实际影响吗？
>
> ——引自埃斯皮纳斯的《文学回忆》

文学的影响与社会和文明的发展是分不开的。正是因为想象力已经触及了广袤无垠的未知世界，生命才如此。布莱克写道，"想象的世界就是永恒的世界。"人通过这种神圣的能力，无论获得了什么永久的兴趣和价值，也只有当人学会认识并进入想象的世界时，他才能真正触及人类生活中最重要的根本。艺术很容易被滥用，就像众神赐予的所有最好的礼物一样，艺术仍然是文明中最崇高、最持久的力量，而文学则是它最直接的体现。只有当我们抛弃了肮脏、卑鄙和蔑视时，我们才会进入文学书籍的世界。只有当我们能够把握与生俱来的权力时，也只有当我们记住我们不单单是尘世间的灵动之物，而是时代的继承人时，我们才会通过书籍找到并拥有人类的宝藏。

V
FALSE METHODS

The most common intellectual difficulty is not that of the lack of ideas, but that of vagueness of ideas. Most persons of moderately good education have plenty of thoughts such as they are, but there is a nebulous quality about these which renders them of little use in reasoning. This makes it necessary to define what is meant by the Study of Literature, as in the first place it was necessary to define literature itself. Many have a formless impression that it is something done with books, a sort of mysterious rite known only to the initiated, and probably a good deal like the mysteries of secret societies, —more of a theory than an actuality. Others, who are more confident of their powers of accurate thinking, have decided that the phrase is merely a high-sounding name for any reading which is not agreeable, but which is recommended by text-books. Some take it to be getting over all the books possible, good, bad, and indifferent; while still others suppose it to be reading about books or their authors. There are plenty of ideas as to what the study of literature is, but the very diversity of opinion proves that at least a great many of these must be erroneous.

In the first place the study of literature is not the mere reading of books. Going on a sort of Cook's tour through literature, checking off on lists what one has read, may be amusing to simple souls, but beyond that it means little and effects little. As the question to be asked in regard to a tourist is how intelligently and how observantly he has traveled, so the first consideration in regard to a reader is how he reads.

The rage for swiftness which is so characteristic of this restless time has been extended to fashions of reading. By some sort of a vicious perversion, the old saw that he who runs may read seems to have been transposed to "He who reads must run". In other words there is too often an assumption that the intellectual distinction of an individual is to be estimated by the rapidity with which he is able to hurry through the volumes he handles. Intellectual assimilation takes time. The mind is not to be enriched as a coal barge is loaded. Whatever is precious in a cargo is taken carefully on board and carefully placed. Whatever is delicate and fine must be received delicately, and its place in the mind thoughtfully assigned.

One effect of the modern habit of swift and careless reading is seen in the impatience with which anything is regarded which is not to be taken in at a glance. The modern reader is apt to insist that a book shall be like a theatre-poster. He must be able to take it all in with a look as he goes past it on a wheel, and if he cannot he declares that it is obscure. W. M. Hunt said, with bitter wisdom, "As print grows cheap, thinkers grow scarce." The enormous increase of books has bred a race of readers who seem to feel that the object of reading is not to read but to have read; not to enjoy and assimilate, but to have turned over the greatest possible number of authors. This idea of the study of literature is as if one selected as the highest social ideal the afternoon tea, where the visitor is presented to numberless strangers and has an opportunity of conversing rationally with nobody.

第五讲　错误的方法

最常见的智力障碍并非观念的缺乏，而是观念的模糊性。大多数受过良好教育的人都有很多这样的想法，但这些想法带有一种模糊的性质，使它们在论断中几乎没有用处。这就使得有必要定义文研读的含义，正如首先有必要定义文学本身一样。许多人有一种无形的印象，认为它与书有关，是一种初学者才知道的神秘仪式，可能颇似秘密社团的奥秘——与其说它是现实，不如说是一种理论。其他对自己准确思维能力更有信心的人认为，对于任何不令人愉快但教科书推荐的读物来说，这个词只是一个冠冕堂皇的名称。有些人认为文学研读就是遍览所有可能的书，好的、坏的和不感兴趣的书统统都可以；还有一些人认为是阅读有关书籍或作者的细节。关于文学研读是什么，有很多观点，但观点的多样性恰好表明，其中至少有不少肯定是错误的。

首先，文学研读不只是读书，进行某种詹姆斯·库克式的文学航海，核对已读过的清单。对简单的人来说可能很有趣，但除此之外，它意义不大，效果甚微。就游客而言，要问的是他如何带着智慧和敏锐的观察力在旅行，因此，一个读者首先要考虑的是怎样去阅读。

对快速阅读的狂热追求是这个躁动不安时代的一个显著特征，它已经波及了阅读方式。由于某种严重的曲解，过去的格言说，跑步的人可以阅读，现在似乎已被转换为"读者必须跑步"。换句话说，人们常常假设一个人的智力特征可以通过他快速浏览处理卷宗的速度来衡量。智力同化需要花费时间，头脑不能像驳船装载煤炭那样去得到充实。货物中任何珍贵的东西都须小心地搬上船并仔细放置。任何微妙和精致的东西，都必须小心翼翼地接纳，并小心谨慎地分配其在大脑中的位置。

快速和粗心阅读的现代习惯的一个影响可见于，人们对任何不能看一眼就能明白的东西缺乏耐心。现代读者倾向于坚持认为一本书应像一幅戏剧海报，当他坐车经过它时，必须能够看一眼就明白一切，如果他做不到，他就会宣称该海报晦涩难懂。W. M. 亨特睿智而尖刻地说道："印刷品变得便宜了，思想家却变得稀缺了。"书籍的大量增加，孕育了一个个庞大的读者群，他们似乎觉得阅读的目的不是阅读，而是读过，不是为了享受和同化，而是为了尽可能多地翻阅作家。这种文学研读的观点，就好像有人选择下午茶为最高的社会理想，在那里来访者被引荐给数不清的陌生人，并有机会与那些无足轻重的人理性地交谈。

A class of self-styled students of literature far more pernicious than even the record-breaking readers is that of the gossip-mongers. These are they who gratify an innate fondness of gossip and scandal under the pretext of seeking culture, and who feed an impertinent curiosity in the name of a noble pursuit. They read innumerable volumes filled with the more or less spicy details of authors; they perhaps visit the spots where the geniuses of the world lived and worked. They peruse eagerly every scrap of private letters, journals, and other personal matter which is available. For them are dragged to light all the imperfect manuscripts which famous novelists have forgotten to burn. For them was perpetrated the infamy of the publication of the correspondence of Keats with Miss Brawne; to them Mrs. Stowe appealed in her foul book about Byron, which should have been burned by the common hangman. It is they who buy the newspaper descriptions of the back bedroom of the popular novelist and the accounts of the misunderstanding between the poet and his washerwoman. They scent scandal as swine scent truffles, and degrade the noble name of literature by making it an excuse for their petty vulgarity. The race is by no means a new one. Milton complained of it in the early days of the church, when, he says: —

> With less fervency was studied what St. Paul or St. John had written than was listened to one that could say, "Here he taught, here he stood, this was his stature, and thus he went habited," and, "O happy this house that harbored him, and that cold stone whereon he rested, this village where he wrought a miracle."

Schopenhauer, too, has his indignant protest against this class: —

> Petrarch's house in Arqua, Tasso's supposed prison in Ferrara, Shakespeare's house in Stratford, Goethe's house in Weimar, with its furniture, Kant's old hat, the autographs of great men, —these things are gaped at with interest and awe by many who have never read their works.

All this is of course a matter of personal vanity. Small souls pride themselves upon having these things, upon knowing intimate details of the lives of prominent persons. They endeavor thus to attach themselves to genius, as burrs cling to the mane of a lion. The imagination has nothing to do with it; there is in it no love of literature. It is vanity pure and simple, a common vulgar vanity which substitutes self-advertisement and gossip-mongering for respect and appreciation. Who can have tolerance for the man whose proudest boast is that he was in a crowd presented to some poet whose books he never read; for the woman who claims attention on the ground that she has from her seamstress heard particulars of the domestic infelicities of a great novelist; or for the gossip of either sex who takes pride in knowing about famous folk trifles which are nobody's business but their own?

比打破阅读速度纪录的读者更致命的是，一类自封为文学学生的八卦贩子。这些人以追求文化为借口，满足了人们对八卦和丑闻的天生爱好，以崇高的追求为名满足了无礼的好奇心。他们阅读了难以计数的关于作者或多或少下流细节的书卷；他们也许会拜访一些世界上的天才们生活和工作过的地方；他们急切地细读每一份私人信件、日记和其他可用的个人资料，正如他们将一些著名小说家忘记烧掉的尚未完善的手稿强行曝光。他们因发表济慈与布劳恩小姐的信件而臭名昭著；或因那本早该被刽子手焚毁的关于拜伦的脏书，斯托夫人起诉了他们。也正是他们购买了报纸上关于流行小说家后卧室的描述以及诗人和洗衣妇之间发生误会的报道。他们像猪嗅到松露一样嗅出丑闻，为他们的小气粗俗编造借口，并以此来败坏文学的崇高名声。

这一类人绝不是新出现的一类人。弥尔顿就曾抱怨过教会早期出现的这一类型的人，他说：

> 研究圣保罗或圣约翰所写著作的热情还不如到听人们说的：
> "他曾经在这里执教，他就站在这里，这就是他的身高，因此他养成了习惯，"并且，"哦，多么幸福，这是庇护他的房子，这是他在上面休息的冰冷的石头，这就是他创造出奇迹的那个村庄。"

叔本华也对这个阶层提出了愤慨的抗议：

> 这是彼特拉克在阿尔夸的房子、塔索曾在费拉拉待过的所谓的监狱、莎士比亚在斯特拉福德的房子；这是歌德在魏玛的房子，里面还有家具；这是康德的旧帽子、伟人们的签名——这些东西让许多从未读过他们作品的人充满兴致，甚至被惊得目瞪口呆。

当然，这一切都是个人虚荣心的问题。卑微的灵魂以拥有这些东西为荣，以了解名人生活的私密细节而深感自豪。他们竭力贴近这些天才作家，就像毛刺粘在狮子的鬃毛上一样。想象力与它无关，也不存在对文学的真正热爱。它是纯粹的虚荣心，一种普遍的庸俗的虚荣心，它用自我标榜和八卦代替了尊重和赏识。他最能引以为豪的是，在一大群人中他被引荐给某一位他从未读过其作品的诗人；那个女人想引起别人注意，于是宣称从裁缝那儿听到了关于一位伟大小说家家门不幸的细节；或者那些喜欢八卦男女之事的人以了解一些名人琐事而沾沾自喜。谁能忍受得了这些人？

A good many text-books encourage this folly, and there are not a few writers who pass their useless days in grubbing in the dust-heaps of the past to discover the unessential and unmeaning incidents in the lives of bygone worthies. They put on airs of vast superiority over mortals who scorn their ways and words; they have only pitying contempt for readers who suppose that the works of an author are what the world should be concerned with instead of his grocery bills and the dust on his library table. Such meddlers have no more to do with literature than the spider on the eaves of kings' houses has to do with affairs of state.

It is not that all curiosity about famous men is unwholesome or impertinent. The desire to know about those whose work has touched us is natural and not necessarily objectionable. It is outside of the study of literature, save in so far as it now and then—less often, I believe, than is usually assumed—may help us to understand what an author has written; yet within proper limits it is to be indulged in, just as we all indulge now and then in harmless gossip concerning our fellows. It is almost sure to be a hindrance rather than a help in the study of literature if it goes much beyond the knowledge of those circumstances in the life of an author which have directly affected what he has written. There are few facts in literary history for which we have so great reason to be devoutly thankful as that so little is known concerning the life of the greatest of poets. We are able to read Shakespeare with little or no interruption in the way of detail about his private affairs, and for this every lover of Shakespeare's poetry should be grateful.

The study of literature, it must be recognized farther, is not the study of the history of literature. The development of what are termed " schools" of literature; the change in fashions of expression; the modifications in verse-forms and the growth and decay of this or that phase of popular taste in books, are all matters of interest in a way. They are not of great value, as a rule, yet they will often help the reader to a somewhat quicker appreciation of the force and intention of literary forms. It is necessary to have at least a general idea of the course of literary and intellectual growth through the centuries in order to appreciate and comprehend literature, —the point to be kept in mind being that this is a means and not in itself an end. It is necessary, for instance, for the student to toil painfully across the wastes of print produced in the eighteenth century, wherein there is little really great save the works of Fielding; and where the reader has to endure a host of tedious books in order properly to appreciate the manly tenderness of Steele, the boyishly spontaneous realism of Defoe, the kindly humanity of Goldsmith, and the frail, exquisite pipe of Collins. The rest of the eighteenth century authors most of us read chiefly as a part of the mechanics of education. We could hardly get on intelligently without a knowledge of the polished primness of Addison, genius of respectability; the vitriolic venom of Swift, genius of malignity; the spiteful perfection of Pope, genius of artificiality; or the interminable attitudinizing of Richardson, genius of sentimentality. These authors we read quite as much as helps in understanding others as for their own sake. We do not always have the courage to acknowledge it, but these men do not often touch our emotions, even though the page be that of Swift, so much the greatest of them. We examine the growth of the romantic spirit through the unpoetic days between the death of Dryden and the coming of Blake and Coleridge and Wordsworth; and from such examination of the history of literature we are better enabled to form standards for the actual estimate of literature itself.

　　很多教科书鼓励了这种愚蠢行为，并且仍有不少作家在尘封的往事中寻找逝去的贤者生活中无关紧要和毫无意义的事件，并以此打发索然无味的日子。他们摆出一副优越傲慢的架子，看不起那些嘲讽他们言行的平凡人。对于那些认为世人应该关心作者的作品而不是关心杂货账单和图书馆桌子上的灰尘的读者，他们只有怜悯的蔑视。这种爱管闲事的人与文学无关，就像王宫屋檐上的蜘蛛与国事无关一样。

　　总是对名人抱有好奇心并非全都是不健康或无礼的。想要了解用其作品打动我们的人，这是一件很自然的事，并不一定令人反感。尽管它已超出文学研读的范围，但除了偶尔——我相信，比通常假设的要少——可以帮助我们理解作者所写的内容。然而，在适当的范围内，也不妨沉迷于这些文学本身以外的事，就如同我们时不时会迷上关于我们同伴的无害闲话一样。如果文学本身以外的事远远超出了直接影响作家写作的环境的知识，它几乎肯定会成为文学研读中的障碍而不是帮助。文学史上，能让我们有充分理由虔诚地表达感激的事实并不多见，我们对一些最伟大诗人的生平知之甚少。我们对莎士比亚的私人事务了解很少，或因那些关于诗人私事的细节并没带来干扰，我们依然能阅读莎士比亚，对此，每一位莎士比亚诗歌爱好者都应心存感激。

　　必须进一步承认，文学研读不是文学史研读。所谓文学"学派"的发展、表达方式的改变、诗词形式的变化、书籍流行品味的阶段性兴衰，在某种程度上这些都是令人感兴趣的话题。虽然它们通常没有多大价值，但往往可以帮助读者更快地了解文学表现形式的力量和意图。为了欣赏和理解文学，至少有必要对几个世纪以来文学和知识的发展过程有一个大致的了解——要记住的一点是，这是一种手段，而不是目的本身。例如，学生有必要在十八世纪生产的印刷品废弃物上花一番功夫，其中除了菲尔丁的作品之外，几乎没有真正伟大的作品。读者必须忍受大量枯燥乏味的书籍，才能正确欣赏斯蒂尔的男子气概中的温柔、笛福小孩子般的自发性现实主义、戈德史密斯的善良人性以及柯林斯脆弱而精致的烟斗。我们大多数人阅读十八世纪剩余的其他作者，主要是将其作为教育方法的一部分来阅读。如果不了解爱迪生的一本正经而又受人尊敬的天才，我们几乎无法不拘形式地深入下去。斯威夫特的恶意刻薄，恶毒的天才；教皇的恶意完美，虚伪的天才；或理查森没完没了的装腔作势，多愁善感的天才。很大程度上，我们读到的这些作者不仅有助于了解作家本人，也有助于了解他人。我们并不总是有勇气承认这一点，但这些人很少能够触动我们的情感，即便那一时期是斯威夫特的时期，他们当中最伟大的人。从德莱顿去世一直到布莱克、柯尔律治和华兹华斯到来的这段时间是缺乏诗意的日子，我们可以通过这段时间的作家来考察浪漫主义精神的成长。从文学史的这种考察中，我们能够更好地为真正评价文学本身构建标准。

There is a wide and essential difference between really entering into literature and reading what somebody else has been pleased to say of it, no matter how wise and appreciative this may be. Of course, the genuine student has small sympathy with those demoralizing *flippancies* about books which are just now so common in the guise of smart essays upon authors or their works; those papers in which adroit literary hacks write about books as the things with which they have meddled most. The man who reads for himself and thinks for himself realizes that these essayists are the gypsy-moths of literature, living upon it and at the same time doing their best to destroy it; and that the reading of these petty imitations of criticism is about as intellectual as sitting down in the nursery to a game of "Authors".

Even the reading of good and valuable papers is not the study of literature in the best sense. There is much of profit in such admirable essays as those, for instance, of Lowell, of John Morley, or of Leslie Stephen. Excellent and often inspiring as these may be, however, it is not to be forgotten that as criticisms their worth lies chiefly in the incitement which they give to go to the fountain-head. The really fine essay upon a masterpiece is at its best an eloquent presentment of the delights and benefits which the essayist has received from the work of genius; it shows the possibilities and the worth within the reach of all. Criticisms are easily abused. We are misusing the most sympathetic interpretation when we receive it dogmatically. In so far as they make us see what is high and fine, they are of value; in so far as we depend upon the perceptions of the critic instead of our own, they are likely to be a hindrance. It is easier to think that we perceive than it is really to see; but it is well to remember that a man may be plastered from head to feet with the opinions of others, and yet have no more genuine ideas of his own than has a bill-board because it is covered with posters. Genuine emotion is born of genuine conviction. A reader is really touched by a work of art only as he enters into it and comprehends it sympathetically. Another may point the way, but he must travel it for himself. Reading an imaginative work is like wooing a maiden. Another may give the introduction, but for real acquaintance and all effective love-making the suitor must depend upon himself if he would be well sped. Critics may tell us what they admire, but the vital question is what we in all truth and sincerity admire and appreciate ourselves.

　　无论可能是多么明智和值得赞赏，真正涉入文学与阅读别人乐于谈论的东西之间存在着广泛而本质的区别。当然，诚实的学生很少认同那些关于书籍的令人沮丧的轻率评价，这些轻率的写作打着评论作家或作品的美文的幌子，如今已变得非常普遍。这些论文出自雇佣文人的灵巧之手，他们在文章中写了很多关于书籍的东西，大行干涉文学之事。为自己读书，为自己思考的人会意识到，这些散文家是文学的五毒蛾，以文学为生，同时又竭尽全力毁掉文学。阅读这些文学批评的蹩脚模仿，其智力水平差不多就像坐在托儿所里玩"作家"游戏一样。

　　即使阅读优秀且有价值的论文，也算不上是最好意义上的文学研读。诸如洛厄尔、约翰·莫利或莱斯利·斯蒂芬，这些令人钦佩的作家的散文是大有裨益的。然而，尽管这些散文可能非常出色且常给我们带来启发和灵感，但不应忘记，作为批评，其价值主要应在于能够激励人们追本溯源。关于名著的真正精美的散文充其量是散文家阅读文学名著的乐趣和裨益的生动表达，揭示了所有人都能实现的可能性和价值。批评很容易被滥用。当我们教条式地接受批评时，那就说明我们正在滥用最有同情心的解释。文学批评能够使我们发现什么是高尚和美好的东西，这便是批评的价值所在。如果我们依赖于批评家的看法，而无法做出自己的判断，评论家的评论很有可能成为一种累赘。人们很容易认为，我们能够感知到的胜过了实际看到的，但务必切记，虽然一个人可以拿别人的意见把自己从头到脚掩饰起来，但他自己的真实想法也多不过海报板上的想法，因为上面贴满了海报。真正的情感源于真正的说服力，读者只有进入艺术作品并以一种共情的心态去理解作品，才能真正为艺术作品所感动。一个人可能会给你指明一条路，但这条路，还必须得你自己去走。阅读富有想象力的作品就像追求一个少女，一个人可能会做介绍，但为了真正的相识和所有的亲热，求婚者必须依靠他自己才能顺利实现。批评家可能会告诉我们他们欣赏什么，但至关重要的问题是，我们在所有真实和真诚中如何赞赏和欣赏我们自己。

VI
METHODS OF STUDY

We have spoken of what the study of literature is not, but negations do not define. It is necessary to look at the affirmative side of the matter. And first it is well to remark that what we are discussing is the examination of literature, —literature, that is, in the sense to which we have limited the term by definition: "The adequate expression of genuine emotion." It is not intended to include trash, whether that present itself as undisguised rubbish or whether it mask under high-sounding names of Symbolism, Impressionism, Realism, or any other affected nomenclature whatever. It has never been found necessary to excuse the existence of the masterpieces of literature by a labored literary theory or a catchpenny classification. It is generally safe to suspect the book which must be defended by a formula and the writers who insist that they are the founders of a school. There is but one school of art— the imaginative.

"But," it may be objected, "in an age when the books of the world are numbered by millions, when it is impossible for any reader to examine personally more than an insignificant portion even of those thrust upon his notice, how is the learner to judge what are worthy of his attention?" To this it is to be answered that there are works enough universally approved to keep the readiest reader more than busy through the span of the longest human life. We shall have occasion later to speak of especial authors and of especial books. Here it is enough to say that certainly at the start the student must be content to accept the verdict of those who are capable of judging for him. Herein lies one of the chief benefits to be derived from critics and essayists. As the learner advances, he will find that as his taste and appreciation advance with them will develop an instinct of choice. In the end he should be able almost at a glance to judge rightly whether a book is worthy of attention.

In the meanwhile he need not go astray if he follow the lead of trustworthy experts.

In accepting the opinions of others it is of course proper to use some caution, and above all things it is important to be guided by common sense. The market is full of quack mental as well as of quack physical nostrums. There is a large and enterprising body of publishers who seem persuaded that they have reduced all literature to a practical industrial basis by furnishing patent outsides for newspapers and patent insides for aspiring minds. In these days one becomes intellectual by prescription, and it is impossible to tell how soon will be advertised the device of inoculation against illiteracy. Common sense and a sense of humor save one from many dangers, and it is well to let both have full play.

第六讲　文学研读方法

我们已经谈过文学研读不是什么，但否定并没有给出文学的定义。所以有必要考虑事情肯定的一面。首先要谈论的是，我们正在讨论的是考察文学——文学，也就是说，我们根据定义限定了这个术语："真实情感的充分表达"。其目的旨在不包括各种垃圾文学，那些未加掩饰的垃圾，冠以象征主义、印象派、现实主义大名的垃圾或任何专门术语的垃圾。从来没有必要用严谨的文学理论或廉价花哨的分类来为文学名著的存在寻找借口。通常完全可以怀疑，如果一本书一定要用一个准则和由那些认定自己是某一流派创始人的作家来维护其声誉，那么，这本书肯定值得怀疑，因为这里只有一种艺术流派——想象派。

有人可能会提出反对理由，"但是，在一个书籍数以百万计的时代，任何读者无法亲自考察哪怕是微不足道的一部分书籍，甚至也无法考察那些必须关注的部分书籍，那么，学习者如何判断什么是他值得关注的?"对此，肯定的答案是，关注那些已得到普遍认可的作品，它们足以让一个聪明的读者在人类最长的一生中保持终日忙碌。稍后，我们将有机会谈到一些特别的作者和书籍。在这里可以说，起步阶段时，一个学生必须满足于接受那些有能力为他做出判断的人的定论。这便是评论家和散文家能带来的主要好处之一。伴随学习者的提升，他的品位和鉴赏力同样会得到提高，会培养出一种选择的才能。到最后，他应该几乎一眼就能判断出一本书是否值得关注。同时，如果他以可信赖的专家为榜样，便不至于误入歧途。

在接受他人意见时，慎重行事当然是恰当的，但尤其重要的是要以常识为指导。市场上充斥着冒充内行的精神病患者和江湖游医骗人的秘方。有一大群雄心勃勃的出版商似乎相信，通过向报纸提供特许的外观并未为有抱负的文人提供特许的内在动力，他们已将所有文学沦为实用产业的基础了。如今，凭借某种诀窍，人们可以博古通今，而且说不清多久以后，就会宣传通过接种文盲疫苗的方式预防孤陋寡闻了。常识和幽默感使人免于许多危险，可取的是让两者都得到淋漓尽致的发挥。

I have spoken earlier in these talks of the pleasure of literary study. One fundamental principle in the selection of books is that it is idle to read what is not enjoyed. For special information one may read that which is not attractive save as it serves the purpose of the moment; but in all reading which is of permanent value for itself, enjoyment is a prime essential. Reading which is not a pleasure is a barren mistake.

The first duty of the student toward literature and toward himself is the same—enjoyment. Either take pleasure in a work of art or let it alone.

It is idle to force the mind to attend to works which it does not find pleasurable, and yet it is necessary to read books which are approved as the masterpieces of literature. Here is a seeming contradiction; but it must be remembered that it is possible to arouse the mind to interest. The books which are really worth attention will surely attract and hold if they are once properly approached and apprehended. If a mind is indolent, if it is able to enjoy only the marshmallows and chocolate caramels of literature, it is not to be fed solely on literary sweetmeats. Whatever is read should be enjoyed, but it by no means follows that whatever can be enjoyed should be read. It is possible to cultivate the habit of enjoying what is good, what is vital, as it is easy to sink into the stupid and slipshod way of caring for nothing which calls for mental exertion. It requires training and purpose. The love of the best in art is possessed as a gift of nature by only a few, and the rest of us must labor for it. The full appreciation of the work of a master-mind comes to no one without effort. The reward of the student of literature is great, but his labor also is great. Literature is not like an empty public square, which even a blind beggar may cross almost unconsciously. It more resembles an enchanted castle beset with spell-infested forests and ghoul-haunted mountains; a place into which only that knight may enter who is willing to fight his way through dangers and difficulties manifold; yet a place, too, of infinite riches and joys beyond the imaginings of dull souls.

It is a popular fallacy that art is to be appreciated without especial education. Common feeling holds that the reader, like the poet, is born and not made. It is generally assumed that one is endowed by nature with an appreciation of art as one is born with a pug nose. The only element of truth in this is the fact that all human powers are modified by the personalequation. One is endowed at birth with perceptions fine and keen, while another lacks them; but no matter what one's natural powers, there must be cultivation. This cultivation costs care, labor, and patience. It is, it is true, labor which is in itself delightful, and one might easily do worse than to follow it for itself without thought of other end; but it is still labor, and labor strenuous and long enduring.

It is first necessary, then, to make an endeavor to become interested in whatever it has seemed worthwhile to read. The student should try earnestly to discover wherein others have found it good. Every reader is at liberty to like or to dislike even a masterpiece; but he is not in a position even to have an opinion of it until he appreciates why it has been admired. He must set himself to realize not what is bad in a book, but what is good. The common theory that the critical faculties are best developed by training the mind to detect shortcomings is as vicious as it is false. Any carper can find the faults in a great work; it is only the enlightened who can discover all its merits. It will seldom happen that a sincere effort to appreciate a good book will leave the reader uninterested. If it does, it is generally safe to conclude that the mind is not ready for this particular work. There must be degrees of development; and the same literature is not adapted to all stages.

在这些谈话中，我早些时候曾谈到文学研读的乐趣。选择书籍的一个基本原则便是，阅读不喜欢的书籍劳而无功。除非服务于重要目的或特定信息的需要，人们才会阅读那些缺乏吸引力的书籍。但若要使阅读对自身具有永久价值，享受阅读至关重要。认为阅读不是一种乐趣的观点，是一种荒谬的错误。

学生对文学和对自己的首要责任是相同的——享受文学。要么享受艺术作品的乐趣，要么别碰它。

强迫一个人去关注不喜欢的作品是枉费心机，但阅读被认为是文学名著的书籍却是十分必要的。这是一个看似矛盾的地方，但须记住，激发思想兴趣是可能的。如果能正确接近和理解真正值得关注的书籍，那么它们一定会吸引我们，并使我们持之以恒地去阅读。如果一个人很懒惰，如果他只喜欢文学的棉花糖和巧克力焦糖，就不能仅仅靠文学甜食来喂养他。读什么书就应该享受什么书，但这绝不意味着可以享受的就应该阅读。一个人养成享受美好事物和重要事物的习惯是可以做到的，关键是人们很容易陷入愚蠢的、草率的、漫不经心的境况，因此必须振奋精神。文学阅读必须有训练和目的，热爱艺术精华是天性使然，仅为少数人所拥有，而我们其他人必须为之勤勉笃行。没有人仅用举手之劳就能充分欣赏大师的作品。学习文学的学生的回报是巨大的，但他付出的辛劳也是巨大的。文学不像眼瞎的乞丐也可以随意穿行的、空空如也的公共广场，文学更像是一座中了魔法的城堡，周围魔法滋扰，群山周围的森林食尸鬼出没无常，这是一个须历尽千难万险、奋勇拼搏的骑士才敢涉足的地方，但是这也是一个蕴藏着无穷财富和欢乐的地方，一个超出了愚钝之人想象力的地方。

目前存在一种颇为流行的谬论，认为无须受过特殊教育就可以欣赏艺术。以常人心态看，人们一直坚持认为，读者和诗人一样，是天生的，不是后天造就的。人们通常认为，一个人天生就长着一幅灵敏的哈巴狗鼻子，因此天生就具有艺术鉴赏能力。这一事实唯一真实的基础在于人类的所有能力或因个人因素而改变。一个人天生具有犀利的感知能力，而另一个人则缺乏这些能力，但无论天分如何，都必须通过后天养成。这种养成需要细心、努力和耐心。诚然，努力本身就是令人愉快的事，一个人如不考虑其他结果，不顺其自然，很容易把事情弄糟。但这仍然是一种付出，而且是一种艰辛而持久的付出。

因此，首先必须努力对任何看起来值得一读的东西产生兴趣。学生应该认真尝试去发现其他人认为好的地方。每一个读者都可以随意喜欢或不喜欢一部名著，但在他尚不明白这部作品为什么受到世人赞赏之前，他甚至还无权去发表高谈阔论，他必须意识到的是书中好的地方，而不是书中不好的地方。最好通过训练发现缺陷来培养人的批判性能力，这一通行说法既是错误的，也是虚假的。任何吹毛求疵的人都能在伟大的作品中找到瑕疵，只有那些有见地的人才能发现它的所有价值。认真努力去欣赏一部好书会让读者兴味索然，这样的事情鲜有发生。果真如此的话，通常可以肯定得出这样的结论，也是因为人的大脑还没有为这一特殊的作品做好准备。心智的发展必定程度不一，并且相同的文学并不适用于所有阶段。

If you cannot honestly enjoy a thing you are from one cause or another in no condition to read it. Either the time is not ripe or it has no message for your especial temperament. To force yourself to read what does not please you is like forcing yourself to eat that for which you have no appetite. There may be some nourishment in one case as in the other, but there is far more likely to be indigestion.

An essential condition of profitable reading is that it shall be intelligent. The extent to which some persons can go on reading without having any clear idea of what they read is *stupefyingly* amazing! You may any day talk in society with persons who have gone through exhaustive courses of reading, yet who from them have no more got real ideas than a painted bee would get honey from a painted flower. Fortunately, ordinary mortals are not so bad as this; but is there one of us who is not conscious of having tobogganed down many and many a page without pausing thoroughly to seize and master a single thought by the way?

It is well to make in the mind a sharp distinction between apprehending and comprehending. The difference is that between sighting and bagging your game. To run hastily along through a book, catching sight of the meaning of the author, getting a general notion of what he would convey, —casually apprehending his work, —is one thing; it is quite another to enter fully into the thoughts and emotions embodied, to make them yours by thorough appreciation, —in a word to comprehend. The trouble which Gibbon says he took to get the most out of what he read must strike ordinary readers with amazement: —

> After glancing my eye over the design and order of a new book, I suspended the perusal until I had finished the task of self-examination; till I had resolved in a solitary walk all that I knew or believed or had thought on the subject of the whole work or of some particular chapter; I was then qualified to discern how much the author added to my original stock; and if I was sometimes satisfied by the agreement, I was sometimes armed by the opposition, of our ideas.

It often happens that the average person does not read with sufficient deliberation even to apprehend what is plainly said. If there be a succession of particulars, for instance, it is only the exceptional reader who takes the time to comprehend fully each in turn. Suppose the passage to be the lines in the *"Hymn before Sunrise in the Vale of Chamouni"*: —

> Your strength, your speed, your fury, and your joy,
> Unceasing thunder, and eternal foam.

The ordinary student gets a general and probably a vague impression of cataracts, dashing down from the glacier-heaped hills; and that is the whole of it. A poet does not put in a succession of words like this merely to fill out his line. Coleridge in writing undoubtedly realized the torrent so fully in his imagination that it was as if he were beholding it. "What strength!" was his first thought. "What speed," was the next. "Whatfury; yet, too, what joy!" Then the ideas of that fury and that joy made it seem to him as if the noise of the waters was the voice in which these emotions were embodied, and as if the unceasing thunder were a sentient cry; while the eternal foam was the visible sign of the mighty passions of the "five wild torrents, fiercely glad".

　　如果你不能真正地享受一部作品，那么出于这样或那样的原因，你可能还没有具备阅读它的条件。要么时机不成熟，要么因为你禀赋特殊，这部作品对你没有任何意义。强迫自己阅读不喜欢的东西，就像强迫自己吃没有胃口的食物一样。尽管无论何种情形下，食物都有某些营养，但消化不良的可能性要大得多。

　　有益阅读的一个基本条件是它应该是明智的阅读。有些人可以在不知道自己所读为何的情况下继续阅读的程度令人震惊！任何一天，你可以在社会上与那些经历过详尽阅读课程学习的人交谈，但要从他们那里获得真实想法，就像一只彩绘蜜蜂会从彩绘花朵中吸取蜂蜜一样，好在一般普通人尚不至于这么坏。但是，我们当中有没有一个人没有意识到，已经翻阅了很多很多页书，却没有彻底停顿下来顺便理解并掌握一个观点？

　　有一点可取的是，最好在头脑中明确区分了解（apprehending）和理解（comprehending）。二者的区别就在于：一个只是看一看游戏，另一个是把游戏收入囊中。匆忙地翻阅一本书，了解作者的意思，大致了解他将要传达的内容，随意了解他的作品，是一回事；要完全参透书籍所体现的思想和情感，通过彻底欣赏使它们成为你自己的一部分，这完全又是另外一回事；总之，要领会。吉本曾说，一个读者为了从阅读中获得最大收益，他付出的劳苦一定会让普通读者感到惊讶：

把新书的设计和顺序瞥了一眼，我暂停了细读，直到我完成了自我检查的任务；直到我独自一人散步时，解决了关于整部作品或某个特定章节的所有我所知道、相信或想到的一切；然后我才有资格弄清作者在我原来的储存物中增加了多少；如果我有时会对与我们观点一致的地方感到满意，有时我会对与我们观点相左的地方感到吃惊。

通常情况下，一般人阅读时并没有经过足够的深思熟虑，甚至没能理解清楚书籍中说得一清二楚东西。例如，如果有一连串的细节，只有出类拔萃的读者才会花时间逐一完全理解。假设这是《沙穆里山谷出日前的赞美诗》中的诗句：

> 你的力量，你的速度，你的狂暴和你的喜悦，
> 如雷鸣不息，如飞沫无穷。

普通学生对大瀑布的印象较笼统，甚至可能比较模糊。瀑布从冰川堆积的山丘倾泻而下，然后就是诗的全部了。诗人不会仅仅为了填满他的诗句而使用一连串的词语。毫无疑问，柯勒律治在想象中充分地意识到了这股急流，他仿佛亲眼看见了它。"多么强大的力量！"是他的第一个念头；"多么快的速度！"是下一个；"多么狂暴"，但最后也有"多么快乐！"那种狂暴和那种喜悦的想法让人仿若感到水流的声音就是这些情绪的体现，持续的雷声似有情的呼喊，而不灭的飞沫是"五股狂野的急流，狂暴的喜悦"的强大激情的清晰标志。

In the dirge in "*Cymbeline*", Shakespeare writes: —

> Fear no more the frown o' the great,
> Thou art past the tyrant's stroke;
> Care no more to clothe and eat;
> To thee the reed is as the oak;
> The sceptre, learning, physic, must

All follow this, and come to dust.

As you read, do you comprehend the exquisite propriety of the succession of the ideas? Death has removed Fidele from the possibility of misfortune; even the lords of the world can trouble no longer. Nay, more; it has done away with all need of care for the sordid details of every-day life, food and raiment. All that earth holds is now alike indifferent to the dead; the pale, wind-shaken reed is neither more nor less important than the steadfast and enduring oak. And to this, the thought runs on, must come even the mighty, the sceptred ones of earth. Not learning, which is mightier than temporal power, can save from this; not physic itself, of which the mission is to fight with death, can in the end escape the universal doom.

Hurried over as a catalogue, to take one example more, how dull is the following from Marlowe's " *Jew of Malta*；" but how sumptuous it becomes when the reader gloats over the name of each jewel as would do the Jew who is speaking: —

> The wealthy Moor, that in the eastern rocks
> Without control can pick his riches up,
> And in his house heap pearls like pebble-stones,
> Receive them free, and sell them by the weight
> Bags of fiery opals, sapphires, amethysts,
> Jacinths, hard topaz, grass-green emeralds,
> Beauteous rubies, sparkling diamonds,
> And seld-seen costly stones of so great price
> As one of them indifferently rated,
> And of a carat of this quantity,
> May serve, in peril of calamity,
> To ransom great kings from captivity.

I have not much sympathy with the trick of reading into an author all sorts of far-fetched meanings of which he can never have dreamed; but, as it is only by observing these niceties of language that a writer is able to convey delicate shades of thought and feeling, so it is only by appreciation of them that the reader is able to grasp completely the intention which lies wrapped in the verbal form.

在《辛白林》的挽歌中，莎士比亚写道：

> 不再畏惧权贵的威力，
> 暴君也对你无可奈何，
> 不再为衣食而忧虑，
> 芦苇和橡树一样结果，
> 王侯学者，千行百业，
> 一切必定化为尘埃，无法逃脱。

（朱生豪　译）

当你阅读时，是否理解这一系列思绪的精妙恰当之处？死亡使费德勒幸免于所有不幸的可能性；就算是天下君王，也不能再打扰他了；不，还有更多；死亡消除了对日常生活、食物和衣物惨淡细节的所有忧虑。尘世所拥有的一切现在对死者而言都无关紧要了；苍白的、被风摇晃过的芦苇并不比坚定而恒久的橡树重要。对此，思绪继续前进，甚至地球上强大的、拥有权杖的人也必须来到。比时间更伟大的学问也不可能幸免；就连肩负与死亡抗争使命的医术本身，最终也不能逃脱普遍的厄运。

再举一个例子，马洛的《马耳他的犹太人》中的以下内容匆匆一览是多么乏味！但是读者向每一颗宝石的名字投以爱慕的眼光时，便会像说话的那个犹太人一样感到，这一切已极尽富丽奢华：

> 富有的摩尔人，在东部的岩石中
> 不受控制可以获得他的财富，
> 在他的屋子里堆放的珍珠像鹅卵石，
> 免费领取，按重量出售
> 一袋袋火红的猫眼石、蓝宝石、紫水晶，

风信子石，硬黄玉，草绿色的祖母绿，

美丽的红宝石，闪闪发光的钻石，

还有售卖的昂贵宝石

其中之一，价格任定，

一克拉的这个量，

在灾难的危险中，可以用来

赎回被囚禁的伟大君王。

　　我不太赞同给作家附加意义的那种解读技巧，有的意思过于牵强附会，可能就连作家本人做梦也想不到。但是，由于作者只有通过观察语言的这些细微之处，才能传达出微妙的思想和情感，因此读者也只有通过欣赏那些微妙之处，才能完全领会围裹在言语形式里的意图。

To read intelligibly, it is often necessary to know something of the conditions under which a thing was written. There are allusions to the history of the time or to contemporary events which would be meaningless to one ignorant of the world in which the author lived. To see any point to the fiery and misplaced passage in "*Lycidas*" in which Milton denounces the hireling priesthood and the ecclesiastic evils of his day, one must understand something of theological politics. We are aided in the comprehension of certain passages in the plays of Shakespeare by familiarity with the conditions of the Elizabethan stage and of the court intrigues. In so far it is sometimes an advantage to know the personal history of a writer, and the political and social details of his time. For the most part the portions which require elaborate explanation are not of permanent interest or at least not of great importance. The intelligent reader, however, will not wish to be tripped up by passages which he cannot understand, and will therefore be likely to inform himself at least sufficiently to clear up these.

Any reader, moreover, must to some extent know the life and customs of the people among whom a work is produced. To one who failed to appreciate wherein the daily existence of the ancient Greeks differed from that of moderns, Homer would hardly be intelligible. It would be idle to read Dante under the impression that the Italy of his time was that of to-day; or to undertake Chaucer without knowing, at least in a general way, how his England was other than that of our own time. The force of language at a given epoch, the allusions to contemporary events, the habits of thought and custom must be understood by him who would read comprehendingly.

When all is said there will still remain much that must depend upon individual experience. If one reads in Lowell: —

> And there the fount rises;...
> No dew-drop is stiller
> In its lupin-leaf setting
> Than this water moss-bounded;

One cannot have a clear and lively idea of what is meant who has not actually seen a furry lupin-leaf, held up like a green, hairy hand, with its dew-drop, round as a pearl. The context, of course, gives a general impression of what the poet intended, but unless experience has given the reader this bit of nature-lore, the color and vitality of the passage are greatly lessened. One of the priceless advantages to be gained from a habit of careful reading is the consciousness of the significance of small things, and in consequence the habit of observing them carefully. When we have read the bit just quoted, for instance, we are sure to perceive the beauty of the lupin-leaf with its dew-pearl if it come in our way. The attention becomes acute, and that which would otherwise pass unregarded becomes a source of pleasure. The most sure way to enrich life is to learn to appreciate trifles.

　　为了清楚明白地阅读，通常需要了解书写一件事的前提，如当时的历史或当代事件的暗示，尽管那些事件对不了解作者生活世界的人来说毫无意义。要了解弥尔顿谴责雇佣神职人员和他那个时代邪恶教会的《利西达斯》，人们不得不了解一些神学政治。熟悉伊丽莎白时代舞台和宫廷阴谋，有助于我们理解莎士比亚戏剧中的某些段落。到目前为止，了解一个作家的个人历史以及他那个时代的政治和社会细节有时是一大优势。在最大程度上，需要详细解释的部分并不代表永久兴趣，或者至少不是很重要。然而，明智的读者不希望被无法理解的段落绊倒，因此可能至少需要充分激励自己以扫清这些障碍。

此外，任何读者都必须在一定程度上了解创作作品的作家的生活和习俗。对于没有意识到古希腊人的日常生活与现代人的日常生活有何不同的人来说，荷马的作品是难以理解的。如果以为但丁那个时代的意大利就是今天的意大利，那么阅读但丁的作品将是枉费心机。或者在不知道，至少在一般意义上，乔叟时代的英格兰与我们时代的英格兰不同的情况下接受乔叟的作品也将是徒劳无功的。一个特定时代的语言力量、对当代事件的暗示、思维和风俗习惯，这些都是读者真正读懂作品必须理解的。

话虽如此，仍有许多理解必须取决于个人经验。如果有人在洛厄尔诗歌中读到：

> 那里的泉源涌动；……
> 露珠不再安静
> 在鲁冰花叶
> 比苔藓环绕的水安静；

如果读者没有真正见过毛茸茸的鲁冰花叶，像一只举起的绿色毛茸茸的手，带着像珍珠一样圆润的露珠，就无法清楚而生动地理解这几行诗的含义。当然，语境可以给出诗人意图的一般印象，但除非经验给读者一点自然知识，否则诗的色彩和活力会大打折扣。仔细阅读的习惯所带来的最为珍贵的好处之一便是，意识到小事的重要性，从而养成仔细观察的习惯。例如，当我们阅读刚刚引用的那几行诗句时，如此景正好近在咫尺，我们一定会感受到带着露珠的鲁冰花叶的美丽。注意力变得敏锐，就会成为快乐的源泉，否则一切都会被疏忽。丰富生活最可靠的方法就是去学会欣赏小事。

There is a word of warning which should here be spoken to the overconscientious student. The desire of doing well may lead to overdoing. The student, in his anxiety to accomplish his full duty by separate words, often lets himself become absorbed in them. He drops unconsciously from the study of literature into the study of philology. There have been hundreds of painfully learned men who have employed the whole of their misguided lives in encumbering noble books with philological excrescences. I do not wish to speak disrespectfully of the indefatigable clan characterized by Cowper as:

> Philologists, who chase
> A panting syllable through time and space;
> Start it at home, and hunt it in the dark,
> To Gaul, to Greece and into Noah's ark.

These gentlemen are extremely useful in their way and place; but the study of philology is not the study of literature. It is at best one of its humble bond-slaves. A philologist may be minutely acquainted with every twig in the family-tree of each obsolete word in the entire range of Elizabethan literature, and yet be as darkly and as completely ignorant of that glorious world of poetry as the stokers in an ocean steamer are of the beauty of the sunset seen from the deck. It is often necessary to know the derivation of a term, and perhaps something of its history, in order to appreciate its force in a particular usage; but to go through a book merely to pick out examples for philologic research is like picking to pieces a mosaic to examine the separate bits of glass.

While, moreover, attention to the force and value of details is insisted upon, it must never be forgotten that the whole is of more value than any or all of its parts. The reader must strive to receive the effect of a book not only bit by bit, and page by page, and chapter by chapter, but as a book. There should be in the mind a complete and ample conception of it as a unit. It is not enough to appreciate the best passages individually. The work is not ours until it exists in the mind as a beautiful whole, as single and unbroken as one of those Japanese crystal globes which look like spheres of living water. He who knows the worth and beauty of passages is like an explorer. He is neither a conqueror nor a ruler of the territory he has seen until it is his in its entirety.

I believe that to comparatively few readers does it occur to make deliberate and conscious effort to realize works as wholes. The impression which a book leaves in the thought is of course in some sense a result of what the book is as a unit; but this is seldom sharply clear and vivid. The greatest works naturally give the most complete impression, and the power of producing an effect as a whole is one of the tests of art. The writer of genius is able so to choose what is significant, and so to arrange his material that the appreciative reader cannot fail to receive some one grand and dominating impression. It is hardly possible, for instance, for any intelligent person to fail to feel the cumulative passion of "*King Lear*". The calamities which come upon the old man connect themselves in the mind of the reader so closely with one central idea that it is rather difficult to escape from the dominant idea than difficult to find it. In "*Hamlet*", on the other hand, it is by no means easy to gain any complete and adequate grasp of the play as a unit without careful and intimate study. It is, moreover, not sure that one has gained a full conception of a work as a whole because one has an impression even so strong as that which must come to any receptive reader of "*King Lear*" or "*Othello*". To be profoundly touched by the story is possible without so fully holding the tragedy comprehendingly in the mind that its poignant meaning kindles the whole imagination. We have not assimilated that from which we have received merely fragmentary impressions. The appreciative reading of a really great book is a profound emotional experience. Individual portions and notable passages are at best but as incidents of which the real significance is to be perceived only in the light of the whole.

有一句告诫的话在这里应该说给过分谨慎的学生听。想要做好一件事情的愿望可能会导致做事过头。学生在急于用单独的词语完成他的全部任务时，常会使自己专注于单个的词，进而不知不觉地从学习文学蜕变成了学习语文。有成百上千的饱学之士穷其一生都在用语言学的赘述妨碍高贵的文学书籍，但我不希望对以考珀为典型代表的不知疲倦的家族有所不敬。

> 语言学家追逐
> 一个穿越时空的喘息音节；
> 在家里开始，在黑暗中猎杀它，
> 追到高卢，追到希腊，再进入诺亚方舟。

　　这些先生们在他们的处事方式和位置上都可堪大用，但是语言学的研究不是文学的研读。语言学充其量只是文学卑微的奴隶之一。一位语言学家可能对整个伊丽莎白时代文学中的每个过时词语的族谱中的每一根枝条都极尽熟悉，但对那个辉煌的诗歌世界却一无所知，这就好比远洋轮船中的司炉工一样，对从甲板上看到的日落之美漠然视之。通常需要了解一个术语的派生，也许还需要了解一些关于它的历史，以便了解这个词在特定用法中的作用。但是通览一本书只是为了挑选语言学研究的例子，这就好比把马赛克拼在一起来检查玻璃的碎片。

　　此外，尽管我们强调关注细节的影响和价值，但绝不能忘记整体比任何或所有部分都更有价值。读者必须努力获得一本书的效果，不仅是一点一点，一页一页，一章一章，而是一整本书。在头脑中应该有一个完整而充实的概念，将它作为一个单元。分别欣赏最精华的段落是不够的，除非它作为一个美丽的整体存在于我们的脑海中，否则它还是不属于我们的作品，就像那些看起来像活水球体的日本水晶球一样单一和完整。知道段落的价值和美感的人就像一个探险家，在他所看到的领地完整属于他之前，他既不是征服者也不是统治者。

　　我相信，能够谨慎地、有意识地、努力从整体认识作品的人相对很少。在某种意义上说，一本书在思想中留下的印象当然是其作为一个单元的结果，但这一印象罕有清晰和生动。最伟大的作品自然给人最完整的印象，创造出整体效果的能力是对艺术的考验之一。具有天赋的作家能够选择重要的东西，并因此编排素材，从而使具有欣赏能力的读者不能不接受某种宏大且占据支配地位的印象。例如，任何聪明的人都几乎不可能没有感受到《李尔王》中积蓄起来的激情。老人一身遭受的厄运在读者的脑海中与一个中心思想紧密相连，以至要摆脱这一占主导地位的思想比发现它更困难。另一方面，在《哈姆雷特》中，如果没有仔细和深入的研读，欲将戏剧作为一个单元来获得一个完整和充分的把握绝非易事。进一步来说，一个人所拥有的印象甚至极其强烈，也无法确定他是否获得了作品作为整体的完整概念，任何一个接受《李尔王》或《奥赛罗》的读者一定有同样强烈的印象，被故事深深打动是可能的，但这离不开对悲剧的心领神会，也离不开其深刻的寓意点燃我们整个想象。我们从那些尚未理解的东西中仅仅能获得一些支离破碎的印象，因此欣赏一本真正伟大的书籍是一种深刻的情感体验，个别部分和值得注意的段落充其量只是作为一段小插曲，其真正意义只有比照整体才能充分理解。

The power of grasping a work of art as a unit is one which should be deliberately cultivated. It is hardly likely to come unsought, even to the most imaginative. It must rest, in the first place, upon a reading of books as a whole. Whatever in any serious sense is worth reading once is worth rereading indefinitely. It is idle to hope to grasp a thing as a whole until one has become familiar with its parts. When once the details are clear in the mind, it is possible to read with a distinct and deliberate sense of the share that each passage bears in the entire purpose. It is necessary, and I may add that it is enchanting, to reread until the detached points gather themselves together in the inner consciousness as molecules in a solution gather themselves into a crystal. The delight of being able to realize what an author had in mind as a whole is like that of the traveler who at last, after long days of baffling mists which allowed but broken glimpses here and there, sees before him the whole of some noble mountain, stripped clean of clouds, standing sublime between earth and heaven.

Whatever effect a book has must depend largely upon the sympathy between the reader and the author. To read sympathetically is as fundamental a condition of good reading as is to read intelligently. It is well known how impossible it is to talk with a person who is unresponsive, who will not yield his own mood, and who does not share another's point of view. On the other hand, we have all tried to listen to speakers with whom it was not in our power to find ourselves in accord, and the result was merely unprofitable weariness. For the time being the reader must give himself up to the mood of the writer; he must follow his guidance, and receive not only his words but his suggestions with fullest acquiescence of perception, whatever be the differences of judgment. What Hawthorne has said of painting is equally applicable to literature: —

A picture, however admirable the painter's art, and wonderful his power, requires of the spectator a surrender of himself, in due proportion with the miracle which has been wrought. Let the canvas glow as it may, you must look with the eye of faith, or its highest excellence escapes you. There is always the necessity of helping out the painter's art with your own resources of sensibility and imagination. Not that these qualities shall really add anything to what the master has effected; but they must be put so entirely under his control and work along with him to such an extent that, in a different mood, when you are cold and critical instead of sympathetic, you will be apt to fancy that the loftier merits of the picture were of your own dreaming, not of his creating. Like all revelations of the better life, the adequate perception of a great work demands a gifted simplicity of vision. —*Marble Faun*, xxxvii

把一件艺术品作为一个整体单元来把握的能力是一种应该刻意培养的能力。即使是最有想象力的人，也不太可能不去寻求这种能力。首先，这种能力的培养必须依赖于对书籍的整体阅读。任何严肃意义上的东西都值得阅读一次，也值得不定期的重读。在熟悉一本书的各个部分之前，希望把一本书作为一个整体来把握是徒然的。一旦细节在脑海中变得清晰，就能清楚而从容地阅读每段文字了，由此文字在整个目的中所占的份额也变得清楚起来。重读直到分割的各个点在内心意识中聚集在一起，就像溶液中的分子聚集成晶体一样，这是必要的，而且可以补充地说，这也是很迷人的。能够认识到作者的整体想法是一件令人愉快的事，就像在漫长的令人迷惑的重重迷雾中，只能断断续续瞥见一些光影的旅行者，终于欣喜地看见了没有一丝云彩的天空下，一整座雄伟的高山屹立于天地之间。

　　一本书的效果如何，很大程度上取决于读者和作者之间的共鸣。带着一颗同理心去阅读和睿智的阅读一样，是良好阅读的基本条件。众所周知，与一个反应迟钝、不会屈服于自己情绪、不能分享作者观点的人交谈是不可能的。另一方面，我们试图倾听那些我们尚无能力与之意见一致的演讲者，但结果只是无益的倦怠。目前，读者暂时还必须全身心专注于作者的情绪，必须遵循他的引导，不仅要接受他的话，还要接受他的建议。无论与作者的判断有什么不同，都要在认识上给予作者最充分的默许。霍桑关于绘画的论断同样适用于文学：

　　　　无论画家的艺术多么令人钦佩，他的力量多么惊人，一幅画都需要观众在与所创造的奇迹相称的情况下臣服。让画布尽可能发出光，你必须用信任的眼光去注视，否则你就抓不住它最卓越的品质。总是有必要用自己的感性和想象力来襄助画家的艺术。并不是说这些品质真的会给大师的创造增加任何东西，但这些品质必须完全置于大师的控制之下，并与他一起工作到这样的程度，以至在不同的心情下，当你冷漠和挑剔而不是同情时，你很容易幻想这幅画的崇高价值就是你自己的梦想，而不是他的创造。像所有对美好生活的启示一样，充分感知伟大作品需要具有天赋的简单而纯朴的视觉。

　　　　　　　　　　　　　　　　　　——《大理石牧神》第三十七

Often it is difficult to find any meaning in what is written unless the reader has entered into the spirit in which it was composed. I seriously doubt, for instance, whether the ordinary person, coming upon the following catch of satyrs, by Ben Jonson, is able to find it much above the level of the melodies of *Mother Goose*： —

　　　"*Buz*," quoth the blue fly,
　　　"*Hum*," quoth the bee;
　　　Buz and *hum* they cry,

And so do we.
In his ear, in his nose,
Thus, do you see?
He ate the dormouse;
Else it was he.

If you are not able to make much out of this, listen to what Leigh Hunt says of it: —

It is impossible that anything could better express than this, either the wild and practical joking of the satyrs, or the action of the thing described, or the quaintness and fitness of the images, or the melody and even harmony, the intercourse, of the musical words, one with another. None but a boon companion, with a very musical ear, could have written it. —A Jar of Honey

If the reader has the key to the mood in which this catch is written, if he has given himself up to the sportive spirit in which "rare old Ben" conceived it, it is possible to find in it the merit which Hunt points out; but without thus giving ourselves up to the leadership of the poet it is hardly possible to make of it anything at all. The example is of course somewhat extreme, but the principle is universal.

It is always well in a first reading to give one's self up to the sweep of the work; to go forward without bothering over slight errors or small details. Notes are not for the first or the second perusal so much as for the third and so on to the hundredth. Dr. Johnson is right when he says: —

Notes are often necessary, but they are necessary evils. Let him that is yet unacquainted with the powers of Shakespeare, and who desires to feel the highest pleasures that the drama can give, read every play from the first scene to the last, with utter negligence of all his commentators. When his fancy is once on the wing, let it not stoop to correction or explanation.

One of the great obstacles to the enjoyment of any art is the too conscientious desire to enjoy. We are constantly hindered by the conventional responsibility to experience over each classic the proper emotion. The student is often so occupied in painful struggles to feel that which he has been told to feel that he remains utterly cold and unmoved. It is like going to some historic locality of noble suggestion, where an officious guide moves the visitor from one precious spot to another, saying in effect, "Here such an event happened. Now thrill. Sixpence a thrill, please."

通常很难在所写的内容中找到任何意义，除非读者已经融入创造作品的那种精神境界。譬如，我严重怀疑，一般读者在读到本·琼森创作的抓色狼的诗句时，是否能发现它远远高于《鹅妈妈》的曲调的水平：

> "嗡嗡，"蓝蝇说，
> "嗡嗡，"蜜蜂道。
> 嗡嗡声，他们哭泣，
> 我们也是。
> 在他的耳朵里，在他的鼻子里，
> 这样，你看到了吗？
> 他吃了睡鼠；
> 否则就是他。

如果你不能从中获益，听听李·亨特是如何评论这首诗：

> 没有什么比这首诗更能表达的了，或是色狼狂放不羁纯粹的笑料，或是所描述事物的动作，或是意象的离奇有趣而恰到好处，或是乐词的旋律，甚至和声、交汇，一个接一个。只有具有音乐欣赏能力又情投意合的朋友才能写出这首歌。——《一罐蜂蜜》

如果读者掌握了创作这首轮唱的心情的关键，如果他全身心专注"稀罕的老本"构思这首诗的嬉戏态度，就有可能在其中找到李·亨特指出的优点，但是，如果不这样把自己置于诗人的统御之下，几乎不可能明白任何东西。这个例子当然有些极端，但其原理是普遍的。

在第一次阅读时，全身心地投入初览作品中总是好的，然后再继续前行而不会为轻微的错误或小细节而烦恼。第一次或第二次阅读并不适合做笔记，而第三次阅读时笔记便比较适合，以此类推。约翰逊博士说得在理：

> 笔记通常是必要的，但它们也有必然的弊端。让那些还不了解莎士比亚的能力，并希望感受戏剧所能带来最高乐趣的人，从第一幕到最后一幕阅读每一部戏剧，完全忽略所有评论者。当他的幻想一旦飞翔起来时，不要让它屈就于修正或解释。

享受任何一种艺术的最大障碍之一是耽于享受的欲望。我们经常被传统的责任所阻碍，去体验每一部经典的正确情感。学生经常沉浸在痛苦的挣扎中，要去感受他被告知要感觉到的东西，但他依旧冷若冰霜和无动于衷。这就像去一个具有崇高意义的历史地点。在那里，过于殷勤的导游带领游客参观一个个珍贵的场所。导游煞有介事地说，"这里发生了这样的事件。现在是激动人心的时刻了，请付费六便士。"

For myself, being of a somewhat contumacious character, I have never been able to thrill to order, even if a shilling instead of sixpence were the price of the luxury; and in the same way I am unable to follow out a prescribed set of emotions at the command of a text-book on literature. Perhaps my temperament has made me unjustly skeptical, but I have never been able to have much faith in the genuineness of feelings carried on at the ordering of an emotional programme. The student should let himself go. On the first reading, at least, let what will happen so you are swept along in full enjoyment. It is better to read with delight and misunderstand, than to plod forward in wise stupidity, understanding all and comprehending nothing; gaining the letter and failing utterly to achieve the spirit. The letter may be attended to at any time; make sure first of the spirit. I do not mean that one is to read carelessly; but I do mean that one is to read enthusiastically, joyously, and, if it be possible, even passionately.

The best test of the completeness with which one has entered into the heart of a book is just this keenness of enjoyment. Fully to share the mood of the author is to share something of the delight of creation. It is as if in the mind of the reader this work of beauty and of immortal significance was springing into being. This enjoyment, moreover, increases with familiarity. If you find that you do not care to take up again a masterpiece because you have read it once, you may pretty safely conclude that you have never truly read it at all. You have been over it, it may be, and gratified some superficial curiosity; but you have never got to its heart. Does one claim to be won to the heart of a friend and yet to be willing never to see that friend more?

One may, of course, outgrow even a masterpiece. There are authors who are genuine so far as they go, who may be enjoyed at one stage of growth, yet who as the student advances become insufficient and unattractive. The man who does not outgrow is not growing. One does not healthily tire of a real book, however, until he has become greater than that book. The interest which becomes weary of a masterpiece is more than half curiosity, and at best is no more than intellectual. It is not imaginative. Margaret Fuller confessed that she tired of everything she read, even of Shakespeare. She thereby unconsciously discovered the quality of mind which prevented her from being a great woman instead of merely a brilliant one. She fed her intellect upon literature; but she failed because literature does not reach to its highest function unless its appeal to the intellect is the means of touching and arousing the imagination; because the end of all art is not the mind but the emotions.

就我自己而言，作为一个性格有点桀骜不驯的人，即使奢侈品的价格是一先令而不是六便士，我也从来没有激动得要去购买什么东西。同样，我无法按照文学教科书的命令来遵循规定的情绪。也许是我的性情让我多疑，但我一直无法相信安排煽情节目获得的情感的真实性。

应该放手让学生阅读，至少在第一次阅读时，让会发生的事情使他们陶醉其中，充分享受阅读之乐。了解一切，却仍一无所知，与其在明智的愚蠢中笨拙地摸索前进，不如带着喜悦，甚至带着误读去阅读，获得了字面意义，却完全没精神上的收获。字面意思任何时候都可以处理，但务必确保理解其精神第一。我的意思并不是说，一个人就可以粗心大意地去阅读，我的意思是，一个人应该积极地、快乐地阅读，如果可能的话，甚至是热情地阅读。

一个人参透一本书的核心是否完整，最好的检验就是这种享受的敏锐度。充分分享作者的情感就是分享创作的乐趣。这就好比让这部美丽而具有不朽意义的作品，浮现在读者的脑海中。此外，这种享受会随着熟悉程度而增加。如果你发现因读过一次而不想再拿起一本名著，肯定可以得出这样的结论，你从来没有真正读过它。你曾经非常喜爱这本书，并满足了一些肤浅的好奇心，但你从来没有深入到它的核心。是否有人声称自己赢得了朋友的心，却又不愿意再见那个朋友一面？

当然，随着成长，一个人也会不再喜欢某一部名著了。就某些作家而言，他们是真诚的，在人的成长的某个阶段可能会很受人喜爱，但随着学生年龄增长，他们会变得不那么吸引人，变得欠缺了。没有长大的人就没有成长，然而，直到一个人变得比那本书更伟大之前，他不会非常厌倦一本真正的书。对杰作的兴趣变得乏味，也胜过一半的好奇心，充其量不过是读者的兴趣变得更理智了，已不再富有想象力了。玛格丽特·富勒承认她厌倦所读的一切，甚至是莎士比亚的作品。从而，她不知不觉地发现了使她仅能成为一个才华横溢的女性，而无法成为伟大女性的心理品质。她用文学滋养了智慧，但是她失败了，因为除非文学对智力的吸引力成为一种触动和激发想象力的手段，才能实现其最高功能。所有艺术的终点不是理智而是情感。

It may seem that enough has already been required to make reading the most serious of undertakings; yet there is still one requirement more which is of the utmost importance. He is unworthy to share the delights of great work who is not able to respect it; he has no right to meddle with the best of literature who is not prepared to approach it with some reverence. In the greatest books the master minds of the race have graciously bidden their fellows into their high company. The honor should be treated according to its worth. Irreverence is the deformity of a diseased mind. The man who cannot revere what is noble is innately degraded. When writers of genius have given us their best thoughts, their deepest imaginings, their noblest emotions, it is for us to receive them with bared heads. He is greatly to be pitied who, in reading high imaginative work, has never been conscious of a sense of being in a fine and noble presence, of having been admitted into a place which should not be profaned. Only that soul is great which can appreciate greatness. Remember that there is no surer measure of what you are than the extent to which you are able to rise to the heights of supreme books; the extent to which you are able to comprehend, to delight in, and to revere, the masterpieces of literature.

　　似乎已有足够多的要求使阅读成为一项最严肃的职责。然而，这里还有一项最为关键的要求：不尊重伟大作品的人，不配分享伟大作品的愉悦；无法心甘情愿以某种崇敬态度对待最优秀文学作品的人，也无权染指文学。在最伟大的书籍中，人类的大师们慷慨地邀请他们的同胞与崇高的文学为伴。荣誉应该根据其价值来对待，不敬是病态心灵的畸形表现，不能敬畏高尚之物的人，天生就堕落了。当天才作家给了我们最好的思想、最深刻的想象、最崇高的情感的时候，我们应该坦诚地接受。非常可惜，在阅读富有想象力的作品时，一个人从来没有意识到有一种高贵的存在感，也没能意识到他被允许进入了一个不应被玷污的地方。只有灵魂伟大的人，才能欣赏伟大。谨记，没有什么比至高无上的书籍更能衡量你是一个什么样的人了。你能够在多大程度上理解、欣赏和崇敬一部文学作品决定了你可能达到的高度。

VII
THE LANGUAGE OF LITERATURE

Whatever intelligence man imparts to man, at least all beyond the crudest rudimentary beginnings, must be conveyed by conventions. There must have been an agreement, tacit or explicit, that a certain sign shall stand for a certain idea; and when that idea is to be expressed, this sign must be used. In order that the meaning of any communication may be understood, it is essential that the means of expression be appreciated by hearer as well as by speaker. We have agreed that in English a given sound shall represent a given idea; and to one who knows this tongue the specified sound, either spoken or suggested by letters, calls that idea up. To one unacquainted with English, the sound is meaningless, because he is not a party to the agreement which has fixed for it a conventional significance; or it may awake in his thought an idea entirely different, because he belongs to a nation where tacit agreement has fixed upon another meaning. The word "dot", for instance, has by English-speaking folk been appropriated to the notion of a trifling point or mark; while those who speak French, writing and pronouncing the word in the same way, take it to indicate a "dowry". In order to communicate with any man, it is necessary to know what is the set of conventions with which he is accustomed to convey and to receive ideas.

The principle holds also in art. There is a conventional language in sound or color or form as there is in words. It is broader as a rule, because oftener founded upon general human characteristics, because more directly and obviously borrowed from nature, and because not so warped and distorted by those concessions to utility which have modified the common tongues of men. Indeed, it might at first thought seem that the language of art is universal, but a little reflection will show that this is not the case. The sculpture of the Aztecs, for instance, is in an art language utterly different from that of the sculpture of the Greeks. If you recall the elaborately intricate uncouthness of the gods of old Yucatan, you will easily appreciate that the artists who shaped these did not employ the same artistic conventions as did the sculptors who breathed life into the Venus of Melos, or who embodied divine serenity and beauty in the Elgin marbles. To the Greeks those twisted and thick-lipped Aztec deities, clutching one another by their crests of plumes, or grasping rudely at one another's arms, would have conveyed no sentiment of beauty or of reverence; while it is equally to be supposed that the Aztec would have remained hardly moved before the wonders of Greek sculpture. The Hellenic art conventions, it is true, were more directly founded upon nature, and therefore more readily understood; but even this would not have overcome the fact that one nation had one art language and the other another. Those of you who were at the Columbian Exposition will remember how the music in the Midway Plaisance illustrated this same point. The weird strain of one or another savage or barbaric folk came to the ear with a strangeness which showed how ignorant we are of the language of the music of these dwellers in far lands. To us it was bizarre or moving, but we could form little idea how it struck the hearers to whom it was native and familiar. It was even all but impossible to know whether a given strain was felt by the savage performers to be grave or gay. Of all the varieties of sound which there surprised the ear, that evolved by the Chinese appeared most harsh and unmelodious. The almond-eyed Celestial seemed to delight in a concatenation of crash and caterwauling, mingled in one cacophony at which the nerves tingled and the hair stood on end. Yet it is on record that when in the early days of European intercourse with China, the French missionary Amiot played airs by Rossini and Boieldieu to a Chinese mandarin of intelligence and of cultivation according to eastern standards, the Oriental shook his head disapprovingly. He politely expressed his thanks for the entertainment, but when pressed to give an opinion of the music he was forced to reply, "It is sadly devoid of meaning and expression, while Chinese music penetrates the soul." After we have smiled at the absurdity, from our point of view, of the penetration of the soul by Chinese music, we reflect that after all our music is probably as absurd to them as theirs to us. We perhaps recall the fact that even the cultivated Japanese, with their sensitive feeling for art, and their readiness to adopt occidental customs, complain of the effect of dividing music into regular bars, and making it, as they say, "*chip-chop*, *chip-chop*, *chip-chop*.*" The fact is that every civilization makes its art language as it makes its word language; and he who would understand the message must understand the conventions by which it is expressed.

第七讲　文学语言

　　人类获得的智慧至少超越了最原始的开端，但都必须通过惯例来表达。必须有一个默契或明确的约定，即某个符号代表某个意思。当要表达这个意思时，必须使用这个符号。为了能够理解任何交流的含义，必须使听者和说话的人都能理解这一表达方式。我们已经公认，在英语中一个特定的声音代表一个特定的意思。对于知道这种语言的人来说，特定的声音，无论是说出来的还是由字母暗示的，都可以唤起这个意思。对于不熟悉英语的人来说，这个声音是没有意义的，因为他不是约定俗成意义的协议的一方，或者它可能会在他的思维中唤醒一个完全不同的意思，因为他属于一个默契已经固定在另一种含义上的国家。"点"（dot）这个词，例如，已被说英语的人照搬来表示微不足道的一点或标记的概念，而那些说法语的人，以同样的方式书写和拼读这个词时，用它来表示"嫁妆"（dowry）的意思。为了与任何人交流，有必要知道他所遵循的用来传递和接受意义的一套惯例。

　　在艺术里，这个原则也同样适用。就像在文字中一样，声音或颜色或形式上也存在一种约定俗成的语言。在艺术领域，这一原则适用性更为广泛，因为艺术语言通常建立在人类普遍特征的基础上，更直接、更明显地借用于自然，并且因为这一原则没有屈从于使用而遭曲解和歪曲。的确，乍一看似乎艺术语言是通用的，但稍加思考就会发现事实并非如此。例如，阿兹特克人的雕塑使用的艺术语言与希腊人在雕塑中使用的语言决然不同。如果你回忆起精心设计的古尤卡坦诸神的粗犷，你会很容易意识到，塑造这些神像的艺术家与为梅洛斯的维纳斯注入生命的雕塑家均有所不同，它们缺少希腊艺术家在埃尔金大理石上体现的美感和圣洁的宁静。对希腊人来说，那些扭曲而嘴唇厚厚的、紧紧抓住对方羽冠，或者粗鲁地抓住对方手臂的阿兹特克神祇，并没有传达出任何美感或崇敬之情。而同样可以假设，在希腊雕塑的奇迹面前，阿兹特克人也几乎不会为之动容。确实，希腊艺术惯例更直接地建立在自然之上，因而更容易理解。但即使这样也无法克服一个国家拥有一种艺术语言而另一国家则拥有另一种艺术语言的事实。你们当中曾参观过哥伦比亚博览会的人会记得，大道乐园的音乐是如何揭示了这一相同事实。一个或另一个原始或蒙昧的民族怪异的情调以一种陌生的方式进入耳朵，这表明我们对这些远方居民的音乐语言是多么无知。对我们来说，它很奇特或很感动人，但我们不知道，那种音乐是如何能够打动了那些熟悉它的听众，甚至几乎不可能知道原始的表演者是否认为特定的旋律是严肃的还是欢快的。在各种令人耳目一新的声音中，由中国人创造的声音显得最为粗糙和不和谐。杏眼的天国人似乎对一连串的撞击声和尖叫声感到高兴，这种音乐混杂在一种嘈杂声中，使人头疼，毛骨悚然。但据记载，在欧洲与中国交往的初期，法国传教士阿米奥特向一位富有素养的中国官员演奏了罗西尼和布耶迪厄的音乐，但这位东方人不以为然地摇了摇头，礼貌地表达了对款待的感谢，但当被要求发表关于音乐的看法时，他勉强道："遗憾的是，它缺乏意义和表达，而中国音乐穿透灵魂"。我们对中国音乐能穿透灵魂一说置于一笑，从我们的角度来反思，毕竟我们的音乐对中国人来说可能和他们的音乐一样荒唐。我们也许还记得这样一个事实，即使是那些有教养的、对艺术很敏感的以及愿意接受西方习俗的日本人，也会抱怨将音乐分成常规小节的效果，就像他们说的那样，"切碎，切碎，切碎"。事实上，每一个文明都在创造自己的艺术语言，就像创造自己的文字语言一样，要理解信息的人必须了解表达信息的惯例。

We are apt to forget this fact of the conventionality of all languages. We become so accustomed both to the speech of ordinary intercourse and to that of familiar art, that we inevitably come to regard them as natural and almost universal. No language, however, is natural, unless it be fair to apply that word to the most primitive signs of savages. It is an arbitrary thing, and as such it must be learned. We acquire the ordinary tongue of our race almost unconsciously, and while we are too young to reason about it. We gain the language of art later and more deliberately, although of course we may owe much to our early surroundings in this as in every other respect. The point to be kept in mind is that we do learn it; that it is not the gift of nature. This is of course true of all art; but here our concern is only with the fact that literature has as truly its own peculiar language as music or painting or sculpture, —its language, that is, distinct from the language of ordinary daily or common speech.

The conventions which serve efficiently to convey ordinary ideas and matter-of-fact statements, are not sufficient for the expression of emotions. The man who has to tell the price of pigs and potatoes, the amount of coal consumed in a locomotive engine, or the effect of political complications upon the stock-market, is able to serve himself sufficiently well with ordinary language. The novelist who has to tell of the bewitchingly willful worldliness of Beatrix Esmond, of the fateful and tragic experiences of Donatello and Miriam, the splendidly real impossibilities of the career of D'Artagnan and his three friends, the passion of Richard Feverel for Lucy; the dramatist who endeavors to make his readers share the emotions of Lear and Cordelia, of Caliban and Desdemona, of Viola and Juliet; the poet who would picture the emotions of Pompilia, of Lancelot and Guinevere, of Porphyrio and Madeline, of Prometheus and Asia, —all these require a special language.

我们很容易忘记所有语言都具有规约性这一事实。我们对日常交往的言语和熟悉的艺术言语都已习以为常了，不可避免地认为它们是自然的，几乎也是普遍的。然而，没有一种语言是自然的，除非将这个词语同样应用于野蛮人的最原始的符号。这是一件主观臆断的事情，因此必须学习不同的语言。我们几乎在不知不觉中获得了我们种族的通用语言，而我们还太年轻，无法对此进行推论。后来我们更煞费苦心地获得了艺术语言，当然，在这方面和其他方面一样，我们可能在很大程度上把艺术语言的获得归功于早期所处的环境。要记住一点，我们确实是通过学习获得了这一语言，而不是大自然的恩赐。这当然适用于所有艺术。但在这里，我们只在乎这样一个事实，即文学确实拥有自己独特的语言，就像音乐、绘画或雕塑一样——也就是说，它的语言是区别于日常或普通语言的语言。

能够有效传达一般意义和一般陈述的语言惯例并不足以表达情感。一个人须说出猪肉和土豆的价格，机车发动机消耗的煤量或政治复杂形势对股票市场的影响，他使用一般语言就足以满足需求了。然而，小说家必须用文学语言讲述比阿特丽克斯·埃斯蒙德令人着迷的、任性的世俗生活，多纳泰罗和米里亚姆的命运和悲惨经历，达尔大尼央和他的三个朋友的职业生涯中极其真实的不可能，理查德·费弗勒对露西的热情；戏剧家则需要努力让他的读者分享李尔和科迪莉亚、卡利班和苔丝狄蒙娜、维奥拉和朱丽叶的情感；诗人则要去描绘蓬皮利亚、兰斯洛特和吉纳维尔、蒲飞里奥以及玛德琳的情感，还有普罗米修斯和亚细亚的情感，——所有这些都需要一种特殊的语言。

The conveying from mind to mind of emotion is a delicate task. It is not difficult to make a man understand the price of oysters, but endeavor to share with a fellow-being the secrets of a moment of transcendent feeling, and you have an undertaking so complex, and so all but impossible, that if you can perfectly succeed in it you may justly call yourself the first writer of your age. This is the making of the intangible tangible; the highest creative act of the imagination. The cleverness and the skill of man have been exhausted in devising means to impart to readers the thought and feeling, the passion and emotion, which sway the hearts of mankind. It is not necessary here to go into those devices which belong especially to the domain of rhetoric, —the mechanics of style. They are designated in the old-fashioned text-books by tongue-twisting Greek names which most of us have learned, and which all of us have forgotten. It is not with them that I am here concerned. They are meant to affect the reader unconsciously. It is with those matters which appeal to the conscious understanding that we have now to do; the conventions which are the language of literature as Latin was the language of Casar or Greek the tongue of Pericles.

I have spoken already of the necessity of understanding what is said in literature; this is, however, by no means the whole of the matter. It is of even greater importance to be clearly aware of what is implied. We test the imaginative quality of what is written by its power of suggestion. The writer who has imagination will have so much to say that he is forced to make a phrase call up a whole train of thought, a word brings vividly to the mind of the reader a picture or a history. This is what critics mean when they speak of the marvelous condensation of Shakespeare; and in either prose or verse the criterion of imaginative writing is whether it is suggestive. Imagination is the realizing faculty. It is the power of receiving as true the ideal. It is the accepting as actual that which is conjured up by the inner vision; the making vital, palpitant, and present that which is known to be materially but a dream. That which is written when the poet sees the unseen palpably before his inner eye is so filled with the vitality and actuality of his vision that it fills the mind of the reader as a tenth wave floods and overflows a hollow in the rocks of the shore. When Keats says of the song of *the nightingale* that it is

> The same that oft-times hath
> Charm'd magic casements, opening on the foam
> Of perilous seas in faery lands forlorn,

All the romance and witchery of faery-lore are in this single phrase. The reader feels the glow of delight, the fascination of old tales which have pleased mankind from the childhood of the race. Into two lines the poet has condensed the fragrance of a thousand flowers of folk-lore.

In the best literature what is said directly is often of less importance than what is meant but not said. In dealing with imaginative writers, it is necessary to keep always in mind the fact that the literal meaning is but a part, and often not the greater part. The implied, the indirect, is apt to be that for the sake of which the work is written.

理解情感在心灵之间的传递是一项十分棘手的任务。让一个人了解牡蛎的价格并不算难，但要努力与人分享一瞬间超然感觉的秘密，你要做的事就变得非常复杂了，甚至几乎不可能完成。如果你能在这方面完全成功，便可自称为是你这个时代的第一作家。这是无形变有形之道，是最高想象力的创造性行为。为了设法向读者传达主宰人类心灵的思想和感觉、激情和情感，人类的聪明才智已消耗殆尽。这里没有必要专门考察那些属于修辞领域——风格手法的技巧。在老式教科书中，我们大多数人都学过修辞手法，但可能已忘记了那些聱牙戟口的希腊名字指定的内容。我在这里担心的不是这些方法，因为它们会有目的地对读者施加无意识的影响。正如拉丁语是恺撒的语言，希腊语是伯里克利的语言，我们现在必须做的正是那些需要付诸意识去理解的事情，即文学语言的惯例。

我谈过理解文学作品所表达内容的必要性，然而，这绝不是事情的全部内容。清楚地意识到隐含的内容更加重要。我们要借助暗示的力量来检验所写内容的想象性特征。有想象力的作家被迫要用一个短语唤起整个思路，去表达很多要说的话，或用一个词在读者脑海中呈现一幅生动的画面或历史。这就是评论家在谈论莎士比亚的奇妙而凝练的表达时所指的意思。无论是散文还是诗歌，富有想象力的写作标准就是看它是否具有暗示性。想象力是实现暗示的一种能力，这是接受真正理想的力量。想象力旨在把内在幻觉虚构的东西作为真实的东西来接受，使人们知道在物质上只是一个梦想的东西能变得生机勃勃，令人心跳，并跃然纸上。当诗人在他内心的眼睛面前清晰地看到了看不见的东西时，他所写的东西就会变得充满活力和真实，它可以溢满读者的心灵，就像第十波潮水从海岸岩石中的空洞中溢出。济慈谈及《夜莺之歌》时写道：

> 就是这声音常常
> 在失掉了的仙域里引动窗扉：
> 一个美女望着大海险恶的浪花。

（查良铮　译）

仙侠传说的所有浪漫和巫术都化作为一句诗词。读者会感受到喜悦的光芒和古老传说的魅力。这些传说从人类的童年时代就给人类带来了无尽的喜悦，诗人将民间传说的千花万香浓缩成了两行诗句。

在最好的文学作品里，直接说出来的意思往往不如没有说出来的暗含意义重要。在与富有想象力的作家打交道时，有必要始终牢记这样一个事实，即字面意义只是一部分，通常不是大部分，而隐含的、间接的意义很容易成为作品的创作缘由。

In its earlier stages all language is largely made up of comparisons. The fact that every tongue is full of fossil similes has been constantly commented upon, and this fact serves to illustrate how greatly the force of a word may be diminished if its original meaning is lost sight of. If, in ordinary conversation, to take a common illustration, some old-fashioned body now speaks of a clergyman as a "pastor," it is to be feared that the word connotes little, unless it be a suspicion of rustic seediness in apparel, a certain provincial narrowness, and perhaps a conventional piety. When the word was still in its prime, it carried with it the force of its derivation; it spoke eloquently of one who ministered spiritual food to his followers, as a shepherd ministers to his flock. A pastor may now be as good as a pastor was then, but the title has ceased to do him justice. The freshness and force of words get worn off in time, as does by much use the sharpness of outline of a coin. We need constantly to guard against this tendency of language. We speak commonly enough in casual conversation of "a sardonic smile," but the idea

119

conveyed is no more than that of a forced and heartless grin. As far back as the days of Homer, some imaginative man compared the artificial and sinister smile of a cynic to the distortions and convulsions produced by a poisonous herb in Sardinia; and from its very persistence we may fancy how forcible and striking was the comparison in its freshness. Of course, modern writers do not necessarily keep in mind the derivation of every word and phrase which they employ; but they do at least use terms with so much care for propriety and exactness that it is impossible to seize the whole of their meaning, unless we appreciate the niceties of their language. Ruskin says rightly: —

> You must get yourself into the habit of looking intensely at words, and assuring yourself of their meaning, syllable by syllable, letter by letter.... You might read all the books in the British Museum (if you could live long enough), and remain an utterly " illiterate", uneducated person; but if you read ten pages of a good book, letter by letter, —that is to say, with real accuracy, —you are forevermore in some measure an educated person. —*Of Kings' Treasuries*

Unless our attention has been especially called to the fact, there are few of us who at all realize how carelessly it is possible to read. We begin in the nursery to let words pass without attaching to them any idea which is really clear. We nourish our infant imaginations upon *Mother Goose*, and are content to go all our days in ignorance even of the meaning of a good many of the words so fondly familiar in pinafore days. We are all acquainted with the true and thrilling tale how

> Thomas T. Tattamus took two tees
> To tie two tups up to two tall trees.

But how many of us know what either a "tee" or a "tup" is? We have all been stirred in our susceptible youth by the rhyme wherein is recounted the exciting adventure of the four and twenty tailors who set forth to slay a snail, but who retreated in precipitate confusion when

She put out her horns like a little Kyloe cow;

But it is to be feared that the proportion of us is not large who have taken the trouble to ascertain what a Kyloe cow is. Or take the well-worn ditty:　—

Cross-patch,
Draw the latch,
Sit by the fire and spin.

Have you ever stopped to reflect that "draw the latch" means to pull in the latch-string, and that in the days of homely general hospitality to which this contrivance belonged the image presented by the verse was that of a misanthropic hag, shutting herself off from her neighbors and sulking viciously by her fire behind a door rudely insulting the caller with the empty hole of the latch-string?

　　在早期阶段，所有语言主要是通过比较构成的。世人一直在评论一个事实，即每一种语言都充满了僵化的明喻。这一事实有助于说明，如果一个词的原始含义消失了，这个词的影响力就会被大大削弱。在日常谈话中，可以用一个常见的例子来说明，如现在某些老式的机构称"牧师"（clergyman）为"牧师"（pastor），除非这个单词用于质疑有的人服饰肮脏、土气、迂腐狭隘，或许传统而虔诚，但恐怕它隐含意义很少。当这个词还处于鼎盛时期时，它就具有派生力量，讲述了一个生动的故事，表示一个人能像牧羊人精心照料羊群一样，为他的追随者提供精神食物。现在的牧师可能和那时的牧师一样好，但他已经配不上这个称谓了。文字的新鲜感和力量会随着时间消逝，就如同很多时候硬币使用太多，其轮廓边缘的锐度也会减少。我们应时常提防语言的这一倾向。我们在漫不经心的谈话中经常说"讪笑"一词，但传达的意思不过是一种勉强而薄情的笑容。早在荷马时代，一位富有想象力的人就把愤世嫉俗者的虚伪和邪恶的笑比作撒丁岛的一种毒草所产生的扭曲和抽搐。从它的持久性来看，我们可以想象它的新鲜度是多么富有说服力和惹人注目。当然，现代作家不一定会记住使用的每个单词和短语的派生词。但他们至少在使用术语时非常关注语言的适当性和准确性，除非我们能鉴别出他们语言的精妙之处，我们不可能掌握其全部含义。拉斯金所言极是：

> 你必须让自己养成细致观察单词的习惯，并确定它们的意思，一个音节一个音节地，一个字母一个字母地……你可能会读完大英博物馆的所有藏书（如果你能活得足够长的话），但仍然是一个十足的"文盲"、没有受过教育的人。但是，如果你逐字逐句地阅读一本好书中的十页——也就是说，准确无误地——从某种意义上说，你将永远是一个受过教育的人。
>
> ——《国王的国库》

除非我们特别关注这一事实，否则我们中很少有人能意识到，自己阅读时有多么马虎大意。我们从幼儿园开始，就会在没有附加任何真正清晰意义的情况下，一眼掠过阅读的文字。我们从《鹅妈妈》的儿歌里滋养了我们幼时的想象力，我们整天满足于快乐时光，却对许多甚至在围裙时代如此熟悉的词的含义一无所知。我们都知道那个真实而激动人心的故事：

> 托马斯·T. 塔塔莫斯拿来两个球座
> 把两只公羊绑在两棵高大的树上。

但是我们中有多少人知道"tee"或"tup"是什么？在我们敏感的青年时代，我们都曾被一首诗所震撼，诗中叙述了二十四位裁缝激动人心的冒险故事，他们出发去杀死一只蜗牛，但突如其来的混乱使他们退缩了：

> 她像一头小基洛爱牛一样伸出她的角；

　　只怕是，我们当中能不厌其烦地查明什么是基洛爱牛的人所占的比例并不大。或者拿老掉牙的小曲：

> 缝缝补丁，
> 插上门栓，
> 火炉旁，纺织忙；

　　你有没有停下来想过，"插上门栓"意味着"拉门闩弦"。这个发明物属于热情好客的年代，这节诗文所表现的形象是一个厌世的女巫，把自己关起来远离她的邻居，并在门后面的火旁凶狠地生气，并透过门弦上的洞粗鲁地侮辱来访者。

Perhaps this seems trifling; and it may easily be insisted that these rhymes become familiar to us while we are still too young to think of the exact meaning of anything. The question then is whether we do better when we are older. We are accustomed, very likely, to hearing in common speech the phrase "pay through the nose." Do you know what that means, or that it goes back to the days of the Druids? When you hear the phrase "where the shoe pinches" do you recall Plutarch's story? Does the anecdote of St. Ambrose come to mind when the saying is "At Rome do as the Romans do"? It happens every few years that the newspapers are full of more or less excited talk about a "gerrymander." Does the word bring before the inner eye that uncouth monster wherewith the caricaturist of his day vexed the soul of Governor Gerry? I have tried to select examples which are not remote from the talk of every day. It seems to me that these illustrate well enough how apt we are to accept words and phrases as we accept a silver dollar, with very little idea of the intrinsic worth of what we are getting. This may be made to do well enough in practical buying and selling, but it is eminently unsatisfactory in matters intellectual or æsthetic. In the study of literature approximations are apt to be pretty nearly worthless.

The most obvious characteristic in literary language is that of allusion.

Constantly does the reader of imaginative works encounter allusions to the Bible, to mythology, to history, to folk-lore, and to literature itself. To comprehend an author it is needful to realize fully what he had in mind when using these. They are the symbols of thoughts and feelings which are not to be expressed in ordinary ways. When we are familiar with the matter alluded to we see by the sudden and vivid light which is cast over the page by the comparison or the suggestion how expressive and comprehensive this form of language may be. To the reader who is ignorant the allusion is of course a stumbling-block and a rock of offense. It is like a sentence in an unknown tongue, which not only conceals its meaning but gives one an irritated sense of being shut out of the author's counsels.

也许这些看起来都是些鸡毛蒜皮的小事，但人们轻易就会断言，这些押韵诗在我们还太年轻而无法思考任何事物的确切含义时，我们就已经如数家珍了。那么问题是，我们长大后是否会做得更胜一筹？我们很可能习惯于在普通的演讲中听到"被勒索"这个词语，但你知道这意味着什么？或者它可以追溯到德鲁伊时代？当你听到"困难所在"这句话时，你会想起普鲁塔克的故事？人们用俗话说"入乡随俗"时，你是否会想到圣安布罗斯的轶事？每隔几年，报纸上就会充斥着或多或少激动人心的关于"操纵"的讨论。这个词是否让那个用漫画激怒格里州长的粗野怪物呈现在我们心眼里？我试图选择与日常话题相去不远的例子，于我而言，这些词语很好地说明了，我们是多么容易就接纳了单词和短语，就如同我们接受一枚银圆，但却很少知道得到的东西的内在价值。这在实际买卖中可以做得足够好，但在智力或审美方面却做得明显不尽人意。在文学研读中，知其一不知其二的做法几乎毫无价值。

文学语言最明显的特征是典故。阅读想象性作品时，读者经常会遇到《圣经》、神话、历史、民间传说和文学本身的典故。要理解一个作家，需要充分了解他在使用这些内容时心里的想法。典故是思想和感情的象征，无法用一般的语言表达。每当我们熟悉所暗示的事物时，仿佛耀眼的光倏忽而来，照亮了书的页面，通过比较或暗示，可以发现，这些语言形式包罗万象、意味深长。对于无知的读者来说，这些典故当然就成了绊脚石或跌人的磐石。就如一种未知的语言里一句话，它不仅隐藏了意思，而且给人一种因被排斥在作者忠告外面而被激怒的感觉。

It is probable that in English literature the allusions to the Bible are more numerous than any other. We shall have occasion later to speak of the place and influence of the King James version upon the literature of our tongue, and here we have to do only with those cases in which a scriptural reference is made part of the special language of an author. Again and again it happens that a writer takes advantage of the associations which cluster about a phrase or an incident of the Bible, and by a simple touch brings up in the mind of the understanding reader all the sentiments connected with the original.

With many of the more common of these phrases it is impossible for anyone who associates with educated persons not to be familiar. They have become part and parcel of the common speech of the time. We speak of the "widow's mite", of a "Judas' kiss", of "the flesh-pots of Egypt", of "a still, small voice", of a "Jehu", a "perfect Babel", a "Nimrod", of "bread upon the waters", and of a "Delilah". The phrases have to a considerable extent acquired their own meaning, so that even one who is not familiar with the scriptures is not likely to have difficulty in getting from them a general idea. To the reader who is acquainted with the force and origin of these terms, however, they have a vigor and significance which for others they must lack.

Prose and poetry are alike full of scriptural phraseology. In short, for the understanding of the language of allusion in English literature a knowledge of the English Bible is neither more nor less than essential.

在英国文学中，取自《圣经》的典故很可能比来自其他任何书籍的都多。稍后，我们将有机会讨论钦定版的地位和对我们的语言文学的影响，这里我们只讨论那些将经文引用作为作者特殊语言的部分情况。作家频频利用汇集在《圣经》中的短语或事件的联想，通过简单的手法，在善于理解的读者脑海中呈现出与原著相关的所有情感。

一个人与受过教育的人交往时，须尽量熟悉一些更常见的短语。有些词语已成为那个时代共同言谈的重要组成部分。我们常说起"绵薄之力""犹大的吻""奢侈的生活""良心的呼唤""马夫""不可收拾的混乱局面""好猎手""行善"和"不忠实的女人"。这些短语在相当大的程度上已经获得了它们自己的意义，因此即便是不熟悉圣经的人也不难从中获得一个大致的意思。然而，如果一个读者熟悉这些词语的感染力和起源，这些词语便具有了活力和意义，而对其他人来说必定缺乏这一层意思。

散文和诗歌都充满了圣经用语。简而言之，对于理解英语文学中的典故语言，英语圣经的知识几乎不可或缺。

Another class of allusions frequent in literature is the mythological. Here also we find phrases which have passed so completely into every-day currency that we hear and use them almost without reflecting upon their origin. "Scylla and Charybdis" "dark as Erebus" "hydra-headed" and "Pandora's box" are familiar examples. We speak of "a herculean task" without in the least calling to mind the labors of Hercules, and employ the phrase "the thread of life" without seeming to see the three grisly Fates, spinning in the chill gray dusk of their cave. We have gone so far as to condense a whole legend into a single word, and then to ignore the story. We say "lethean" "mercurial" "aurora" and "bacchanalian" without recalling their real significance. It is obvious how a perception of the original meaning of these terms must impart vividness to their use or to their understanding. There are innumerable instances, more particular, in which it is essential to know the force of a reference to old myths, lest the finer meaning of the author be altogether missed. In *The Wind-Harp* Lowell wrote: —

> I treasure in secret some long, fine hair
> Of tenderest brown....

I twisted this magic in gossamer strings
Over a wind-harp's Delphian hollow.

In the phrase "a wind-harp's Delphian hollow" the poet has suggested all the mysterious and fateful utterances of the abyss from which the Delphic priestess sucked up prophecies, and he has prepared the comprehending reader for the oracular murmur which swells from the instrument upon which have been stretched chordstwisted from the hair of the dead loved one. To miss this suggestion is to lose a vital part of the poem. When Keats writes of "valley-lilies whiter still than Leda's love", unless there come instantly to the mind the image of the snowy swan whose form Jove took to win Leda, the phrase means nothing. The woeful cry in *Antony and Cleopatra*.

The shirt of Nessus is upon me; teach me,
Alcides, thou mine ancestor, thy rage,

It is full of keen-edged horror when one recalls the garment poisoned with his own blood by which the centaur avenged himself on Hercules. In a flash it brings up the picture of the demigod tearing his flesh in more than mortal agony, and calling to Philoctetes to light the funeral pyre that he might be consumed alive. It is not needful to multiply examples since they so frequently present themselves to the reader. The only point to be made is that here we have another well-defined division of literary language.

　　文学中常见的另一类型典故是神话。在这里，我们还发现了一些短语已经完全进入了日常通用语，以至我们听到和使用它们时几乎没有考虑它们的起源。"左右为难""像地狱般黑暗""多头的"和"潘多拉的盒子"都是耳熟能详的例子。我们谈到"一项艰巨的任务"时，不可能丝毫想不起赫拉克勒斯的辛勤劳动；而使用"生命之线"这个词时，却似乎没有看到三个可怕的命运，在洞穴寒冷的灰色黄昏中旋转。我们甚至将整个传说浓缩为一个词，然后忽略了这个故事。我们说"忘河的""反复无常的""晨曦"和"狂欢作乐的"，却有可能想不起它们的真正含义。很明显，对这些词语原始含义的认识，必定使其应用或理解变得更加生动有趣。可以找到无数类似的例子，但还有更特别的是，其中有必要了解引用古老神话产生的力量，以免完全错过作者更精妙的含义。洛厄尔在《风琴》中写道：

> 我偷偷地珍惜一些长而细的头发
> 是最温柔的棕色……
> 我用游丝串起这个魔法
> 放在风琴的德尔菲空洞之上。

用"德尔菲空洞"一语时，诗人暗指德尔菲女祭司从深渊中所有神秘而致命的话语中汲取预言，诗人为读者理解准备了从乐器中涌出的神谕低语，那是从死者所爱之人的头发上拧出来并拉长的和弦。错过这个暗示便失去了这首诗的一个重要部分。当济慈写到"比丽达的爱情还要洁白的百合花"时，除非立刻想起雪天鹅是朱庇特为赢得丽达的爱化身成的天鹅这一形象，否则这句话毫无意义。还有《安东尼与克利奥帕特拉》中悲惨的哭声：

> 涅索斯的衬衫在我身上；教我，
> 阿尔西德斯，你我的祖先，你的愤怒。

当读者回忆起半人半马神用那件沾有自己毒血的衣服向赫拉克勒斯复仇时，会感到那哭声令人不寒而栗。倏然间，一副画面浮现在人们脑海中，半神半人在极度痛苦中撕裂自己的肉体，并呼唤菲罗克忒忒斯点燃火葬柴堆，他可能会被烈火活活吞噬。没有必要增加更多例子，因为它们经常呈现在读者面前。唯一要指出的是，这里我们已对文学语言有了另一个清晰的界定。

Allusion to history is another characteristic form of the language of literature. References to classic story are perhaps more common than those to general or modern, but both are plentiful. Sometimes the form is that of a familiar phrase, as "a Cadmean victory" "a Procrustean bed" "a crusade" "a Waterloo" and so on. Phrases like these are easily understood, although it is hardly possible to get their full effect without a knowledge of their origin. What, however, would this passage in Gray's "*Elegy*" convey to one unfamiliar with English history? —

> Some village Hampden, that with dauntless breast
> The little tyrant of his fields withstood;
> Some mute, inglorious Milton here may rest;
> Some Cromwell, guiltless of his country's blood.

It is necessary to know about the majestic figure of ivory and gold which the Athenian sculptor wrought, or one misses the meaning of Emerson's couplet, —

> Not from a vain or shallow thought
> His awful Jove young Phidias brought.

Shakespeare abounds in examples of this use of allusions to history to produce a clear or vivid impression of some emotion or thought.

> I will make a Star-chamber matter of it.
> —*Merry Wives* , i. 1.
> Though Nestor swear the jest be laughable.
> —*Merchant of Venice* , i. 1.
> Even such a man, so faint, so spiritless,
> So dull, so dead in look, so woe-begone,
> Drew Priam's curtain in the dead of night,
> And would have told him half his Troy was burnt.
> —*2 Henry IV.* , i. 1.

The reader must know something about the Star-chamber, of the gravity and wisdom of Nestor, of the circumstances of the tragic destruction of Troy, or these passages can have little meaning for him.

Sometimes references of this class are less evident, as where Byron speaks of—

The starry Galileo with his woes;

Or where Poe finely compresses the whole splendid story of antiquity into a couple of lines: —

To the glory that was Greece
And the grandeur that was Rome.

If we have in mind the varied and inspiring story of Greece and Rome, these lines unroll before us like a matchless panorama. We linger over them to let the imagination realize the full richness of their suggestion. The heart beats more quickly, and we find ourselves murmuring over and over to ourselves with a kindling sense of warmth and glow: —

To the glory that was Greece
And the grandeur that was Rome.

Poe affords an excellent example of this device of historical allusion carried to its extreme. In *The Fall of the House of Usher*, there is a stanza which reads: —

Wanderers in that happy valley
Through two luminous windows saw
Spirits moving musically
To a lute's well-tunèd law,
Round about a throne, where sitting
(Porphyrogene!)
In state his glory well-befitting,
The ruler of the realm was seen.

If the reader chance to know that in the great palace of Constantine the Great at Constantinople there was a building of red porphyry, which by special decree was made sacred to motherhood, and that here the princes of the blood were born, being in recognition called "porphyrogene," there will come to him the vision which Poe desired to evoke. The word will suggest the regal splendors of the Byzantine court at a time when the whole world babbled of its glories, and will give to the verse a richness of atmosphere which could hardly be produced by any piling up of specific details. The reader who is not in possession of this information can only stumble over the word as I did in my youth, with an aggrieved feeling of being shut out from the innermysteries of the poem. I spoke of this as an extreme instance of the use of this form of literary language, because the knowledge needed to render it intelligible is more unusual and special than that generally appealed to by writers. It is one of those bold strokes which are tremendously effective when they succeed, but which are likely to fail with the ordinary reader.

对历史事件的引用是文学语言的另一种具有特色的形式。对经典故事的引用可能比对一般或现代故事的引用更常见，但两者都十分丰富。有时这种形式是一个熟悉的短语，如"惨胜""强求一律""运动""惨败"等。像这样的短语浅显易懂，但如不知道它们的起源，就很难明白其整体效果。然而，格雷的《墓地挽歌》中的这段话会向不熟悉英国历史的人传达什么？

> 也许有乡村汉普顿在这里埋身，
> 反抗过当地小霸王，胆大，坚决；
> 也许有缄口的弥尔顿，从没有名声，
> 有一位克伦威尔，并不曾害国家流血。

（卞之琳　译）

有必要了解一下雅典雕刻家所创作的象牙和黄金的雄伟形象，否则就会错过艾默生下面这一对句的含义：

> 不是来自徒劳或肤浅的想法
> 他带来了可怕的朱庇特年轻的菲迪亚斯。

莎士比亚的戏剧中有很多这样的例子，它们利用历史典故来使某些情感或思想产生的印象变得清晰和生动。

> 我一定要把这案子闹到"星室"去。
> ——《温莎的风流妇人》，第一幕，第一场
> 即使涅斯托发誓说那笑话很可笑。
> ——《威尼斯商人》，第一幕，第一场
> 正是这样一个人，这样没精打采，
> 这样垂头丧气，这样脸如死灰，
> 这样满心忧伤，在沉寂的深宵揭开普里阿摩斯的帐子，
> 想要告诉他他的半个特洛亚已经烧去。
> ——《亨利四世》（第二部），第一幕，第一场
> （朱生豪　译）

读者必须了解星室、涅斯托的严肃和智慧、特洛伊惨遭毁灭的情形，否则这些段落对他来说意义甚微。

有时类似的引用并不十分清晰，如拜伦所说：

> 满天星斗的带着悲伤的伽利略；

或者如爱伦·坡一样将整个辉煌壮丽的古代故事凝练成两行诗句：

> 致敬希腊的辉煌荣光，
> 致敬罗马的宏伟壮丽。

如果在我们心中想到的是希腊和罗马多姿多彩和鼓舞人心的故事，

这些诗句就像无与伦比的全景一样在我们面前展开。我们流连于这些历史画卷，让想象力充分体现暗示的丰富性。心脏跳得更快，我们不知不觉带着一种热情燃放的感觉一遍又一遍地低声吟诵：

> 致敬希腊的辉煌荣光，
> 致敬罗马的宏伟壮丽。

坡为这种将历史典故发挥到极致的手段提供了一个典范，在《厄舍府的倒塌》中，有一节写道：

> 漫游在欢乐之谷
> 探看两扇明亮的窗户，
> 仙女轻歌曼舞，
> 琴瑟悠悠。
> 她们绕着王位旋转，
> 思想之君荣光万丈，
> 如坐云端，
> 威仪而有帝王风范。

（曹明伦 译）

如果读者恰逢知道，在君士坦丁堡君士坦丁大帝的宫殿中有一座红色斑岩建筑，它是根据特别法令为纪念母亲修建的，并且这里出生的拥有帝王血统的王子，被称为"贵胄"。在这里，读者便会看到坡想要唤起的幻景。这个词将暗示，整个世界都在鼓噪拜占庭辉煌的时候，拜占庭宫廷拥有的富丽堂皇，同时，这一词语将为诗歌营造出一种浓郁的氛围，这是任何具体细节的堆积都难以产生的氛围。离开这些信息，读者只能像我年轻时那样，跌倒在这个词面前，而且还会生出一种被诗的内在奥秘拒之门外的委屈感。这是一个使用这种文学语言的极端例子，因为使其易于理解所需的知识比作家通常所诉求的知识更为异乎寻常和独特。这是那些成功了的卓有成效的浓墨重彩的一笔，但对于一般读者来说，他可能无法领会其中的精妙之处。

After historic allusion comes that to folk-lore, which used to be a good deal appealed to by imaginative writers. Some knowledge of old beliefs is often essential to the comprehension of earlier authors. Suckling, for instance, says very charmingly: —

But oh, she dances such a way!
No sun upon an Easter day
Is half so fine a sight!

The reference, of course, is to the superstition that the sun on Easter morning danced for joy at the coming of the day when the Lord arose. To get the force of the passage, it is necessary to put one's self into the mood of those who believed this pretty legend. In the same way it is only to one who is acquainted with the myth of the lubber fiend, the spirit who did the work of the farm at night for the wage of a bowl of cream set for him beside the kitchen fire, that there is meaning in the lines in *"L'Allegro"*: —

Tells how the grudging goblin sweat
To earn his cream-bowl duly set,
When in one night, ere glimpse of morn,
His shadowy flail hath thresh'd the corn
That ten day-laborers could not end;
And, stretch'd out all the chimney's length,
Basks at the fire his hairy strength;
And crop-full out of doors he flings,
Ere the first cock his matin rings.

There is much of this folk-lore language in Shakespeare, and in our own time Browning has perhaps more of it than any other prominent author. It may be remarked in passing, that Browning, who loved odd books and read a good many strange old works which are not within general reach, is more difficult in this matter of allusion than any other contemporary. References of this class are generally a trouble to the ordinary reader, and especially are young students likely to be unable to understand them readily.

在历史典故之后是民间传说，其数量甚多，富有想象力的作者常常用它们来吸引读者。了解一些旧时信仰的知识对于理解早期作者十分必要。例如，约翰·萨克林非常迷人地说：

> 但是哦，她舞步翩翩！
> 太阳在复活节的那一天
> 美景也折了一半！

当然，这里暗示的是一种迷信，即复活节早晨，太阳为上帝升起日的到来载歌载舞。要想感悟这段诗文的说服力，就必须将自己置身于相信这个美丽传说的情绪中。同样地，只有熟悉笨汉精灵传说的人——一个精灵为了得到放在炉火旁的一碗奶酪作为酬劳，夜里拼命干农活——才会在《欢乐颂》中的诗行里找到意义：

> 又说那个做苦工的精灵流汗干活，
> 怎样为了赚得一碗人家赏给他的奶酪，
> 他在夜里，赶在曙光闪现之前，
> 在阴影中用连枷把麦子打完，
> 这抵得过十个白天劳动的人；
> 然后就躺在地上，这笨拙的精灵，
> 伸开身子，就同壁炉一样长，
> 他取暖靠近炉火旁。
> 然后他吃饱了便往门外跑，
> 趁公鸡还未开始早晨叫。

（赵瑞蕻 译）

莎士比亚戏剧中也存在很多类似民间传说的语言，而在我们这个时代，罗伯特·勃朗宁或许比任何其他著名作家都拥有更多民间传说语言。可以顺便说一句，勃朗宁喜欢古怪的书籍并阅读了众多一般无法接触到的奇怪的古老作品，所以勃朗宁比任何当代作家使用的民间传说语言更晦涩难懂。这一类型的暗示对于普通读者来说通常是一个麻烦，尤其是年轻学子可能无法轻易理解。

The last class of allusions, and one which in books written to-day is especially common, is that which calls up passages or characters in literature itself. We speak of a "quixotic deed"; we allude to a thing as to be taken "in a Pickwickian sense"; we have become so accustomed to hearing a married man spoken of as a "Benedick", that we often forget the brisk and gallant bachelor of *Much Ado about Nothing*, and how he was transformed into "Benedick the married man" almost without his own consent. When an author who weighs his words employs allusions of this sort, it is needful toknow the originals well if we hope to get the real intent of what is written. In "*Il Penseroso*", Milton says: —

> Sometimes let gorgeous Tragedy
> In *sceptered* pall come sweeping by,
> Presenting Thebes or Pelops' line,
> Or the tale of Troy divine.

There should pass before the mind of the reader all the fateful story of the ill-starred house of Labdacus: the horrible history of Œdipus, involved in the meshes of destiny; the deadly strife of his sons, and the sublime self-sacrifice of Antigone; all the involved and passionate tragedies of the descendants of Pelops: Agamemnon, the slaughter of Iphigenia, the vengeance of Clytemnestra, the waiting of Electra, the matricide of Orestes and the descent of the Furies upon him; and after this should come to mind the oft-told tale of Troy in all its fullness. Milton was not one to use words inadvertently or without a clear sense of all that they implied. He desired to suggest all the rich and tragic histories which I have hinted at, to move the reader, and to show how stirring and how pregnant tragedy is when dealing with high themes. In two lines he evokes all that is most potent in Grecian poetry. Or again, when Wordsworth speaks of—

The gentle Lady married to the Moor,
And heavenly Una with her milk-white lamb,

It is not enough to glance at a foot-note and discover that the allusion is to Desdemona, and to the first canto of Spenser's *Faerie Queene*. The reader is expected to be so familiar with the poems referred to that the spirit of one and then of the other comes up to him in all its beauty. An allusion of this sort should be like a breath of perfume which suddenly calls up some dear and thrilling memory.

最后一类典故是当今成书中尤为常见的一类典故。这类典故在文学作品里能够使人回想起文学作品中本身的一些段落或人物。我们会说起"不切实际的行为"；暗示某种东西是一个"在匹克威克的意义上"的东西；我们已经习惯于听到一个已婚男人被称为"本尼迪克"，以至我们经常忘记《无事生非》中活泼而殷勤的单身汉，以及他是如何在几乎未经允许的情况下变成了"已婚男人本尼迪克"。一个用词考究的作家会时常使用这一类典故，如果我们希望了解所写内容的真实意图，就需要很好地了解原著。在《沉思颂》中，弥尔顿写道：

有时候，辉煌的悲剧，
壮丽的黄袍在我眼前闪出，
扮演底比斯或佩罗普斯的家史，
或者神圣的特洛伊的故事。

（赵瑞蕻　译）

　　读者的脑海中应该会浮现出拉布达科斯命运多舛之家的所有命运故事：俄狄浦斯卷入可怕的历史和命运之网；他的儿子们致命的冲突，以及安提戈涅崇高的自我牺牲；珀洛普斯后裔的所有卷入者与激情的悲剧，阿伽门农、伊菲革涅亚的屠杀、克吕泰涅斯特拉的复仇、伊莱克特拉的等待、俄瑞斯忒斯的弑母以及复仇女神的降临。在这之后，读者应会想起人们经常传颂的特洛伊的故事的完整内容。弥尔顿不会无缘无故用一个词，或者也不会在没有弄清楚词语含义前就使用某一词语。他希望把我提示的所有丰富内容和悲惨历史都暗示出来，以打动读者，并展现在处理崇高主题时，悲剧多么令人激情澎湃，多么富有想象力！在下面两行诗句中，华兹华斯唤起了希腊诗歌中最有力的一切。或者再一次，当华兹华斯谈道，

> 温柔的女士嫁给了摩尔人，
> 还有神圣的尤娜和她乳白色的羊羔。

　　匆匆看一下脚注，发现这是暗示苔丝狄蒙娜和斯宾塞的《仙后》的第一章，但这仍远远不够。读者应熟悉所有提及的诗，让其中一首诗的精神和另一首诗的精神以完美的形式走向他。这种典故应该像一股香水的气息，能突然唤起一些弥足珍贵而又激动人心的回忆。

Enough has been said to show that the language of literature is a complicated and in some respects a difficult one. Literature in its highest and best sense is of an importance and of a value so great as to justify the assumption that no difficulties of language are too great if needed for the full expression of the message which genius bears to mankind. In other words, the writer who can give to his fellows works which are genuinely imaginative is justified in employing any conventions which will really aid in expression. It is the part of his readers to acquaint themselves with the means which he finds it best to employ; and to be grateful for the gift of the master, whatever the trouble it costs to appreciate and to enter into its spirit. If we are wise, if we have a proper sense of values, we shall find it worth our while to familiarize ourselves with scriptural phrases, with mythology, history, folk-lore, or whatever will aid us in seizing the innermost significance of masterpieces.

It is important, moreover, to know literary language before the moment comes for using it. Information grubbed from foot-notes at the instant of need may be better than continued ignorance, but it is impossible to thrill and tingle over a passage in the middle of which allusions must be looked up in the comments of the editor. It is like feeling one's way through a poem in a foreign tongue when one must use a lexicon for every second word. The feelings cannot carry the reader away if they must bear not only the intangible imagination but a solidly material dictionary. As has been said in a former page, notes should not be allowed to interrupt a first reading. It is often a wise plan to study them beforehand, so as to have their aid at once. It is certainly idle to expect a vivid first impression if one stops continually to look up obscure points; one cannot soar to the stars with foot-notes as a flying-machine.

One danger must here be noted. The student may so fill his mind with concern about the language that he cannot give himself up to the author. The language is for the work, and not the work for the language. The teacher who does not instruct the student in the meaning and value of allusion fails of his mission; but the teacher who makes this the limit, and fails to impress upon the learner the fact that all this is a means to an end, commits a crime. I had rather intrust a youth to an instructor ill-informed in the things of which we have been speaking, and filled with a genuine love and reverence for beauty as far as he could apprehend it, than to a preceptor completely equipped with erudition, and filled with Philistine satisfaction over this knowledge for its own sake. No amount of learning can compensate for a lack of enthusiasm. The object of reading literature is not only to understand it, but to experience it; not only to apprehend it with the intellect, but to comprehend it with the emotions. To understand it is necessary and highly important; but this is not the best thing. When the gods send us gifts, let us not be content with examining the caskets.

　　我所讲的已经足以说明文学语言是一种复杂的语言，而且在某些方面也是一种极其困难的语言。文学在其最崇高和最美好的意义上具有重要意义和价值，可以证明这样一种假设的合理性：如果需要充分表达天才给人类传递的寓意，语言的困难不会太大。换句话说，能够将真正富有想象力的作品提供给他的同胞的作家，有理由使用任何真正有助于表达的惯例。我们应该对大师的恩赐怀有感恩之心，无论欣赏和领悟它的精神要付出多大的代价，读者都有责任去熟悉他认为最好的方法。如果我们有智慧与正确的价值观，我们就会发现值得付出一番心血去熟悉经书的短语、神话、历史、民间传说，或者任何能帮助理解名著内在意义的东西。

　　此外，重要的是，不要到了要使用文学语言的时候再去了解它。在需要的时刻，马上从脚注中获取信息可能比继续视而不见更明智，但有的段落中的典故必须在编辑的评论中去查找，这样便不会令人感到恐惧和头疼。就如同要在外语诗歌中找到感觉，一个人必须每隔一个单词就使用词典。如果读者不仅要承载无形的想象，还要带上一本实实在在厚重的词典，那么这些感受就无法使读者陶醉于阅读文学作品中。正如前面的某一页所说，不应让做笔记干扰初读。事先研读作品通常是一个明智的计划，以便阅读时能得心应手。如果一个人要不断停顿下来查证含糊不清的要点，以此期待一个生动的第一印象必定徒劳无益。一个人不可能像飞行器一样带着脚注去翱翔星空。

　　这里必须注意到一种危险，即学生可能一门心思去关照语言，而无法潜心于研读作家。语言为作品而存在，而不是作品为语言而存在。一个教师没有教会学生去理解典故的意义和价值，他就算不上完成了自己的使命。但是，如果教师以此作为限制，并且没有让学习者明白这一切是达到目的的手段，那就是一大过失了。我宁愿将一个年轻人托付给一位对我们所谈论的事物一无所知，但能对他理解的美妙之处充满真挚的爱和崇敬的导师，也不愿意托付给一个尽管满腹经纶，但只能满足于知识本身的市侩之士。学识再多也弥补不了热情的缺失。阅读文学的目的不仅是理解，更是体验；不仅要用理智去理解它，更要用情感去理解它。理解这一点势在必行且至关重要，但这还不是最完美的。当众神赐礼时，让我们不要仅仅满足于查验礼盒。

VIII
THE INTANGIBLE LANGUAGE

We have spoken of the tangible language of literature; we have now to do with that which is intangible. Open and direct allusion is neither the more important nor the more common form of suggestion. He who has trained himself to recognize references to things historical, mythological, and so on, has not necessarily become fully familiar with literary language. Phrase by phrase, and word by word, literature is a succession of symbols. The aim of the imaginative writer is constantly to excite the reader to an act of creation. He only is a poet who can arouse in the mind a creative imagination. Indeed, one is tempted to indulge here in an impossible paradox, and to say that he only is a poet who can for the time being make his reader a poet also. The object of that which is expressed is to arouse the intellect and the emotions to search for that which is not expressed. The language of allusion is directed to this end, but literature has also its means far more subtle and far more effective.

Suggestion is still the essence of this, but it is suggestion conveyed more delicately and impalpably. Sometimes it is so elusive as almost to seem accidental or even fanciful. The choice of a single word gives to a sentence a character which without it would be entirely wanting; a simple epithet modifies an entire passage. In Lincoln's "*Gettysburg Address*", for instance, after the so concise and forceful statement of all that has brought the assembly together, the speaker declares "that we here highly resolve that these dead shall not have died in vain". The adverb is the last of which an ordinary mind might have thought in this connection, and yet once spoken, it is the one inevitable and supreme word. It lifts the mind at once into an atmosphere elevated and noble. By this single word Lincoln seems to say, "With the dead at our feet, and the future for which they died before us, lifted by the consciousness of all that their death meant, of all that hangs upon the fidelity with which we carry forward the ideals for which they laid down life itself, we ' *highly* resolve that their death shall not have been in vain.' " The phrase is one of the most superb in American literature. It is in itself a trumpet-blast clear and strong. Or take Shakespeare's epithet when he speaks of "death's dateless night." To the appreciative reader this is a word to catch the breath, and to touch one with the horror of that dull darkness where time has ceased; where for the sleeper there is neither end nor beginning, no point distinguished from another; night from which all that makes life has been utterly swept away. "Death's dateless night!"

第八讲　无形的语言

　　我们已经谈到了文学的有形语言，我们现在要讨论无形的语言。公开和直接的暗示既不是非常重要，也不是很常见的暗示形式。一个人刻意训练自己识别历史、神话等事物的暗示，不一定会完全熟悉文学语言。逐句、逐字，文学是一连串的符号。富有想象力的作家的目标是不断激发读者的创造行为。只有诗人才能激发心灵的创造性想象。的确，人们很容易受到诱惑而沉迷于一个不可能的悖论，并宣称他只是一个可以暂时使读者也成为诗人的诗人。文学表达的目的旨在唤起理智和情感去寻找未表达之物。暗示的语言就是针对这个目的，但文学也有它更微妙、更有效的手段。

　　暗示仍然是这件事的本质，但暗示是以一种更微妙、更难以捉摸的方式传递出来的。有时它变幻莫测，几乎看起来是偶然的，甚至是幻想的。选择一个词会给一个句子一种品质，没有它就会完全缺失，一个简单的表述词可以改变整个段落。例如，在林肯的《葛底斯堡演说》中，简洁有力的声明将集会者聚集起来后，演讲者宣布："我们要在这里下定最大的决心，不让这些死者白白牺牲。"副词是一个普通人可能完全想不到的一个词，但只要说出，它就是一个极其令人信服且至高无上的词，与会者的心情一下子就被提升到了一种崇高的境界。林肯用这个词似乎在说："死者就在我们脚下，他们为之牺牲的未来就在前面，他们的牺牲将鼓舞我们去奋斗，我们将忠实地弘扬他们为之献身的理想，我们'坚决认为他们的死不会白费'。"这句话是美国文学中最出色的名言之一，它吹响了嘹亮而坚定的喇叭声。或者拿莎士比亚在谈及"死亡永夜"时的表述词为例，对于有鉴赏力的读者来说，这是一个能让人屏住呼吸的词语，它使时间停止，暗淡黑暗的恐惧触动了每一个人；对于长眠于此的人来说，时光停滞，暗夜使人恐惧，这里没有开始也没有结束，没有任何区别，生命的一切都被黑夜扫光——一切都笼罩在"死亡永夜"之中！

It is told of Keats that in reading Spenser he shouted aloud in delight over the phrase "sea-shouldering whales". The imagination is taken captive by the vigor and vividness of the image of the great monsters shouldering their mighty way through opposing waves as a giant might push his path through a press of armed men, forging onward by sheer force and bulk. The single word says more than pages of ordinary, matter-of-fact description. The reader who cannot appreciate why Keats cried out over this can hardly be said to have begun truly to understand the effect of the epithet in imaginative writing.

Hazlitt cites the lines of Milton: —

> Him followed Rimmon, whose delightful seat
> Was fair Damascus, on the fertile banks
> Of Abbana and Pharphar, lucid streams;

He comments, "The word lucid here gives to the idea all the sparkling effect of the most perfect landscape." In each of the following passages from Shakespeare the single italicized word is in itself sufficient to give distinction: —

Enjoy the*honey-heavy* dew of slumber.

—*Julius Cæsar*, ii. 1.

When love begins to sicken and decay

It useth an *enforcèd* ceremony.

—*Ib.*, iv. 2.

After life's*fitful* fever he sleeps well.

—*Macbeth*, iii. 2.

据说，济慈在读到斯宾塞用的"背海鲸"这个词时，曾兴奋得大呼小叫。巨大的怪物用其强大的鲸背划开水路，就像一个巨人可能要顶着全副武装人员的压力推开一条道路。充满活力和生动的形象征服了人们的想象力，仅仅一个词就可胜过几页平淡无奇、刻板生硬的描写。如果读者不能理解济慈为何为此大喊大叫，那么很难说他已经开始真正理解表述词在想象性写作中的作用。

威廉姆·哈兹利特曾引用弥尔顿的台词：

> 跟着他的是临门，他欢娱的座席
> 在亚巴拿，法珥清澈溪流肥沃的
> 两岸上秀色可餐的大马士革；

（金发燊　译）

他评论说，"这里的'清澈'一词赋予了最完美风景的所有闪光效果。"在莎士比亚的以下每一段中，单个斜体字本身就足以区分：

> 尽情享受甜蜜安稳的睡眠
> 　　　　——《尤利乌斯·恺撒》第二幕，第一场
> 当爱开始生病和腐烂
> 它就用一种强制的礼节。
> 　　　　——《尤利乌斯·恺撒》第四幕，第二场
> 经过人生的一阵热病，他现在睡得好好的。
> 　　　　——《麦克白》第三幕，第二场

（朱生豪　译）

It would lead too far to enter upon the suggestiveness which is the result of skillful use of technical means; but I cannot resist the temptation to call attention to the great effect which may result from a wise repetition of a single word, even if that word is in itself commonplace. I know of nothing else in all literature where so tremendous an effect is produced by simple means as by the use of this device is given in the familiar lines: —

> To-morrow, and to-morrow, and to-morrow,
> Creeps in this petty pace from day to day
> To the last syllable of recorded time.
> —*Macbeth* , v. 5.

The suggestion of heart-sick realization of the following of one day of anguish after another seems to sum up in a moment all the woe of years until it is almost more than can be borne.

In many passages appreciation is all but impossible unless the language of suggestion is comprehended. To a dullard there is little or nothing in the line of Chaucer: —

> Up roos the sonne, and up roos Emelye.

It is constantly as important to read what is not written as what is set down. Lowell remarks of Chaucer, "Sometimes he describes amply by the merest hint, as where the Friar, before setting himself softly down, drives away the cat. We know without need of more words that he has chosen the snuggest corner." The richest passages in literature are precisely those which mean so much that to the careless or the obtuse reader they seem to mean nothing.

The great principle of the need of complete comprehension of which we have spoken before meets us here and everywhere. It is necessary to read with a mind so receptive as almost to be creative: creative, that is, in the sense of being able to evoke before the imagination of the reader those things which have been present to the inner vision of the writer. The comprehension of literary language is above all else the power of translating suggestion into imaginative reality.

When we read, for instance: —

Like waiting nymphs the trees present their fruit;

The line means nothing to us unless we are able with the eye of the mind to see the sentient trees holding out their branches like living arms, tendering their fruits. When Dekker says of patience: —

'Tis the perpetual prisoner's liberty,
His walks and orchards;

We do not hold the poet's meaning unless there has come to us a lively sense of how the wretch condemned to life-long captivity may by patience find in the midst of his durance the same buoyant joy which swells in the heart of one who goes with the free step of a master along his own walks and through his richly fruited orchards.

深入探讨巧妙运用写作技巧所产生的暗示性有时也会过头，因为这些词语的合理重复，可以产生我们简直无法拒绝的巨大效果的诱惑，即便这个词本身早已司空见惯。我从未听说过，在所有文学作品中，简单的方法会产生如此巨大的效果，如同下面熟悉的台词中，这种方法产生的效果可见一斑：

明天，明天，再一个明天，
一天接着一天地蹑步前进，
直到最后一秒钟的时间

——《麦克白》第五幕，第五场

一天接一天的痛苦使人苦恼不叠，暗示性的语言似乎瞬间就把多年让人不堪忍受的苦痛一一道尽。

在许多段落中，除非了解暗示性的语言，否则欣赏几乎是不可能的。对于一个笨蛋来说，乔叟的这一行诗句很少或根本没有意义：

太阳升起来了，埃梅利也起床了。

阅读未写出的内容与阅读已写在纸页上的内容同等重要。洛厄尔这样评价乔叟道："有时他用最纯粹的暗示就能描写得十分充分，比如修士轻轻地坐下之前赶走了猫。无需用更多言语，我们便知道作者选择了温暖舒适的角落。"准确地说，文学中最丰富的段落恰恰是那些蕴意充足的段落，但对粗心或愚钝的读者来讲，这些暗示似乎毫无意义。

我们之前曾说过，需要完全理解这一重要原则无论在何处都能满足我们的阅读需求。读者有必要以一种乐意接受的心态去阅读，唯有如此才能富有创造性。创造性即是能够在想象之前召唤那些已经出现在作者内在想象力中的东西。对文学语言的理解首要的便是将暗示转化为想象性现实的力量。

例如，当我们读到：

树木像等待的仙女一样呈上它们的果实。

这一行诗句对我们没有任何意义，除非我们能够用心灵的眼睛看到，有灵性的树木像活生生的手臂一样伸出树枝，温柔地呈上果实。当德克尔谈到耐心时写道：

这是囚徒永远的自由，
他的散步和果园。

我们无法抓住诗人的意思，除非有一种身临其境的感受，即被判处终身囚禁的可怜之人，在监禁期间如何凭借耐心找到了同样的轻松惬意。这种感觉在他的心中洋溢，仿佛他能像主人那样沿着自己的步道信步而行，并穿过一片果实累累的果园。

Almost any page of Shakespeare might be given bodily here in illustration. Take, for instance, the talk of Lorenzo and Jessica as in the moonlit garden at Belmont they await the return of Portia.

> *Lor.*　The moon shines bright. In such a night as this,
> When the sweet wind did gently kiss the trees,
> And they did make no noise, —in such a night
> Troilus, methinks, mounted the Trojan walls,
> And sighed his soul toward the Grecian tents,
> Where Cressid lay that night.
> *Jes.*
> In such a night
> Did Thisbe fearfully o'ertrip the dew,
> And saw the lion's shadow ere himself,
> And ran dismayed away.
> *Lor.*
> In such a night
> Stood Dido with a willow in her hand
> Upon the wild sea-banks, and waved her love
> To come again to Carthage.
> *Jes.*
> In such a night
> Medea gathered the enchanted herbs
> That did renew old Æson.

几乎莎士比亚书写的任何一页都可以给出具体的示例。以罗兰佐和杰西卡的谈话为例，在贝尔蒙特月光下的花园中，他们正等待波西亚的归来。

> 罗兰佐：
> 好皎洁的月色！
> 微风轻轻地吻着树枝，

不发出一点声响；

我想正是在这样一个夜里，

特洛伊罗斯登上了特洛亚的城墙，

遥望着克瑞西达所寄身的希腊人的营幕，

发出他的内心中的悲叹。

杰西卡：

正是在这样一个夜里，

提斯柏心惊胆战地踩着露水，

去赴她情人的约会，

因为看见了一头狮子的影子，

吓得远远逃走。

罗兰佐：

正是在这样一个夜里，

狄多手里执着柳枝，

站在辽阔的海滨，

招她的爱人回到迦太基来。

杰西卡：

正是在这样一个夜里，

美狄亚采集了灵芝仙草，

使衰迈的埃宋返老还童。

（朱生豪　译）

　　The question is how this is read. Do we go over the enchanting scene mechanically and at speed，as if it were the account of a political disturbance on the borders of Beloochistan? Do we take in the ideas with crude apprehension，satisfied that we are doing our duty to ourselves and to literature because the book which we are thus abusing is Shakespeare? That is one way not to read. Again，we may，with laborious pedantry，discover that all the stories alluded to in this passage are from Chaucer's *Legends of Good Women*"；that for a single particular Shakespeare has apparently gone to Gower，but that most of the details he has invented himself. We may look up the accounts of the legendary personages mentioned, compare parallel passages in which they are named, and hunt for the earliest reference to the willow as a sign of woe. There is nothing necessarily vicious in all this. It is a sort of busy idleness which is somewhat demoralizing to the mind, but it is not criminal. It has, it is true, no especial relation to the genuine and proper enjoyment of the poetry. That is a different affair! The reader should luxuriate through the exquisite verse, letting the imagination create fully every image, every emotion. The sense should be steeped in the beauty of that garden, softly distinct in the golden splendors of the moon; there should come again the feeling which has stolen over us on some June night, so lovely that it seemed impossible but that dreams should come true, and in sheer delight of the time we have involuntarily sighed, "In such a night as this!" —as if all that is bewitching and romantic might happen when earth and heaven were attuned to harmony so complete. We should take in the full mood of the lines: —

> When the sweet wind did gently kiss the trees,
> And they did make no noise.

The image of the amorous wind, subduing its riotous glee lest it be overheard, and stealing as it were on tiptoe to kiss the trees, warm and willing in the sweet-scented dusk, makes in the mind the very atmosphere of the sensuous, luscious, moonlit garden at Belmont. We are ready to give our fancy over to the mood of the lovers, and with them to call up the potent images of folk immortal in the old tales: —

> In such a night
> Troilus, methinks, mounted the Trojan walls,
> And sighed his soul toward the Grecian tents,
> Where Cressid lay that night.

If we share the imaginings of the poet, we shall seem to see before us the sheen of the weather-stained Grecian tents, silvered by the moonlight there below the wall where we stand, —we shall seem to stretch unavailing arms toward that far corner of the camp where Cressid must be sleeping, —we shall feel a sigh swell our bosom, and our throat contract.

> In such a night
> Did Thisbe fearfully o'ertrip the dew,
> And saw the lion's shadow ere himself,
> And ran dismayed away.

The realizing reader moves with timorous eagerness to meet Pyramus, feeling under foot the dew-wet grass and on the cheek the soft night wind, and suddenly, with that awful chill of fright which is like an actual grasp upon the heart, to see the shadow of the lion silhouetted on the turf. He sees with the double vision of the imagination the shrinking, terror-smitten Thisbe, arrested by the shadow at her feet, while also he seems to look through her eyes at the beast which has called up her gaze from the shade to the reality. He trembles with her in a brief-long instant, and then flees in dismay.

　　问题是如何去阅读以上示例。我们是否机械地、快速地浏览那些迷人的场景，好像这只是有关俾路支省边界的政治骚乱的一篇报道？因为我们误读的书正是莎士比亚的作品，难道我们浅尝辄止的理解，便可以满足对自己，对文学的应尽之责了吗？那不是阅读文学的正确方式。再者，阅读时凭借费劲卖弄学问，我们可能会发现这段文字中提到的所有故事，都暗指乔叟的《好妇人的传说》，因为那个特指的莎士比亚显然曾去过高尔，但大部分细节都是他自己杜撰出来的。我们可以查阅所提到的传奇人物的记述，比较他们被命名的相同段落，并搜寻最早提到柳树作为悲哀标志的出处。在所有这一切中，没有什么必然是恶意的。这是一种无所事事的忙碌，虽让人有些泄气，但它不算是犯罪。事实上，它与真正合理欣赏诗歌没有特别的关系。完全是另一回事了！读者应该尽情享受精美的诗歌，让想象充分创造出每一个形象，每一种情感。感觉应该融入月亮金色光辉中隐约闪现的美丽花园中。在六月的某个夜晚，那种不知不觉出现的感觉还会再次袭来，它是如此可爱，似又遥不可及，但梦想终会成真。在这个万分惊喜的时刻，我们不由自主地叹道："正是在这样的一个夜里！"——当地球和天堂完美地融入一体时，仿佛所有迷人和浪漫的事情都会发生。我们应该充分理解这些台词透露出的情绪：

> 微风轻轻地吻着树枝，
> 不发出一点声响；

多情的风这一形象压抑着它的狂喜，以免泄露天机，仿佛悄悄地踮着脚亲吻树木，在芬芳的黄昏中温暖而多情。这一切在脑海中营造出了月光下贝尔蒙特花园充满感性、迷人的氛围。我们情愿去幻想情侣们的心境，并与他们一起回想古老传说中民间流传的诸神无比健硕的形象：

> 我想正是在这样一个夜里，
> 特洛伊罗斯登上了特洛亚的城墙，
> 遥望着克瑞西达所寄身的希腊人的营幕，
> 发出他的内心中的悲叹。

如果我们去分享诗人的想象，似乎便会在面前看到，日晒雨淋已经变色的希腊住营地的光彩，我们伫立于洒满银色月光的城墙下。我们似乎将徒劳的手臂伸向那个营地远处的角落，在那里克瑞西达一定正在酣睡——我们心潮起伏，惊叹不已。

> 正是在这样一个夜里，
> 提斯柏心惊胆战地踩着露水，
> 去赴她情人的约会，
> 因为看见了一头狮子的影子，
> 吓得远远逃走。

意识到这一点的读者既羞怯又急迫地想见到皮拉摩斯，去感受露水打湿的脚下的草地和脸颊上柔和的夜风，突然全身不寒而栗，就像心仿佛被抓住了一样，猛然间瞧见草地上狮子的倒影。他用想象的双重视觉看到了，被她脚下的阴影吓得惊恐万状的提斯柏，同时他似乎也透过她的眼睛瞧见了那头将她的视线从阴影中拉回现实的野兽。他因她在短暂的一瞬间颤抖，然后惊慌失措地逃跑了。

Now all this is almost sure to seem to you to be rather closely allied to that pest of teachers of composition which is known as "fine writing". I realize that my comment obscures the text with what is likely to seem a mist of sentimentality. There are two reasons why this should be so, —two, I mean, besides the obvious necessity of failure when we attempt to translate Shakespeare into our own language. In the first place, the feelings involved belong to the elevated, poetic mood, and not at all to dry lecturing. In the second place, and what is of more importance, these emotions can be fairly and effectively conveyed only by suggestion. It is not by specifying love, passion, hate, fear, suspense, and the like, that an author brings them keenly to the mind; but by arousing the reader's imagination to create them. It follows that in insisting upon the necessity of understanding what is connoted as well as what is denoted in what one reads, I am but calling attention to the fact that this is the only way in which the most significant message of a writer may be understood at all. The best of literature must be received by suggestion or missed altogether.

现在，在你看来，这一切几乎肯定与被称为"佳作"的作文老师令人讨厌的东西密切相关。我意识到，我的评论似乎可能给文本蒙上一层多愁善感的薄雾，使文本变得模糊不清了。我的意思是指，除了试图将莎士比亚的作品翻译成我们自己的语言时必然失败之外，还有两个原因。首先，卷入的情感属于高尚的、诗意的情绪，完全不属于那种听枯燥的讲座时所有的情绪。其次，更重要的是，只有通过暗示才能清楚有效地传达这些情感。作者并不是靠详细具体地说明爱、激情、仇恨、恐惧、悬念等，将情感敏锐地带进读者脑海里，而是依靠激发读者的想象力来创造出这些情感。因此，在所读内容上，要坚持理解所指意义和暗示意义的必要性。我只是提醒注意这样一个事实，即这是理解作者最重要寓意的唯一方式。最好的文学作品必须通过暗示才能被接受，否则什么也得不到。

Often ideas which are essential to the appreciation of even the simplest import of a work are conveyed purely by inference. Doubtless most of you are familiar with Rossetti's poem "*Sister Helen*". A slighted maiden is by witchcraft doing to death her faithless lover, melting his waxen image before the fire, while he in agony afar wastes away under the eyes of his newly wedded bride as the wax wastes by the flame. Her brother from the gallery outside her tower window calls to her as one after another the relatives of the dying man come to implore her mercy. The first is announced in these words: —

> Oh, it's Keith of Eastholm rides so fast,...
> For I know the white mane on the blast.

There follows the plea of the rider, and again the brother speaks: —

> Here's Keith of Westholm riding fast,...
> For I know the white plume on the blast.

When the second suppliant has vainly prayed pity, and the third appears, the boy calls to his sister: —

> Oh, it's Keith of Keith now that rides fast,...
> For I know the white hair on the blast.

We see first a rider who is not of importance enough to overpower in the mind of the boy the effect of his horse, and we feel instinctively that some younger member of the house has been sent on this errand. Then comes the second brother, and the boy is impressed by the knightly plume, by the trappings of the rider rather than by his personality. An older and more important member of the family has been dispatched as the need has grown greater. It is not, however, until the old man comes, with white locks floating on the wind, that the person of the messenger seizes the attention; it is evident that the head of the house of Keith has come, and that a desperate climax is at hand.

When one considers the care with which writers arrange details like this, of how much depends upon the reader's comprehending them, one knows not whether to be the more angry or the more pitiful in thinking of the careless fashion in which literature is so commonly skimmed over.

通常，观念对理解即便最简单意义都是必不可少的，但这种观念纯粹是通过推理来传达的。毫无疑问，大多数人都熟悉罗塞蒂的诗《海伦修女》。一个受人冷落的少女凭借巫术正欲杀死了她不忠的情人，在火前融化他的蜡像。当蜡像被火焰融化，远方的他受尽煎熬，渐渐在新娘的眼前融化掉。新娘的兄弟从塔窗外长廊上呼喊着少女，一个又一个垂死者的亲属前来恳求她的怜悯。第一个前来的人用这些话宣布：

> 哦，来自东边小岛的基思骑得这么快，……
> 因我知道疾风中的白色鬃毛。

随之而来的是骑手的恳求，另一个兄弟再次开口：

> 这是来自西边小岛的基思骑得很快，…
> 因我知道疾风中的白色羽状物。

当第二个祈求者徒劳地祈求怜悯时，第三个祈求者出现了，男孩呼叫道：

> 哦，现在骑得快的正是基思的基思，……
> 因我知道疾风中的白发。

　　我们首先看到第一个骑手的重要性在男孩的脑海中还不足以压倒那匹马留下的印象，我们本能地感觉到家里的某位年轻成员被派来跑腿了。然后是二哥，骑士的羽毛令男孩印象深刻，但给男孩留下深刻印象的是骑手的装饰物，而不是骑手的个性。随着需要愈加紧迫，一位年长且更重要的家庭成员被派来了。然而，直到那位在风中白发飘飘的老者到来，才引起了信使的人注意，很明显，基思家的首领驾临了，一场绝望的高潮迫近了。

　　当我们考虑到作家如此细心地安排这些细节时，在多大程度上要取决于读者对它们的理解，因为人们不知道，在想到文学如此普遍被一掠而过的粗心阅读方式时，是更愤怒还是更觉可怜。

It is essential, then, to read carefully and intelligently; and it is no less essential to read imaginatively and sympathetically. Of course, the intelligent comprehension of which I am speaking cannot be reached without the use of the imagination. No author can fulfill for you the office of your own mind. In order to accompany an author who soars it is necessary to have wings of one's own. Pegasus is a sure guide through the trackless regions of the sky, but he drags none up after him. The majority of readers are apt unconsciously to assume that a work of imaginative literature is a sort of captive balloon in which any excursionist who is in search of a novel sensation may be wafted heavenward for the payment of a small fee. They sit down to some famous book prepared to be raised far above earth, and they are not only astonished but inclined to be indignant that nothing happens. They feel that they have been defrauded. The reputation of the masterpiece they regard as a sort of advertisement from which the book cannot fall away without manifest dishonesty on the part of somebody. They are there; they are ready to be thrilled; the reputation of the work guarantees the thrilling; and yet they are unmoved. Straightway they pronounce the reputation of that book a snare and a delusion. They do not in the least appreciate the fact that they have not even learned the language in which the author has written. Literature shows us what we may create for ourselves; it suggests and inspires; it awakens us to the possibilities of life; but the actual act of creation must every mind do for itself. The hearing ear and the responsive imagination are as necessary as the inspired voice to utter high things. You are able appreciatively to read imaginative works when you are able, as William Blake has said: —

> To see the world in a grain of sand,
> And a heaven in a wild flower;
> Hold infinity in the palm of your hand,
> And eternity in an hour.

The language of literature is in reality a tongue as foreign to every-day speech as is the tongue of the folk of another land. It is necessary to learn it as one learns a foreign idiom; and to appreciate the fact that even when it is acquired what we read does not accomplish for us the possibilities of emotion, but only points out the way in which we may rise to them for ourselves.

因此，仔细而明智地阅读是必不可少的，带着想象力和同情心去阅读也同等重要。当然，如果不使用想象力，就无法达到我所说的明智的理解。没有一个作家可以为你完成你自己内心应尽的职责。陪伴一个飞翔的作者，必须有自己的翅膀。飞马是穿越天空无迹可寻区域的可靠向导，但他身后并没有拖拽任何东西。大多数读者都不自觉地倾向于假定，一部富有想象力的文学作品是一个受控制的气球，任何一个寻求新奇感觉的远足者都可以在支付少量费用后被带到天空。他们面向某一名著静坐下来，准备飞上高空，但他们不仅感到惊讶，而且还刻意为没有发生任何事情而感到愤慨，他们觉得自己受到了欺骗。他们认为名著的声誉是某种宣传广告，如果不表现出某人的不诚实，这本书就不会从广告中消失。读者都到了，并已经准备好为之而激动。

作品的名声保证可以惊险刺激，然而他们却无动于衷。他们直接宣称那本书的名声是圈套和妄想。他们丝毫没有意识到这一事实，即他们甚至还没有理解作者用于写作的语言。文学向我们展示了可以为自己创造什么，它暗示和启发我们，使我们意识到生活的各种可能性，但真正的创造行为必须是每个人都为自己创造。倾听的耳朵和灵敏的想象力与言说高尚事物的激励之声一样必要。当你有能力时，尽可能带着赞赏的态度去阅读富有想象力的作品，正如威廉·布莱克曾说：

> 从一粒沙子看到一个世界，
> 从一朵野花看到一个天堂，
> 把握在你手心里的就是无限，
> 永恒也就消融于一个时辰。

　　实际上，相对于日常语言来说，文学语言就像另一国家人们使用的语言一样，是一种陌生的语言，有必要像学外语习语一样学习文学语言，而且也有必要理解这样一个事实，纵使获得了我们所阅读的内容，我们也不一定能实现表达情感的可能性，但文学语言却指出了一条达到这些可能性的途径。

IX
THE CLASSICS

The real nature of a classic is perhaps to the general mind even more vague than that of literature. As long as the term is confined to Greek and Roman authors, it is of course simple enough; but the moment the word is given its general and legitimate application the ordinary reader is apt to become somewhat uncertain of its precise meaning. It is not strange, human nature being what it is, that the natural instinct of most men is to take refuge in the idea that a classic is of so little moment that it really does not matter much what it is.

While I was writing these talks, a friend said to me, "I know what I would do if I were to speak about literature. I would tell my audience squarely that all this talk about the superiority of the classics is either superstition or mere affectation. I would give them the straight tip that nobody nowadays really enjoys Homer and Chaucer and Spenser and all those old duffers, and that nobody need expect to." I disregarded the slang, and endeavored to treat this remark with absolute sincerity. It brought up vividly the question which has occurred to most of us how far the often expressed admiration of the classics is genuine. It is impossible not to see that there is a great deal of talk which is purely conventional. We know well enough that the ordinary reader does not take Chaucer or Spenser from the shelf from year's end to year's end. It is idle to deny that the latest novel has a thousand times better chance of being read than any classic, and since there is always a latest novel the classics are under a perpetual disadvantage. How far, then, was my friend right? We live in an age when we dare to question anything; when doubt examines everything. We claim to test things on their merits; and if the reverence with which old authors have been regarded is a mere tradition and a fetish, it is as well that its falsity be known.

Is it true that the majority of readers find the works of the great writers of the past dull and unattractive? I must confess that it is true. It is one of those facts of which we seldom speak in polite society, as we seldom speak of the fact that so large a portion of mankind yield to the temptations of life. It is more of an affront, indeed, to intimate that a man is unfamiliar with Shakespeare than to accuse him of having foully done to death his grandmother. Whatever be the facts, we have tacitly agreed to assume that every intelligent man is of course acquainted with certain books. We all recognize that we live in a society in which familiarity with these works is put forward as an essential condition of intellectual, and indeed almost of social and moral, respectability. One would hesitate to ask to dinner a man who confessed to a complete ignorance of " *The Canterbury Tales*" ; and if one's sister married a person so hardened as to own to being unacquainted with " *Hamlet*" , one would take a good deal of pains to prevent the disgraceful fact from becoming public. We have come to accept a knowledge of the classics as a measure of cultivation; and yet at the same time, by an absurd contradiction, we allow that knowledge to be assumed, and we accept for the real the sham while we are assured of its falsity. In other words, we tacitly agree that cultivation shall be tested by a certain criterion, and then allow men unrebuked to offer in its stead the flimsiest pretext. We piously pretend that we all read the masterpieces of literature while as a rule we do not; and the plain fact is that few of us dare rebuke our neighbors lest we bring to light our own shortcomings.

第九讲　文学经典

对于一般人来说，经典的真正本质也许比文学的本质更加模糊。只要该术语仅限于希腊和罗马作家，当然就足够简单了，但是一当这个词被赋予其普遍和合法的应用，一般读者马上便很容易对其确切含义感到有些不确定。这并不奇怪，人的本性就如此，大多数人的本能是从一个观点中寻求慰藉，把经典视如过眼云烟，因而并不会很在乎经典究竟是什么。

在我写这些演讲的时候，一个朋友对我说："如果我要谈文学，我知道会怎么做。我会坦率地告诉听众，所有这些关于经典优越性的论调要么是迷信盲从，要么是故弄玄虚。我会直截了当地提醒他们，如今没有人真正喜欢荷马、乔叟和斯宾塞以及所有那些老朽之人，而且没有人可以期待人们会去喜欢。"我鄙视这样的粗话，并努力以赤诚之心来对待他的这番言论。这样的话鲜明地提出了一个大多数人想到的问题，长久以来人们对经典的膜拜在多大程度上是真实的？不可能看不出，人们的许多言论纯属套话。但我们很清楚地知道，一般读者并没有年复一年地从书架上取走乔叟或斯宾塞的书。如果拒绝承认阅读最新小说的机会比阅读经典小说的机会要好上一千倍，这也无用，因为总会有最新小说出现，经典永远都处于不利地位。那么，我的朋友说对了多少？我们生活在一个敢于质疑任何事情且怀疑检验一切的时代。我们声称要根据事物的价值来检验事物，如果人们对过去的作家怀有的崇敬之心仅仅是一种习惯和一种迷恋，那么人们也应该了解它的虚假性。

是不是大多数读者真的发现过去的伟大作家的作品枯燥乏味，缺乏吸引力？我必须承认这是真实的。这是我们在上流社会中很少谈论的事实之一，正如我们很少谈论这样一个事实，即相当大一部分人屈服于生活的诱惑。事实上，暗示一个人不熟悉莎士比亚，比指控他卑鄙地谋杀了他的祖母更具侮辱性。不管事实如何，我们都默认了这种说法，每一个有才智的人理所当然地熟悉某些书籍。我们都承认，我们生活在这样一个社会中，熟悉这些作品被认为是证明一个人聪明才智的基本条件。实际上，它几乎是在社会和道德上受人尊敬的一个基本条件。如果一个人要邀请一位自己承认对《坎特伯雷故事集》一无所知的人共进晚餐，他会显得很犹豫；如果有人的姐姐嫁给了一个不熟悉《哈姆雷特》而又冷酷无情的人，我们会千方百计阻止这件不体面的事公之于众。我们承认经典知识是衡量一个人修养的尺度，但同时我们又以一种荒谬的矛盾心态，认定这种知识是虚假的，我们既已确信这种知识是虚假的，却又把虚假的理解为真实的。换言之，我们既已默认要以某种标准检验人们的修养，但又允许人们无可非议地提供于己有利的最不足信的借口。我们虚伪的假装都阅读过文学名著，而通常情况下，我们并未读过。我们中很少有人敢非议邻居，以免曝光自己的缺陷，这是一个有目共睹的事实。

Such a state of things is sufficiently curious to be worth examination; and there would also seem to be some advisability of amendment. If it is not to be supposed that we can alter public sentiment, we may at least free ourselves from the thralldom of superstition. If this admiration of the classics which men profess with their lips, yet so commonly deny by their acts, is a relic of old-time prejudice, if it be but a mouldy inheritance from days when learning was invested with a sort of supernatural dignity, it is surely time that it was cast aside. We should at least know whether in this matter it is rational to hold by common theory or by common practice.

In the first place it is necessary to supply that definition of a classic which is so generally wanting. In their heart of hearts, concealed like a secret crime, many persons hide an obstinate conviction that a classic is any book which everybody should have read, yet which nobody wishes to read. The idea is not unallied to the notion that goodness is whatever we do not wish to do; and one is as sensible as the other. It has already been said that the object of the study of literature is to enjoy and to experience literature; to live in it and to thrill with its emotions. It follows that the popular idea just mentioned is neither more nor less sensible than the theory that it is better to have lived than to live, to have loved than to love. Whatever else may be said, it is manifest that this popular definition of a classic as a book not to read but to have read is an absurd contradiction of terms.

Equally common is the error that a classic is a book which is merely old. One constantly hears the word applied to any work, copies of which have come down to us from a former generation, with a tendency to assume that merit is in direct proportion to antiquity. To disabuse the mind from this error nothing is needed but to examine intelligently the catalogue of any great library. Therein are to be found lists of numerous authors whose productions have accidentally escaped submergence in the stream of time, and are now preserved as simple and innocuous diet for book-worms insectivorous or human. These writ which should be left in decent quiet to die from simple inanition. Mere age no more makes a classic of a poor book than it makes a saint of a sinner.

上述情形足以令人好奇，值得一探究竟，并且这里似乎也存在纠正这一情形的合理性。如果不认为可以改变公众情绪，我们至少可以摆脱迷信的束缚。如果人们口口声声地宣扬经典，但行为上却普遍否认；如果这只是旧时偏见的遗产；如果它只是具有某种超自然尊严知识时代霉迹斑斑的继承物，那么现在肯定是该把它扔在一边的时候了。至少我们应该知道，在这件事上，按一般理论或通行做法是否合理而且站得住脚。

首先，有必要给人们提供一个普遍需要的经典定义。许多人在内心深处隐藏着一种顽固的信念，即经典是任何人都应该阅读但没有人愿意阅读的书。这个想法与善行是人们不愿意做的事情的想法一脉相承，这一想法和另一个想法一样合理。前面已经说过，文学研究的目的是享受和体验文学，是活在其中并为之动情。由此可见，刚才提到的流行观点与活过不如活着，爱过不如爱的看法一样不理智。不管怎么说，很明显，将经典书籍定义成一本无须阅读但已读过的书是一个措辞上荒谬的矛盾。

同样，常见的一个谬见认为经典不过就是一本旧书。人们经常听到这个词语用于指任何作品，一册册的书是都是从前一代人传给我们的，人们通常认为其价值与古老直接成正比。要打消这种错误认识，无须做其他的事情，只消理智地细阅任何一家大图书馆的书目即可。其中可以发现许多作者的名单，他们的作品在岁月的长河里意外地逃脱了被湮灭，现在作为啃噬纸张的书虫或人类简单无害的膳食保存下来了。有些著作不是经典，但有一群忙碌的闲人尽心竭力地维护这些没有足够生命力来维持自己生活的书籍，并将它们展示在公众面前——总而言之，编辑起着医院护士的作用，照料那些身体虚弱的文学遗老，让它们能安详地离去。单凭时间并不能使一本糟糕的书成为经典，就如同时间也无法使一个罪孽深重的人变成圣人一样。

A classic is more than a book which has been preserved. It must have been approved. It is a work which has received the suffrages of generations. Out of the innumerable books, of the making of which there was no end even so long ago as the days of Solomon, some few have been by the general voice of the world chosen as worthy of preservation. There are certain writings which, amid all the multitudinous distractions of practical life, amid all the changes of custom, belief, and taste, have continuously pleased and moved mankind, —and to these we give the name Classics.

A book has two sorts of interest; that which is temporary, and that which is permanent. The former depends upon its relation to the time in which it is produced. In these days of magazines there is a good deal of talk about articles which are what is called timely. This means that they fall in with some popular interest of the moment. When a war breaks out in the Soudan, an account of recent explorations or travels in that region is timely, because it appeals to readers who just then are eager to increase their information concerning the scene of the disturbance. When there is general discussion of any ethical or emotional topic, the novel or the poem making that topic its theme finds instant response. Often a book of no literary merit whatever speeds forward to notoriety because it is attached, like a barnacle on the side of a ship, to some leading issue of the day. Books which are really notable, too, may owe their immediate celebrity to connection with some vital topic of the day. Their hold upon later attention will depend upon their lasting merit.

The permanent interest and value of a book are precisely those qualities which have been specified as making it literature. As time goes on all temporary importance fails. Nothing becomes more quickly obsolete than the thing which is merely timely. It may retain interest as a curious historic document. It will always have some value as showing what was read by large numbers at a given period; but nobody will cherish the merely timely book as literature, although in its prime it may have had the widest vogue, and may have conferred upon its author a delicious immortality lasting sometimes half his lifetime. Permanent interest gives a book permanent value, and this depends upon appeal to the permanent characteristics and emotions of humanity.

While the temporary excitement over a book continues, no matter how evanescent the qualities upon which this excitement depends, the reader finds it difficult to realize that the work is not genuine and vital. It is not easy to distinguish the permanent from the momentary interest. With the passage of time extraneous attractions fade, and the work is left to depend upon its essential value. The classics are writings which, when all factitious interests that might have been lent to them by circumstances are stripped away, are found still to be of worth and importance. They are the wheat left in the threshing-floor of time, when has been blown away the chaff of sensational scribbling, noisily notorious productions, and temporary works of what sort soever. It is of course not impossible that a work may have both kinds of merit; and it is by no means safe to conclude that a book is not of enduring worth simply because it has appealed to instant interests and won immediate popularity. "Don Quixote" on the one hand, and "Pilgrim's Progress" on the other, may serve as examples of works which were timely in the best sense, and which yet are permanent literature.

一部经典不仅是一本被留存下来的书，也是一部获得了几代人认可的书。在浩如烟海的书籍中，远至所罗门时代，经典的创造一直在延续，其中仅有少量书籍为世人普遍的声音选定为有保存价值的书籍。在实际生活的各种纷扰中，在变化多端的习俗、信仰和品位中，有些著作自始至终给人类带来欢乐，并不断感动人类，我们将这些著作命名为经典。

一本书有两种兴趣：一种是暂时兴趣，一种是永恒兴趣。前者取决于它产生的时间。在杂志盛行的日子里，存在大量关于所谓的应时文章的讨论。这意味着这些文章符合当下的某些流行兴趣。当苏丹爆发战争时，针对最近在该地区的探险或旅行的描述便是非常应时的，因为这些文章可以吸引当时渴望能增加有关骚乱现场信息的读者。当人们普遍谈论伦理或情感话题时，以该话题为主题的小说或诗歌便会得到即时回应。通常，一本毫无文学价值的书会迅速变得小有名气，因为它就像附在船舷上甲壳动物，紧贴在当下某个主要争议的问题上。真正引人注目的书籍也可能将一夜成名归功于与当今一些重大话题的联系，但这样的书籍至于以后能否吸引人们的关注，将取决于它们持久的价值。

准确地说，一本书的永恒兴趣和价值正是那些使其成为文学的特有品质。随着时间的推移，所有暂时的重要性都将失去。如果某一事物只是适合时宜的，那么它会很快成为过时。作为一个稀奇的历史文件，它可能会保留兴趣，毕竟它总会具有一定的价值。一本这样的书可以表明在特定时期曾为大量读者阅读，尽管在其流传最为广泛的时候，或许已赋予其作者一种极为珍贵的不朽，有时甚至会延续一个人的大半生，但没有人会像珍惜文学一样珍视这样的应时之书。永恒的兴趣赋予一本书永恒的价值，而这要取决于它对人类永恒特征和情感的诉求。

虽然对一本书的暂时兴趣仍在延续，但无论这种兴趣所依赖的品质消失得如何迅疾，读者都很难意识到这本书不是真实的、富有生命活力的。将永恒的兴趣与暂时的兴趣区分开来并不容易。随着时间的流逝，无关紧要的吸引力会渐渐消失，但作品要留待其本身价值来决定。经典著作是当所有可能因环境为之增彩的人为兴趣被剥离后，仍然具有价值和重要性的著作。轰动一时的涂鸦、声名狼藉的作品和各种临时作品的糠壳被吹走后，留在时间打谷场上的小麦即是经典。一部作品兼具这两种优点当然不是不可能的。仅仅因为一本书吸引了一时兴趣并立即赢得了人气，就断定一本书没有持久的价值，这绝对不够慎重。一方面有《堂吉诃德》，另一方面有《天路历程》，这两部作品均可以作为最应时的作品，同时又是永恒的文学作品的例证。

The important point is that in the classics we have works which, whether they did or did not receive instant recognition, have by age been stripped of the accidental, and are found worthy in virtue of the essential that remains. They are books which have been proved by time, and have endured the test.

The decision what is and what is not literature may be said to rest with the general voice of the intellectual world. Vague as the phrase may sound, it really represents the shaping power of the thought of the race. It is true that here as in all other matters of belief the general voice is likely to be a confirmation and a repetition of the voice of the few; but whether at the outset indorsed by the few or not, a book cannot be said to be fairly entitled to the name "classic" until it has received this general sanction. Although this sanction, moreover, be as intangible as the wind in a sail, yet like the wind it is decisive and effective.

The leaders of thought, moreover, have not only praised these books and had their judgment indorsed by the general voice, but they have by them formed their own minds. They are unanimous in their testimony to the value of the classics in the development of the perceptions, intellectual and emotional. So universally true is this that to repeat it seems the reiteration of a truism. The fact of which we have already spoken, the fact that those who in theory profess to respect the classics, do yet in practice neglect them utterly, makes it necessary to examine the grounds upon which this truism rests. If the classics are the books which the general voice of the best intelligence of the race has declared to be permanently valuable, if the highest minds have universally claimed to have been nourished and developed by them, why is it that we so often neglect and practically ignore them?

重要的一点是，在经典中我们有一些作品，无论是否得到了即时的认可，随着时间的流逝，偶然性已经被剥离了，但由于它们保留了经典的本质而被认为有价值。这些经典都为时间所证明，且经受住了时间的考验。

决定什么是文学，什么不是文学，可以说，取决于知识界的普遍声音。虽然这句话听起来很模糊，但它确实代表了塑造人类思想的力量。的确，就像在所有其他信仰问题中一样，普遍的声音不过是确认和重复少数人的声音。但是，无论一开始一本书是否会受到少数人的认可，在获得普遍认可之前，尚不能说一本书有资格被授予"经典"的称号。这种认可虽然像吹在风帆上的风儿一样无形，但又像风一样关键而有效。

此外，思想的先行者不仅赞扬这些书，并通过普遍的声音来支持他们的判断，而且他们通过这些书籍形成了自己的思想。他们一致确认经典在认识能力、智力和情感发展中的价值。这一判断是普遍正确的，但反复提及似乎又是旧调重弹。我们已经说过的一个事实，即那些在理论上自称尊重经典的人，但实际上却完全置经典于不顾，因此我们有必要去检查这种老生常谈的判断依据的理由。如果经典是人类最优秀智慧的普遍声音认定的具有永久价值的书籍；如果具有最高才智的人普遍声称受经典的滋养才得以发展，为什么我们还经常忽略它们，甚至对它们完全置之不理？

In the first place there are the obstacles of language. There are the so to say technical difficulties of literary diction and form which have been somewhat considered in the preceding talks. There are the greater difficulties of dealing with conceptions which belong to a different mental world. To a savage, the intellectual and emotional experiences of a civilized man would be incomprehensible, no matter in how clear speech they were expressed. To the unimaginative man the life of the world of imagination is pretty nearly as unintelligible as to the bushman of Australian wilds. The men who wrote the classics wrote earnestly and with profound conviction that which they profoundly felt; it is needful to attain to their elevation in point of view before what they have written can be comprehended. This is a feat by no means easy for the ordinary reader. To one accustomed only to facile and commonplace thoughts and emotions it is by no means a light undertaking to rise to the level of the masters. Readers to whom the rhymes of the "poet's corner" in the newspapers, for instance, are thrillingly sweet, are hardly to be expected to be equal to the emotional stress of Shelley's "*Prometheus Unbound*"; it is not to be supposed that those who find "*Over the Hills to the Poor-House*" soul-satisfying will respond readily to the poignant pathos of the parting of Hector and Andromache. The admirers of "*Curfew must not ring to-night*" and the jig-saw school of verse in general are mentally incapable of taking the attitude of genuinely imaginative work. The greatest author can do but so much for his reader. He may suggest, but each mind must for itself be the creator. The classics are those works in which the geniuses of the world have most effectively suggested genuine and vital emotions; but every reader must feel those emotions for himself. Not even the music of the spheres could touch the ear of a deaf man, and for the blind the beauty of Grecian Helen would be no more than ugliness. As Mrs. Browning puts it: —

> What angel but would seem
> To sensual eyes, ghost-dim?

The sluggish mind is incapable of comprehending, the torpid imagination incapable of realizing; and the struggle to attain to comprehension and to feeling is too great an exertion for the mentally indolent.

阅读经典的障碍首先来自语言。可以这么说，文学用词和形式上的技巧困难在前面的讨论中已经有所考虑。处理属于不同精神世界的概念则愈加困难。对于一个原始人来说，文明人的智力和情感体验，无论以多么清晰的语言来表达都令他们无法理解。对于缺乏想象力的人来说，想象世界的生活几乎就像对澳大利亚荒野中的丛林人一样，令人茫然不解。经典书写者认真而具有说服力地把深切感受的东西付诸笔端，在理解他们所写的内容之前，需要先达到他们视角的高度，这对于普通读者来说绝对是一个难以企及的任务。对于一个只习惯于简单而平凡思想和情感的人来说，提升到大师的水平绝非易事。例如，对那些读过报纸上"诗人角落"令人心醉神迷的诗歌的读者，很难期待他们的情绪能与读雪莱的《解放了的普罗米修斯》时体验的情感压力相提并论。不应该认为，那些发现《翻山越岭到穷人家》就灵魂满足的人，会轻易对赫克托尔和安德洛马赫离别的凄美悲痛做出回应。崇拜《今晚宵禁不会响起》和诗歌拼图的读者，对真正富有想象力的作品，在精神上一般不可能持有正确的态度。最伟大的作家可以为读者做很多事情，他可能会提出丰富的建议，但每个有才智的人本身必须是创造者。经典是天才作家有效揭示真实和充满活力的情感的作品，但每个读者都必须自己去感受这些情感。即使是天籁之音也无法打动聋人的耳朵，对于盲人来说，希腊海伦的美丽不过是丑陋。正如勃朗宁夫人所说：

> 天使看起来像什么
> 在情欲的眼睛里的鬼魅？

呆滞的头脑无法领悟，麻木的想象力也无法达到。对于精神懈怠的人来说，获得理解和感受的斗争颇费周折。

It is no less true, that to the mind unused to high emotions the vivid life of imaginative literature is disconcerting. The ordinary reader is as abashed in the presence of these deep and vibrant feelings which he does not understand, and cannot share, as would be an English washerwoman to whom a duchess paid a ceremonious afternoon call. The feeling of inadequacy, of being confronted with an occasion to the requirements of which one is utterly unequal, is baffling and unpleasant to the last degree. In this difficulty of comprehending, and in this inability to feel equal to the demands of the best literature, lies the most obvious explanation of the common neglect of the classics.

It is also true that genuine literature demands for its proper appreciation a mood which is fundamentally grave. Even beneath the humorous runs this vein of serious feeling. It is not possible to read Cervantes or Montaigne or Charles Lamb sympathetically without having behind laughter or smiles a certain inner solemnity. Hidden under the coarse and roaring fun of Rabelais lurk profound observations upon life, which no earnest man can think of lightly. The jests and "excellent fooling" of Shakespeare's clowns and drolls serve to emphasize the deep thought or sentiment which is the real import of the poet's work. Genuine feeling must always be serious, because it takes hold upon the realities of human existence.

It is not that one reading the classics must be sad. Indeed, there is nowhere else fun so keen, humor so exquisite, or sprightliness so enchanting. It is only that human existence is a solemn thing if viewed with a realization of its actualities and its possibilities; and that the great aim of real literature is the presentation of life in its essentials. It is not possible to be vividly conscious of the mystery in the midst of which we live and not be touched with something of awe. From this solemnity the feeble soul shrinks as a silly child shrinks from the dark. The most profound feeling of which many persons are capable is the instinctive desire not to feel deeply. To such readers real literature means nothing, or it means too much. It fails to move them, or it wearies them by forcing them to feel.

同样真实的是，对于那些还不习惯高尚情感的人来说，富有想象的、文学创造的、栩栩如生的生活令他们困惑不安。面对那些无法理解的、无法分享的、深刻而充满活力的感情时，一般读者会感到羞愧难当，这就好比一位英国洗衣妇在下午接受了公爵夫人的隆重探访一样。面对这一要求完全不对等的场合，不实在的感觉令她疑惑和不愉快。人们普遍轻视经典的最明确原因就在于，理解困难和无法与最优秀文学作品的要求相匹配。

诚然，正确欣赏真正的文学需要一种极为严肃的情绪，即使在幽默的情绪下也贯穿着这种严肃的感觉。如果在笑声或微笑背后没有某种内心的庄严，就不可能在阅读塞万提斯或蒙田或查尔斯·兰姆的作品时，产生情感共鸣。隐藏在法国作家拉伯雷粗俗和咆哮的乐趣之下，潜藏着对生活的深刻洞察，这是任何一个严肃的人都无法轻视的。莎士比亚创造的小丑和表演者的玩笑以及那些"绝妙的愚弄"都起着强调深刻的思想或情感的作用，这也是诗人作品的真正意义所在。真正的感情必须始终是严肃的，因为它根植于人类生存的现实。

阅读经典并非一定会让人感到难过。的确，除了在经典中，没有其他地方可找到如此深刻的乐趣，如此敏锐的幽默，如此迷人的活力。仅从现实可能性来观察，人的存在是一件严肃的事情，真正文学的伟大目标旨在呈现生活的本质，一个人不可能清楚地意识到了生活其中的奥秘而不为之感到敬畏。在这种庄严的气氛里，软弱的人会退缩，就像一个愚蠢的小孩从黑暗中畏缩那样。许多人能够有最深刻的情感体验，恰恰是其本能的欲望未曾深刻的感受过。对这样的读者来说，真正的文学要么毫无意义，要么意义重大，他们从未感动过，即使强迫他们去感受，他们也会失去热情。

Yet another reason for the neglect of the classics is the irresistible attractiveness which belongs always to novelty, which makes a reader choose whatever is new rather than anything which has been robbed of this quality by time. Every mind which is at all responsive is sensitive to this fascination of that which has just been written. What is new borrows importance from the infinite possibilities of the unknown. The secret of life, the great key to all the baffling mysteries of human existence, is still just beyond the bound of human endeavor, and there is always a tingling sense that whatever is fresh may have touched the longed-for solution to the riddle of existence. This zeal for the new makes the old to be left neglected; and while we are eagerly welcoming novelties which in the end too often prove to be of little or no value, the classics, of tried and approved worth, stand in forlorn dust-gathering on the higher shelves of the library.

A. Conan Doyle is reported as saying in a speech before a literary society: —

> It might be no bad thing for a man now and again to make a literary retreat, as pious men make a spiritual one; to forswear absolutely for a month in the year all ephemeral literature, and to bring an untarnished mind to the reading of the classics. —*London Academy*, December 5, 1896

The suggestion is so good that if it does not seem practical, it is so much the worse for the age.

　　漠视文学经典的另一个原因来自新生事物不可抗拒的吸引力，它驱使读者选择新的东西，而不是选择被时间掠去了特有品质的东西。每一个反应敏捷的头脑都对刚刚写成的作品的魅力最为敏感。新事物从未知的无限可能性中乞求重要性。生命的奥秘，人类存在的令人费解的秘密的关键，这些人生奥秘仍然超出了人类努力的范围，然而，令人激动的是，新生事物好像已触摸到了人们渴望已久的谜语的谜底。对新事物的热情使旧事物遭到厌弃，当我们热切欢迎最终往往被证明价值甚微或毫无价值的新奇事物时，久经考验且被认可的经典作品却在图书馆凄凉的被束之高阁，在那儿蒙尘受辱。

　　据报道，亚瑟·柯南道尔在一个文学社团的演讲中曾说：

> 对于一个人来说，一次又一次进行文学静修可能不算是件坏事，这如同虔诚的人进行精神修炼一样。在一年中的一个月内发誓放弃所有昙花一现的文学作品，并带着纯洁的心灵去阅读经典。
>
> ——《伦敦学院》，1896 年 12 月 5 日

　　这个建议非常合理，如果它看起来不切实际，那对这个时代来说就更糟糕了。

X

THE VALUE OF THE CLASSICS

It is sufficiently evident that the natural inclinations of the ordinary man are not toward imaginative literature, and that unless there were strong and tangible reasons why it is worthwhile to cultivate an appreciation and a fondness for them, the classics would be so little read that they might as well be sent to the junk-shop at once, save for the occasional mortal whom the gods from his birth have endowed with the precious gift of understanding high speech. These reasons, moreover, must apply especially to the classics as distinguished from books in general. Briefly stated, some of them are as follows: —

The need of a knowledge of the classics for the understanding of literary language has already been spoken of at some length. This is, of course, a minor and comparatively extraneous consideration, but it is one not to be left wholly out. It is not difficult, however, to get a superficial familiarity with famous writings by means of literary dictionaries and extract books; and with this a good many persons are apparently abundantly content. The process bears the same relation to the actual study of the originals that looking at foreign photographic views does to traveling abroad. It is undoubtedly better than nothing, although it is by no means the real thing. It gives one an intellectual understanding of classic and literary allusions, but not an emotional one. Fully to appreciate and enjoy the allusions with which literature is filled, it is essential to have gained knowledge directly from the originals.

One reason why references to the classics are so frequent in literary language, is that in these writings are found thought and emotional expression in their youth, so to say. Even more important than learning the force of these allusions is the coming in contact with this fresh inspiration and utterance. That into which a man steps full grown can never be to him the same as that in which he has grown up. We cannot have with the thing which we have known only in its complete form the same intimate connection as with that which we have watched from its very beginnings. To that with which we have grown we are united by a thousand delicate and intangible fibres, fine as cobweb and strong as steel. The student who attempts to form himself solely upon the literature of to-day misses entirely the childhood, the youth, the growth of literary art. He comes full grown, and generally sophisticated, to that which is itself full grown and sophisticated. It is not possible for him to become himself a child, but he may go back toward the childhood of emotional expression and as it were advance step by step with the race. He may feel each fresh emotional discovery as if it were as new to him as it was in truth new for the author who centuries ago expressed it so well that the record has become immortal.

第十讲 经典的价值

　　不言而喻，常人不喜欢想象性文学乃是天性使然，除非有强烈而切实的理由说明值得培养对经典的欣赏和喜爱，或因个别凡人天生就被诸神赋予了理解精妙语言的宝贵才能，除此之外，鲜有人阅读经典，倒不如把经典书籍立即送到古董店去。进而，以下理由必须特别适用于与一般书籍不同的经典。简而言之，其中一些理由如下：

　　为了理解文学语言必须了解关于经典的知识，这一点已经讲得很详细了。当然，这是一个次要且相对无关的考虑，但也不应完全忽略这一点。然而，借助文学辞典和摘录，对名著有一个粗浅的认识并不困难，能做到这一点，很多人显然已经心满意足了。这个过程与实际研读原著的关系与观看外国摄影师的风景照和出国旅行的关系并无二致。毫无疑问，这总比什么都没有好得多，但它绝不是真实的东西，因为这样的方式只能使人从知识上去理解经典和文学典故，而不是情感上的理解。要充分欣赏和享受文学中丰富的典故，直接从原著中掌握已有知识是必不可少的。

　　文学语言中如此频繁的引用经典的一个原因，可以这么说，就在于人们从这些作品中发现了他们年轻时的思想和情感表达。比了解这些典故的力量更重要的是能够接触鲜活的灵感和话语。对一个人来说，他步入完全成熟的状态永远不同于他成长的状态。我们了解一些事物是以其完整形式呈现的，而有的事物只是我们从其一开始观察到的，我们与两种事物联系的亲密程度迥然不同。一千根纤细无形的细丝将我们连接在一起，细如蜘蛛网，坚固如钢铁。学习者如果试图仅仅依靠当今的文学来塑造自己，就完全错过了的文学艺术的童年、青年以及发展时期。他已经完全长大成人，通常已深谙世故了，而对文学本身而言，它也已完全成熟并发展到了更高阶段。一个成人不可能把自己变成一个小孩，但他可以回到情感表达的童年，仿佛是与人类一道渐渐进步。他可能会觉得每一次新的情感发现对他来说都是全新的，实际上，对一个作家而言，也是全新的，因为几个世纪前就已经有作家出色地表达了这样的情感体验，并已使之成为不朽的记载。

I do not know whether what I mean is fully clear, and it is of course difficult to give examples where the matter is so subtle. It is certain, however, that any reader of early literature must be conscious how in the simplicity and naïveté of the best old authors we find things which are now hackneyed and all but commonplace said with a freshness and conviction which makes them for the first time real to us. Many emotions have been so long recognized and expressed in literature that there seems hardly to be a conceivable phase in which they have not been shown, and hardly a conceivable phrase in which they have not been embodied. It appears impossible to express them now with the freshness and sincerity which belonged to them when they were first imprisoned in words. So true is this that were it not that the personal impress of genius and the experience of the imaginative writer always give vitality, literature would cease from the face of the earth, and become a lost art.

It is the persuasion and vividness of first discovery which impart to the folk-song its charm and force. The early ballads often put to shame the poetry of later days. The unsophisticated singers of these lays had never been told that it was proper for them to have any especial emotions; they had never heard talk about this feeling or that, and art did not consciously exist for them as other than the spontaneous and sincere expression of what really moved them. That which they felt too strongly to repress, they said without any self-consciousness. Their artistic forms were so simple as to impose no hindrance to the instinctive desire for revealing to others what swelled in their very hearts. The result is that impressiveness and that convincingness which can come from nothing but perfect sincerity. Innumerable poets have put into verse the sentiments of the familiar folk-song, *"Waly, Waly"*; yet it is not easy to find in all the list the same thing said with a certain childlike directness which goes to the heart that one finds in passages like this: —

> O waly, waly, but love be bonny
> A little time while it is new;
> But when 'tis auld, it waxeth cauld,
> And fades awa' like morning dew!

What later singer is there who has surpassed in pathos that makes the heart ache the exquisite beauty of *"Fair Helen"*?

> I would I were where Helen lies;
> Night and day on me she cries;
> Oh, that I were where Helen lies
> On fair Kirconnell Lea!...
> I would I were where Helen lies;
> Night and day on me she cries;
> And I am weary of the skies,
> Since my love died for me.

　　我不知道要表达的意思是否完全清楚了，如此微妙之处很难一一举例说明。然而，可以肯定的是，任何早期文学的读者都必定清楚，在过去最优秀作家的纯朴和天真中，我们发现了现在已经成为陈词滥调，几乎习以为常的东西，而他们却能用新颖别致的手法，令人信服地表达出来，使我们一开始感觉它们是真的。许多情感在文学中早已得到认可和表达，以至几乎每一个阶段都得到了充分表现，同样，几乎每一个短语都得到了完美体现。他们一开始就把语言禁锢在了囚笼里，现在似乎已不可能找到新颖和真切的言语来表达那些情感了。如果不是天才的个人印象和富有想象的作家的经验一直赋予文学以活力，文学便会从地球表面消失，成为一门终结了的艺术。

　　正是第一次发现的说服力和生动性，才给予了民歌魅力和力量。早期的民谣常常令后期的诗歌蒙羞。那些淳朴的歌手从来没有被告知过，应该拥有何种特殊的情感才算合适。他们从来没有听说过这种或那种感觉，艺术对他们来说并不是自觉的存在，真正打动他们的是自发而真实的情感表达。对于他们而言，情感太强烈而无法压抑，就能毫无自我意识地把它们表达出来。他们的艺术形式极其简单，没有什么能阻止向他人吐露激荡在内心深处情感的本能愿望，答案就在于深刻的印象和说服力只能来自完美的真挚。无数诗人将民歌《天呀！天呀!》中熟悉的情感融进了诗歌，然而，在所有的书单中都不容易找到同样的东西，唯有在这样的诗节中才能找到那种以小孩子般的直率直入人心的情感：

　　　　哦，天呀！天呀！但爱有多美好
　　　　当它还新鲜，就只一会儿；
　　　　但当它变老了，它就会变冷，
　　　　像晨露一样消失！

　　有哪位后世的歌手超越了《美少女海伦》的哀婉，造就了令人心痛的凄切之美？

> 我愿我在海伦躺着的地方；
> 她日日夜夜在我身旁哭泣；
> 哦，我在海伦安睡的地方
> 在美丽的科康内尔草地上！…
> 我愿意我在海伦被埋葬的地方；
> 她日日夜夜在我身旁哭泣；
> 我厌倦了天空，
> 因为我的爱为我而死。

The directness and simplicity which are the charm of folk-song and ballad are far more likely to be found in early literature than in that which is produced under conditions which foster self-consciousness. They belong, it is true, to the work of all really great writers. No man can produce genuinely great art without being completely possessed by the emotions which he expresses; so that for the time being he is not wholly removed from the mood of the primitive singers. Singleness of purpose and simplicity of expression, however, are the birthright of those writers who have been pioneers in literature. It is chiefly in their work that we may hope to experience the delight of finding emotions in the freshness of their first youth, of gaining something of that realization of perception which is fully only his who first of mortal men discovers and proclaims some new possibility of human existence.

Another quality of much importance in primitive writings and the early classics is complete freedom from sentimentality. As certain parasites do not attack young trees, so sentimentality is a fungus which never appears upon a literature until it is well grown. It is not until a people is sufficiently cultivated to appreciate the expression of emotions in art that it is capable of imitating them or of simulating that which it has learned to regard as a desirable or noble feeling. As cultivation advances, there is sure to be at length a time when those who have more vanity than sentiment begin to affect that which it has come to be considered a mark of high cultivation to feel. We all know this vice of affectation too well, and I mention it only to remark that from this literature in its early stages is far more apt to be free than it is in its later and more consciously developed phases.

The blight which follows sentimentality is morbidity; and one of the most important characteristics of the genuine classics is their wholesome sanity. By sanity I mean freedom from the morbid and the diseased; and the quality is one especially to be prized in these days of morbid tendencies and diseased eccentricities. There is much in many of the classics which is sufficiently coarse when measured by later and more refined standards; but even this is free from the gangrene which has developed in over-ripe civilizations. Rabelais chose the dunghill as his pulpit; in Shakespeare and Chaucer, Homer, in the Bible there are many things which no clean-minded man would now think of saying; but there is in none of these any of that insane pruriency which is the chief claim to distinction of several notorious contemporary authors. Neither is there in classic writers the puling, sentimental, sickly way of looking at life as something all awry. The reader who sits down to the Greek poets, to Dante, to Chaucer, to Molière, to Shakespeare, to Cervantes, to Montaigne, to Milton, knows at least that he is entering an atmosphere wholesome, bracing, and manly, free alike from sentimentality and from all morbid and insane taint.

直接和简单是民歌及民谣的魅力所在，这些品质在早期文学中比在自我意识养成的条件下产生的文学作品中更容易找到。它们确实属于所有真正伟大作家的作品。如果要表达的情感不能彻底征服一个人，他就无法创作出真正伟大的艺术，因而作家暂时还无法完全脱离原始歌手所有的那种心境。然而，目的单一和表达简单是那些文学先驱者与生俱来的权利。正是在这些先驱们的作品中，或许我们可以期盼体验到一种快乐，因为从中可以寻找到他们风华正茂时充满朝气的情感世界，也可以收获感知实现带来的东西———一种完全只属于凡人发现和称颂的人类生活的新的潜能。

在远古著作和早期经典中，另一个非常重要的品质是完全摆脱了多愁善感的情愫。由于某些寄生虫不会攻击幼树，多愁善感像一种真菌，在它没有成熟之前，也不会出现在文学作品里。只有当一个民族具备足够修养来欣赏艺术中的情感表达时，这个民族才能够模仿这些情感，才会模仿那些被认为值得拥有或高尚的情感。随着人们修养的提高，终会有一些虚荣心胜过真正情感的人，他们开始伪装已公认标志着更高修养的情感。我们都非常了解这种矫揉造作的恶习，我提到它只是为了说明，早期阶段的文学比后期以及更有自觉意识发展阶段的文学享有更多自由。

多愁善感带来的一大祸害就是文学中的病态。真正的经典最重要的特征之一是健康的理智。我所说的理智是指远离病态和病态的人。在这些病态倾向和病态怪癖的时代，健康的理智这一品质尤其值得推崇。用后来更缜密的标准来衡量时，许多经典存在一些粗俗的东西，但即便如此，我们过度成熟的文明也不曾患上坏疽病。拉伯雷选用"粪山粪海"作为他的讲道坛；在莎士比亚、乔叟、荷马和《圣经》中，有许多东西是心灵纯洁的人现在都没想到要表达的。但在这些作品中，并不存在任何荒唐淫乱之念，而这正是几个恶名昭著的当代作家的自称与众不同的主要手段。在经典作家那里，哀鸣、多愁善感、扭曲的病态眼光，这些病态的怪癖全都没有。坐拥希腊诗人、但丁、乔叟、莫里哀、莎士比亚、塞万提斯、蒙田、弥尔顿的读者起码应该知道，他正在进入一个健康、令人振奋且充满男性气概的艺术氛围，这里没有多愁善感，也免去了受各种病态及精神错乱的腐蚀。

Besides a knowledge of literary language, we must from the classics gain our standards of literary judgment. This follows from what has been said of temporary and permanent interest in books. Only in the classics do we find literature reduced to its essentials. The accidental associations which cluster about any contemporary work, the fleeting value which this or that may have from accidental conditions, the obscurity into which prejudice of a particular time may throw real merit, all help to make it impossible to learn from contemporary work what is really and essentially bad or good. It is from works which may be looked at dispassionately, writings from which the accidental has been stripped by time, that we must inform ourselves what shall be the standard of merit. It is only from the classics that we may learn to discriminate the essential from the incidental, the permanent from the temporary; and thus gain a criterion by which to try the innumerable books poured upon us by the inexhaustible press of to-day.

Nor do we gain only standards of literature from the classics, but standards of life as well. In a certain sense standards of literature and of life may be said to be one, since our estimate of the truth and the value of a work of art and our judgment of the meaning and value of existence can hardly be separated. The highest object for which we study any literature being to develop character and to gain a knowledge of the conditions of being, it follows that it is for these reasons in especial that we turn to the classics. These works are the verdicts upon life which have been most generally approved by the wisest men who have lived; and they have been tested not by the experiences of one generation only, but by those of succeeding centuries. For wise, wholesome, and comprehensive living there is no better aid than a familiar, intimate, sympathetic knowledge of the classics.

除文学语言的知识，我们还必须从经典中取得文学判断的标准。这是从人们所说的对书籍的暂时和永久兴趣产生的必然结果。只有在经典中，我们才能发现文学被简化到了极致。当代作品充斥着各种偶然联系，也充满着偶然条件下这个或那个作品可能拥有的短暂价值，并且特定时期的歧见可能使文学真正的价值陷于似是而非的境地，所有这些因素使人们无法从中了解，当代作品哪些属于真正和本质上优秀的文学，哪些是低劣的文学。我们只有冷静地看待文学作品，让岁月抹去作品中的偶然性，才能知道什么是价值的标准。只有从经典中，才能学会从偶然性中鉴别出本质，从瞬间中鉴别出永恒，并由此赢得一个标准去检验当今不知疲倦的印刷机倾泻在我们身上的不计其数的书籍。

我们从经典中获得的不仅是文学的标准，而且还有生活的标准。在某种意义上，文学和生活的标准可以说是一体的，因为我们对艺术作品的真实性和价值的评价与对生活的意义和价值的判断密不可分。

我们研读任何文学的最高目的是陶冶性格并了解我们的生存状态，因此，正是出于这些特殊的原因，我们转向了经典。经典作品是对生活的判断，为那些曾经享受过人生的最具智慧的人普遍认可。经典作品不仅接受过一代人经验的考验，而且还要经受后几个世纪的考验。对于智慧、健康和全面的生活，没有比熟悉、亲切、富有同情心的经典知识更能助我们一臂之力的了。

XI
CONTEMPORARY LITERATURE

We speak of the classics, of ancient literature, and of contemporary literature, but in reality, all literature is one. We divide it into sections for convenience of study, but it is a notable error to forget that it is consecutive from the dawn of civilization to the present. It is true that in applying the term to works of our own time it is both customary and necessary to employ the word with a meaning wider than that which it has elsewhere. It is often difficult to distinguish in contemporary productions that which is of genuine and lasting merit from that which is simply meretricious and momentary, and still harder to force others to recognize such distinction when made. It is therefore inevitable that the name literature should have a broader signification than when applied to work which has been tested and approved by time.

There are few things more perplexing than the attempt to choose from the all but innumerable books of our own day those which are to be considered as genuine. If we are able to keep vividly in mind what qualities make a thing literature, it is possible to have some not inadequate idea of what contemporary writings most completely fulfill the given conditions. We are able to speak with assurance of the work of a Tennyson or a Browning; and to feel that we have witnessed the birth of classics of the future. Beside these, however, stand the enormous multitude of books which are widely read, much talked about, and voluminously advertised; books which we cannot openly dispraise without the risk of being sneered at as captious or condemned as conceited. There are the poems which publishers inform the public in column-long advertisements, bristling with the testimonials of men and women who make writing their business, are the finest productions since Shakespeare; there are the novels which prove themselves to be works of genius by selling by the hundreds of thousands of copies and very likely being given to the purchasers of six bars of some patent soap; there are the thin and persecuted looking volumes of "prose poems" or rhyming prose which are looked upon by small bands of devoted followers as the morsel of leaven which is to leaven the whole lump; there are, in short, all those perplexing writings which have merit of some kind and in some degree, yet to decide the genuine and lasting merit of which might tax the wisdom and the patience of a Solomon of Solomons.

第十一讲　当代文学

　　我们说古典文学、古代文学、当代文学，但实际上所有的文学都是一体的。为便于研读，我们将其分成几个部分，但绝对不可忘记，文学是如何从文明的开端逐渐演变至今的。的确，在将文学一词应用于我们这个时代的作品时，依照惯例，有必要赋予其更广泛的意义。在当代作品中，通常很难区分真正具有持久价值的作品，还是华而不实、昙花一现的作品，也很难在做出这种区分时强迫他人承认这种区别。因此，当文学的名称用于经过时间检验认可的名著时，应该具有更广泛的意义。

　　想从当今无垠书海中选出真正有价值的书更是难上加难。如果我们能够清楚地认识到真正成就文学作品的那些特性，就可能大概明白当代作品中哪些最符合规定的要求。如果遇到某个像丁尼生或勃朗宁这样作家的作品，我们就能肯定地指出其作品的价值，并能预感它们将成为未来的经典。然而，除此之外，还有大量被广泛阅读、谈论和大力宣扬的书籍，这些都是不能公开批评的书，否则就可能有人嘲笑我们是吹毛求疵、狂妄自负。出版商在长篇广告中向公众宣传一些诗歌，堆砌了对这些以写作为业的男男女女的溢美之词，甚至说他们的作品是自莎士比亚以来最优秀的作品。有些小说以数十万册的销量证明自己是天才的作品，而且还要强调其读者都是有品位的。有些看起来很单薄，但很有反叛意味的"散文诗"或押韵散文，被一小群虔诚的追随者视为用来发酵一整块面团的一小块酵母。简而言之，所有这些令人困惑的著作都具有某种类型和某种程度的优点，但尚未确定是否具有真实且永恒的价值，这些书将考验真正的智者的智慧和耐心。

I have already spoken of the effect which temporary qualities are sure to have in determining the success of an author. The history of books is full of instances of works which have in their brief day filled the reading world with noisy admiration, but which have in the end been found destitute of enduring merit. While transient fame is at its height, while enthusiastically injudicious admirers are praising and judiciously enthusiastic publishers are reechoing their plaudits, it is a well-trained mind that is able to form a sound and rational judgment, and to distinguish between the ephemeral and the abiding. The only hope lies in a careful and discriminating application of standards deduced from the classics. He who desires to judge the books of to-day must depend upon comparison with the books of yesterday. He must be able to feel toward the literature of the past as if it were of the present, and toward that of the present as if it were of the past.

It is not to the popular verdict upon a work that one can look for aid in deciding upon real merit. In time the general public accepts the verdict of the few, but at first it is the noisy opinion of the many, voluble and undiscriminating, which is heard. The general public is always affected more by the accidental than by the permanent qualities of a work, and it is more often imposed upon by shams than touched by real feeling. It is easy to recognize conventional signs for sentiment, and it is not difficult for the ordinary reader to persuade himself that he experiences emotions which are explicitly set forth for him. Popular taste and popular power of appreciation are not inaccurately represented by those eminently successful journals which in one column give the fashions and receipts for cake and in the next detailed directions for experiencing all the sensations of culture. Sentimentality is always more instantly and more widely effective than sentiment. Sentimentality finds a ready response from the fact that it only calls upon us to seem, while sentiment demands that for the time being at least we shall be.

It is necessary here to say that I do not wish to be misunderstood. I do not mean in the least to speak with scorn or contempt of the lack of power justly to discriminate and to appreciate which comes from either natural disability or lack of opportunities of cultivation. Narrowness of comprehension and appreciation is a misfortune, but it is not necessarily a fault. I mean only to point out that it is a thing to be outgrown if possible. Of the pathos of lives which are denied their desire in this I am too keenly aware to speak of such otherwise than tenderly. For the young women who put their sentiments up in curl-papers and the young men who wax the mustaches of their minds I have no patience whatever; but for those who are seeking that which seems to them the best, even though they blunder and mistakenly fall prostrate before Dagon, the great god of the Philistines, it is impossible not to feel sympathy and even admiration. In what I have been saying of the fallibility of popular opinion I have not meant to cast scorn on any sincerity, no matter where it is to be found; but merely to point out that the general voice of the public, even when sincere, is greatly to be distrusted.

　　我已经说过，暂时的品质肯定能促使一个作者的成功。在书籍的历史中，不乏在阅读界短暂成功的例子，这些书都曾受到热捧，但最终却被证明缺乏经久不衰的价值。当某本书短暂的名气达到顶峰时，当狂热的不明智的崇拜者不断赞美时，当聪明而积极的出版商不断吆喝时，这时候只有训练有素的头脑才能够做出正确合理的判断，才能区分其短暂的或持久的价值。唯有从经典中找寻标准，并小心公正地运用这些标准，才有可能更好地做出判断。想要评判当今的作品，就必须同过去的作品进行比较，还必须有能力将过去的文学作品带入当今时代，并将当今的文学作品置于过去来酌量。

　　想要判断一部作品的真正价值，我们不能依靠大众的评价。随着时间的推移，大众会接受少数人的判断，但大家首先听到的是许多滔滔不绝且没有鉴赏力的读者的意见。普通大众总是更容易受到作品的偶然而非永久的品质的影响，并且容易被假象欺骗，而不是为真情实感所打动。我们很容易就能识别出表达情感的惯用符号，但普通的读者却很容易感同身受，且并不知道这是作者的刻意诱导。那些非常成功的期刊也不能代表大众品味和大众欣赏力，它们往往在一个专栏中大谈蛋糕的时尚和收益，又在下一个专栏细细讨论如何体验不同的文化。情绪总是比情感更即时、更广泛。情绪是一种即时的反应，因为它只需要我们表现出来的样子，而情感体现的是我们当下的真实自我。

这里有必要解释一下，因为我不想被误解。无论是因为天生的障碍还是缺乏后天的培养而没有公正区分和欣赏能力的人，我都丝毫没有嘲笑或蔑视的意思。领悟和欣赏的狭隘是一种不幸，但并不一定是一种过失。我的意思只是要指出，如果可能的话，这是一件须用阅历来超越的事情。对于拒绝去感受艺术感染力的人们，我会非常热切地而非温和地谈论此话题。不过，对于那些把心思都花在卷头发的年轻女人和给胡须打蜡的年轻男人，我是没有任何耐心的。对于那些不断寻求美好事物的人，即使他们愚蠢地、错误地俯伏在非利士人的大衮神面前，我也无法不为之感到同情甚至钦佩。在谈论流行观点的不可靠性时，我并不是要蔑视任何真诚，无论是哪里来的真诚。我只想指出公众的普遍声音，即使是真诚的，也是非常不可信的。

Whatever contemporary literature may be, however mistaken may be the popular verdict, and however difficult it may be for the most careful criticism to determine what is of lasting and what of merely ephemeral merit, the fact remains that it is the voice of our own time, and as such cannot be disregarded. To devote attention exclusively to the classics is to get out of sympathy with the thought of our own generation. It is idle to expend energy in learning how to live if one does not go on to live. The true use of literature is not to make dreamers; it is not to make the hold upon actual existence less firm. In the classics one learns what life is, but one lives in his own time. It follows that no man can make his intellectual life full and round who does not keep intelligently in touch with what is thought and what is written by the men who are alive and working under the same conditions.

Contemporary literature is the expression of the convictions of the time in which it is written. The race having advanced so far, this is the conclusion to which thinkers have come in regard to the meaning of life. Contemporary literature is like news from the front in war-time. It is sometimes cheering, sometimes depressing, often enough inaccurate, but continually exciting. It is the word which comes to us of the progress of the eternal combat against the unknown forces of darkness which compass humanity around. There are many men who make a good deal of parade of never reading books of their own time. They are sometimes men of no inconsiderable powers of intellect and of much cultivation; but it is hardly possible to regard them as of greater contemporary interest than are the mummies of the Pharaohs. They may be excellent in their day and generation, but they have deliberately chosen that their generation shall be one that is gone and their day a day that is ended. They may be interesting relics, but relics they are. It is often wise to wait a time for the subsiding of the frenzy of applause which greets a book that is clever or merely startling. It is not the lover of literature who reads all the new books because they are new, any more than it is he who neglects the old because they are old; but if we are alive and in sympathy with our kind, we cannot but be eager to know what the intellectual world is thinking, what are the fresh theories of life, born of added experience, what are the emotions of our own generation. We cannot, in a word, be in tune with our time without being interested in contemporary literature.

It is here that the intellectual character of a man is most severely tested. Here he is tried as by fire, and if there be in him anything of sham or any flaw in his cultivation it is inevitably manifest. It is easy to know what to read in the classics; they are all explicitly labeled by the critics of succeeding generations. When it comes to contemporary work a reader is forced largely to depend upon himself. Here he must judge by his individual standards; and here he both must and will follow his own inclinations. It is not always possible for a man accurately to appraise his mental advancement by the classics he reads, because his choice may there be influenced by conventional rather than by personal valuation; but if he will compare with the established classics the books which he genuinely likes and admires among the writings of his own time, he may come at an estimate of his mental state as fair as a man is ever likely to form of himself.

　　无论当代文学是什么，无论流行的判断是多么错误，无论对于最谨慎的评判来说要区分持久的和短暂的价值有多么困难，我们必须意识到这都是我们这个时代的声音。只关注经典，就是对我们这一代人的思想失去同情。如果一个人不继续生活，那么花费精力学习如何生活是无用的。文学的真正用途不是造梦，也并不是让大家脱离真实世界。人们通过阅读经典了解生活是什么，但也同时真实地生活在自己的时代。因此，如果一个人不明智地去了解那些与他在相同条件下活着和工作的人们所想和所写，就不可能拥有完善而丰盈的精神世界。

　　当代文学是对当下时代信念的表达。人类已经取得了长足的进步，这是思想家们对生命意义得出的结论。当代文学就像战时前线的新闻，它有时令人欢呼，有时令人沮丧，常常不够准确，但仍然令人兴奋。这个词是一个向我们传达人类与未知黑暗势力进行永恒战斗的进程的词。有许多人大肆宣扬自己从不读自己这个年代的书，他们有时候就是文雅过头，智慧不足的那类人，很难觉得他们比法老的木乃伊更具有当代影响。他们可能在那个时期，甚至那个年代都很优秀，但他们却有意认为自己的年代已是过去的年代，自己的那个时期是已经结束了的时期。他们可能是有趣的遗物，但那也就只是遗物而已。对待一本精巧的或者惊人的书，通常明智地做法是等待热烈的掌声平息。因书籍新而只读新书的人，和因书旧而只读旧书的人一样，都不是真正的文学爱好者。只要我们还活着并同情我们的同类，就不能不渴望知道知识界在想什么，新的生活道理是什么，有着不同生活经验的我们这一代人的情感又是什么。总之，如果对当代文学不感兴趣，我们就无法与时代保持同步。

　　读当代文学，一个人的智慧水平将会受到最严峻的考验，他会经受烈火般的考验，若存在任何虚伪或修为上的缺陷，难免都会暴露出来。由于已经有成功的书评做过详细的分析，想知道经典作品的内容很简单。但读当代作品很大程度上就只能依靠自己了。读当代文学，必须用自己的标准来判断，必须也必然遵循自己的意愿。一个人并不总是可以通过他阅读的经典来准确地评价他的精神进步，因为他的选择可能会受到传统而不是个人评价的影响，但是，如果他将自己真正喜欢和欣赏的同时代的书籍与被认可的经典作品进行比较，他就可能对自己的精神世界有着较为公正的认识，就像是认识一个全新的自我一样。

It is, then, easy to see that there is a good deal of danger in dealing with current work. It is necessary to be in sympathy with the thought of the day, but it is only too common to pay too dear for this. It is extremely hard, for instance, to distinguish between genuine literary taste and curiosity when writings are concerned which have the fresh and lively interest which attaches to those things about which our fellows are actually talking and thinking. It is of course allowable to gratify a healthy curiosity, but it is well to recognize that such reading is hardly likely to promote mental growth. There is no law, civil or moral, against indulging the desire to know what is in any one of those books which are written to be talked about at ladies' luncheons; and it is not impossible that the readers who give their time to this unwholesome stuff would be doing something worse if they were not reading it. The only point upon which I wish to insist is that such amusement is neither literary nor intellectual.

There is, moreover, the danger of allowing the mind to become fixed upon the accidental instead of the permanent. I have spoken of the fact that the temporary interest of a book may be so great as to blind the reader to all else. When *Uncle Tom's Cabin* was new, it was practically impossible for the readers of that day to see in it anything but a fiery tract against slavery. To-day who reads *Ground Arms—The Story Of A Life* without being chiefly impressed with its arguments against war? It is as controversial documents that these books were written. If they have truth to life, if they adequately express human emotion, they will be of permanent value after this temporary interest has passed. The danger is that the passing interest, which is natural and proper in itself, shall blind us to false sentiment, to unjust views of life, to sham emotion. We are constantly led to forget the important principle that books of our own time must be judged by the standards which are afforded by the books which are of all time.

There has never been a time when self-possession and sound judgment in dealing with contemporary literature were more important than they are to-day. The immeasurably prolific press of the nineteenth century is like a fish-breeding establishment where minnows are born by the million a minute. There are so many books that the mind becomes bewildered. The student who might have the strength of mind to form an intelligent opinion of five books is utterly incapable of doing the same by five thousand. We are all constantly led on to read too many things. It has been again and again remarked that our grandfathers were better educated than their grandsons because they knew thoroughly the few works which came in their way. We have become the victims of over-reading until the modern mind seems in danger of being destroyed by literary gluttony.

因此，不难发现想要讨论当代作品是很有风险的。我们有必要抱着一颗同情心去理解这个时期的思想，却又很容易为此付出很高的代价。例如，当涉及与我们的同胞正在谈论和思考的事物相关的新鲜而活泼的作品时，很难区分真正的文学品味和好奇心。满足健康的好奇心当然是可以的，但也最好认识到这样的阅读不太可能促进精神进步。无论是法律上还是道德准则上，都没有明确反对大家渴望了解女士们在午餐会上谈论的那些书的内容。那些把时间花在这些不健康的东西上的读者，如果没有读到这些东西，也可能做出一些更糟糕的事情。我唯一想强调的是，这种消遣的东西既不是文学也不是知识。

此外，还有一种危险，就是让头脑专注于偶然的事物而不是永恒的事物。我已经谈到过这样一个事实，即对一本书的短暂兴趣点可能如此之大，以至读者对其他一切视而不见。当《汤姆叔叔的小屋》刚出版时，当时的读者就觉得这是一本反对奴隶制的小册子，至于其他什么也看不到。今天谁读了《放下武器——一个生命的故事》不是只记住了它对战争的批判？这些书的本意是体现争议性。如果它们忠于生活，如果它们充分表达了人类的情感，那么在这种短暂的兴趣过去之后，将具有永久的价值。危险在于，一时的兴趣本身是自然而然的，却会使我们看不到不真实的情感、不公正的生活观和虚假的情感。我们经常被引导忘记一个重要的原则，即必须根据所有时代的书籍提供的标准来判断我们这个时代的书籍。

在讨论当代文学时，自我控制和正确判断从未像今天这样重要。十九世纪超级高产的出版社就像一个养鱼场，每分钟有数百万条小鱼出生。书太多了，脑子都糊涂了。一个学生可能有智力对五本书籍做出一个明智的判断，但要对五千本书籍形成明智的判断就完全做不到了。我们不断被引导阅读太多的东西。越来越多的人评论说，我们的祖辈比我们接受的教育更好，因为他们对读到的那些少量的作品了如指掌。我们已经成为过度阅读的受害者，而且现代思想似乎有被贪食文学摧毁的风险。

It is well in dealing with contemporary work to be especially self-exacting in insisting that a book is not to be read once which is not to be read a second time. This may seem to be a rule made merely for the sake of having a proper theory, yet it is to be taken literally and observed exactly. It is true that the temptation is so great to read books which are talked about, that we are all likely to run through a good many things which we know to be really unworthy of a single perusal, and of course to go over them again would be a waste of more time. Where to draw the line between the permanent and the ephemeral is a point which each must settle for himself. If, on the whole, it seems to a man well to pay the price in time and in the risk of forming bad mental habits, it is his right to do this, but pay the price he must and will.

It is hardly possible to discuss contemporary literature without speaking of that which is not literature—the periodicals. One of the conditions of the present time which most strongly affects the relations of ordinary readers to reading in general is the part which periodicals of one sort or another play in modern life. The newspaper enters so intimately into existence to-day that no man can escape it if he would, and with innumerable readers it is practically the sole mental food. It is hardly necessary to say that there is no more relation between the newspaper and literature than there would be between two persons because they both wear hats. Both books and journals are expressed in printed words, and that is about all that there is in common. It is necessary to use the daily paper, but its office is chiefly a mechanical one. It is connected with the purely material side of life. This is not a fault, any more than it is the fault of a spade that it is employed to dig the earth instead of being used to serve food with. It is not the function of the newspapers to minister to the intellect or the imagination in any high sense. They fulfill their mission when they are clean and reliable in material affairs. What is beyond this is a pretense at literature under impossible conditions, assumed to beguile the unwary, and harmless or vicious, according to circumstances. It is seen at its worst in the Sunday editions, with their sheets as many—as autumnal leaves that strow the brooks in Vallombrosa.

It is safe to say that for the faithful reader of the Sunday newspaper there is no intellectual salvation. Like the Prodigal Son, he is fain to fill his belly with the husks which the swine do eat, and he has not the grace even to long for the more dignified diet of fatted calf.

在面对当代文学作品时，我们可以严谨地坚持一个标准，那就是如果这本书不值得读第二遍，那它也不值得读第一遍。这似乎只是为了有一个正确的理论而制定的规则，但它应该被认真理解并严格遵守。确实，大家都很想阅读公众热议的书籍，我们也很容易去浏览许多我们知道真的不值得细读的书，当然也知道再一遍一遍地去读就会浪费更多时间。在永久和短暂之间划清界限是每个人必须自己解决的问题。总的来说，如果一个人愿意付出时间并冒着形成不良心理习惯的风险，那么他有权这样做，但他也必须且自愿为之付出代价。

讨论当代文学几乎不可能不谈非文学的东西——期刊。当今对普通读者与一般阅读的关系影响最大的状况之一就是，不同类型的期刊在现代生活中产生的作用。期刊已经深入现代人的生活，就算有人愿意逃离它，也无法逃离，因为它几乎是无数读者的唯一的精神食粮。期刊和文学之间并无过多联系，就像不是两个人都戴着帽子就有必然联系一样，这一点无须赘述。书籍和期刊都用印刷文字表达，这就是它们所有的共同点。我们有必要读每日时报，但这样的阅读是机械的。它只与生活的物质方面有关。这不是报纸的错，就像铁锹被用来挖土而不是用来盛食物一样，这也不是铁锹的错。报纸的功能不是为精神或想象力提供任何高级别的服务。在处理物质事务时能公正可靠，报纸就完成了它们的使命。除此之外，是在不真实的条件下伪装成文学，以便根据情况来哄骗粗心、有恶意或者无恶意的人。可以看出，周日版尤为糟糕，一张张报纸多得如同飘在瓦隆布罗萨旅游胜地小溪上的秋叶。

可以肯定地说，对于周日报纸的忠实读者来说，得不到任何精神上的提升。就跟流浪汉一样，宁愿用猪食填饱肚子，也不愿追求体面的肥牛大餐。

The newspaper habit is pretty generally recognized as demoralizing, and in so far it may be in a literary point of view less dangerous than the magazine habit. The latter is often accompanied by a self-righteous conviction that it is a virtue. There is a class who take on airs of being of the intellectual elect on the strength of reading all the leading magazines; who are as proud of having four serials in hand at once as a society belle of being able to drive as many horses; who look with a sort of pitying contempt upon persons so old-fashioned as to neglect the magazines in favor of books, and who in general are as proudly patronizing in their attitude toward literature as they are innocent of any connection with it. This is worse than too great a fondness for journalism, and of course this is an extreme type; but it is to be feared that at their best the magazines represent mental dissipation.

It is true that genuine literature is often published in periodicals; and there are many editors who deeply regret that the public will not allow them to print a great deal more. As things are, real literature in the magazines is the exception rather than the rule. The general standard of magazine excellence is the taste of the intellectually*nouveaux riches* —for persons who have entered upon an intellectual heritage which they are not fitted rightly to understand or employ are as common as those who come to material wealth under the same conditions. It is to this class, which is one of the most numerous, and still more one of the most conspicuous in our present civilization, that most of the magazines address themselves. The genuinely cultivated reader finds in the monthlies many papers which he looks through as he looks through the newspaper, for the sake of information, and less often he comes upon imaginative work. The serials which are worth reading at all are worthy of being read as a whole, and not in the distorted and distorting fashion of so many words a month, according to the size of the page of a particular periodical. Reading a serials is like plucking a rose petal by petal; the whole of the flower may be gathered, but its condition is little likely to be satisfactory. While the magazines, moreover, are not to be looked to for a great deal of literature of lasting value, they not only encourage the habit of reading indifferent imitations, but they foster a dangerous and demoralizing inability to fix the attention for any length of time. The magazine-mind is a thing of shreds and patches at best; incapable of grasping as a whole any extended work. Literature holds the mirror up to nature, but the magazine is apt to show the world through a toy multiplying-glass, which gives to the eye a hundred minute and distorted images.

读期刊的习惯被普遍认为是令人沮丧的，到目前为止，从文学的角度来看，它可能不如读杂志的习惯危险。后者往往伴随着一种自以为是的信念，认为这是一种美德。有一类人靠阅读所有主流杂志的实力，装出自己是知识精英的姿态，就如同能驾驭尽可能多的骏马的社会名流一样，他们为自己同时能读四本杂志而自豪，他们以一种怜悯的眼光看待那些只看书籍不看杂志的老派人物，不愿意跟文学扯上联系，总觉得自己比读文学的更高尚。这比过于热爱新闻报的人还要糟糕，当然这是一种极端的类型，但令人担心的是，杂志在很大程度上代表了精神上的消遣。

　　诚然，真正的文学往往发表在期刊上，并且有很多编辑对公众不允许他们大量刊载文学内容而深感遗憾。事实上，杂志中的真正文学是一种例外而非常规。杂志卓越的一般标准是为了迎合知识新贵的品位——因为那些并不怎么理解或使用的知识遗产的人与那些在相同条件下获得物质财富的人一样普遍。大多数杂志都针对这个阶层，它是我们如今文明中人数最多的阶层之一，也是最引人注目的阶层之一。真正有教养的读者阅读月刊，就像浏览报纸一样，为了获取信息，而不是为了培养想象力。值得一读的连载小说必然值得完整地去阅读，而不是按照特定期刊的页面大小，每个月把那么多字用奇怪的排版方式呈现出来。阅读连载小说就像一瓣一瓣地采摘玫瑰花瓣，尽管整朵花可以被采摘下来，但最后花的样子就没法令人满意了。阅读杂志就更加无法感受到文学的持久价值了，杂志不仅会让读者养成阅读平庸中立的文学仿制品的习惯，而且还会培养一种危险的、令人沮丧的无法长时间集中注意力的行为。满脑子的杂志充其量只是零碎的东西，无法从整体上掌握任何完整的作品。文学是真实世界的镜像，但杂志却更像是用玩具放大镜来看世界，它给眼睛带来的是短暂的体验和扭曲的映像。

It may seem that I do scant justice to the magazines. It is certainly to be remembered that in the less thickly settled parts of this great inchoate country, where libraries are not, the magazine is often a comfort and even an inspiration. It is to be acknowledged that, with the enormous mass of half-educated but often earnest and sincere souls, the periodical has done and may still do a great deal of good. The child must play with toys before he is able to grasp the tools of handicraft, and enjoyment of the chromo may be a healthy and legitimate stage on the way to an appreciation of the masters of painting. It is not a reproach to call a man a toy-vender or a maker of chromos; nor do I see that what I have been saying is to be interpreted as reflecting on the makers of periodicals. It must be remembered that the

publication of a magazine is a business enterprise in the same sense that the
selling of carpets or calicoes is a business enterprise. The manufacturer of
magazines must please the general public with what he prints, as the
manufacturer must satisfy the ordinary buyer by the designs of his fabrics. In
either case it is the taste of the intellectual*bourgeoisie* which is the standard of
success. The maker of periodicals can no more afford to appeal to the taste of
the cultivated few than can the thrifty maker of stuffs. What is sold in the
open market must be adapted to the demands of the open market. It is simply
legitimate business prudence which keeps most magazines from attempting to
print literature. They publish, as a rule, all the literature that the public
will have, —modified, unhappily, by the difficulty of getting it to publish
in a world where literature cannot be made to order. A book, it is to be
remembered, is a venture; a magazine is an enterprise. The periodical must
pay or it must be discontinued.

　　The moral of the whole matter is that the only thing to do is to accept
magazines for what they are; neither to neglect them completely, nor to give
them that abundant or exclusive attention which they cannot even aim under
existing conditions at deserving. They may easily be dangerous intellectual
snares; but the wise student will often find them enjoyable, and sometimes
useful.

　　看起来似乎对杂志缺乏公正的评价。当然要记住，在这个伟大的
尚未完全发展的国家中人口稀少的地区，没有图书馆，杂志往往是一
种安慰，甚至是一种激发灵感的东西。应该承认，我们有着许多受教
育有限却非常认真且诚恳的人，期刊已经发挥了很大的作用，现在应
该依然大有益处。孩子必须先玩玩具，然后才能掌握手工艺工具，学
会欣赏真正的绘画之前，也必然先经过健康且合理的欣赏石版画的阶
段。把一个人称作玩具商贩或石版画制造商算不上是一种指责，并且
我也看不出我说的可以理解为是对期刊制造商的非难。但我们必须记
住，出版杂志就像卖地毯或印花布一样，是一种商业活动。杂志出版
商必须用他的印刷品取悦大众，就像纺织品制造商必须设计出让普通

买家满意的面料。对于二者来说，成功的标准都是符合中产阶级的品位。就像制造商要节约材料一样，期刊出版商也无法满足少数受教育人群的口味。在公开市场上销售的东西必须适应公开市场的需求。纯粹是出于合理的商业谨慎，大多数杂志并不会尝试刊登文学作品。一般来说，他们只刊登符合大众口味的改良过的文学，但遗憾的是在无法定制文学的杂志圈，要刊登文学是很难的。请记住，一本书就是一次冒险活动，而杂志是一次商业活动。期刊必须有收益，否则将会停刊。

　　我们讨论这件事的意义在于，明白我们唯一要做的就是接受杂志的本来面目，既不完全忽视它们，也不给予它们过多的或专门的关注，因为在现有条件下它们也不值得。它们很容易成为危险的精神陷阱，但聪明的学生往往会发现它们很有趣，有时也很有用。

XII

NEW BOOKS AND OLD

The quality of "timeliness" is one of the things which makes it especially difficult to distinguish among new books. There is on this day an ever increasing tendency to treat all topics of popular discussion in ways which profess to be imaginative, and especially in the narrative form. The novel with a theory and the poem with a purpose are so enveloped with the glamour of immediate interest that they appear to be of an importance far beyond that which belongs to their real merit. Curiosity to know what these books have to say upon the questions which most deeply interest or most vitally affect humanity is as natural as it is difficult to resist. The desire to see what a book which is talking about is doubly hard to overcome when it is so easily excused under the pretense of gaining light on important questions. Time seems to be proving, however, that the amount of noise made over these theory-mongering romances is pretty nearly in adverse ratio to their worth. We are told in *Scripture* that wisdom called in the streets, and no man regarded, but the opposite seems to be true of the clamors of error. The very vehemence of these books is the quality which secures their attention; and it is impossible wholly to ignore them, and yet to keep in touch with the time.

It is more difficult to evade pretentious and noisily worthless writings because of the great ingenuity of the advertising devices which force them upon the attention. The student of genuine literature naturally does not allow himself to be led by these, no matter how persuasive they may be. The man who bases his choice of books upon the advertisements is like him who regulates the health of his family by the advice of a patent-medicine almanac. It is not easy, however, to escape entirely from the influence of advertising. If we have seen a book talked about in print, been confronted with its title on a dazzling poster, if it has been recommended by the chief prize-fighter in the land, or damned by the admiration of Mr. Gladstone, we are any of us inclined to read it, just to see what it is like. The ways by which new publications are insinuated upon the attention are, too, so impalpably effective, so cunningly unexpected, that we take our opinion from them without realizing that we have not originated it. The inspiration and stress of the soul which in Greece begot art, bring forth in our day advertising, and no man can wholly escape its influence.

第十二讲　新书和旧书

　　"及时性"这个特性是造成新书特别难以区分的因素之一。在今天，有一种方式越来越倾向于以自称富有想象力的方式来对待所有讨论的流行话题，尤其是在叙事形式上。有理论的小说和有目的的诗都被眼前利益的魅力所笼罩，以至它们的重要性似乎远远超出了作品具有的真正价值。人们好奇地想知道，这些书对人类最感兴趣或对人类影响最大的问题有什么说法，这种好奇心是自然而然的，也是难以抗拒的。看一看人们谈论的一本书是什么样子的愿望愈发难以抑制，因为这一愿望以了解重要问题为借口很容易获得开脱。然而时间似乎证明，这些散布理论的浪漫故事所引起的鼓噪与它们的价值几乎成反比。《圣经》告诉我们，智慧在上街呼唤，却没有人会在意，但谬见的喧嚣似乎恰恰相反。这些书的热烈程度在于其特有的品质能确保引人瞩目，因此如完全忽略这些书籍，就无法与时代保持联系。

　　人们越来越难以躲避那些自命不凡但毫无价值的作品，这是由于广告手段极为巧妙，迫使人们去关注那些作品。但不管广告手段多么具有说服力，真正学习文学的学生自然不允许自己被它们牵着鼻子走。根据广告来选择书籍的人，与根据专利医学年鉴的建议来管控家人健康的人如出一辙。然而，要完全摆脱广告的影响并不是一件易事。如果我们看到一本尚在印刷中的书被谈论，在令人眼花缭乱的海报上看到它的书名，如果这本书赢得了这个国家首席职业拳击手的推荐，或者被令人钦佩的格莱斯顿先生骂得一文不值，那么，只是为了看看它是什么样的，我们便可能成为倾向于去阅读这本书的其中一人。新出版物引起人们注意的方式出奇有效，令人难以琢磨，以至我们由此高谈阔论，却没意识到它并非我们首创。灵魂的感召和压力孕育了希腊的艺术，也催生了今天的广告艺术，没有人能完全摆脱它的影响。

Innumerable are the methods by which authors, whose sole claim to genius is this skill in advertising, keep themselves and their books before the public. Eccentricities of manner and of matter are so varied as to provoke wonder that mental fertility of resource so remarkable should not produce results really great and lasting. Some writers claim to be founders of schools, and talk a good deal about their "modernity," a word which really means stale sensationalism revamped; others insist in season and out of season that they have discovered the only true theory of art, and that literature is only possible upon the lines which they lay down. It is unfortunately to be observed that the theory invariably follows the practice; that they first produce queer books, and then formulate a theory which excuses them. Still others call attention to themselves by a variety of artifices, from walking down Piccadilly mooning over a sunflower to driving through the Bois de Boulogne in brocade coat, rose-pink hat, and cravat of gold-lace, like Barbey d'Aurevilly. No man ever produced good art who worked to advertise himself, and fortunately the day of these charlatans are usually short. I have spoken in another place of the danger of confounding an author and his work; and of course, this peril is especially great in the case of writers of our own time. I may add that the parading of authors is a vice especially prevalent in the nineteenth century. Mrs. Leo Hunter advertises herself, and incidentally the celebrities whom she captures, and the publishers not infrequently show a disposition to promote the folly for the sake of their balance-sheet. If Apollo and the Muses returned to Earth they would be bidden instantly to one of Mrs. Hunter's

Saturday five o'clock, and a list of the distinguished guests would be in the Sunday papers. That is what many understand by the encouragement of literature.

Another method of securing notice, which is practiced by not a few latter-day writers, is that of claiming startling originality. Many of the authors who are attempting to take the kingdom of literary distinction by violence lay great stress upon the complete novelty of their views or their emotions. Of these, it is perhaps sufficient to say that the men who are genuine insist that what they say is true, not that they are the first to say it. In all art that is of value the end sought is the work and not the worker. Perhaps most vicious of all these self-advertisers are those who force themselves into notice by thrusting forward whatever the common consent of mankind has hitherto kept concealed. The trick is an easy one. It is as if the belle who finds herself a wall-flower at a ball should begin loudly to swear. She would be at once the centre of observation.

　　有的作家声称他们唯一的天才就是广告技巧，凭借数不胜数的技巧，就可使自己和他们的书籍家喻户晓。特异的方式和如此千奇百怪的内容，令人诧异于为什么如此显赫的精神想象力资源没有催生出真正伟大而永恒的成果。一些作家自诩某一学派的创始人，经常大肆谈论学派的"现代性"——翻新了陈腐的煽情主义。另一些作家时不时地坚持认为，已经发现了唯一真正的艺术理论，并且文学只有在他们规划的路线上才能成为可能。不幸地看到，理论总是追随实践。他们首先出版一些古怪的书籍，然后提出一套理论来为他们辩护。还有一些人通过各种巧妙之法吸引人们的注意。从漫步在皮卡迪利大街凝视向日葵，到身着锦缎外套、佩戴玫瑰粉色帽子和金色蕾丝领结驱车穿过布洛涅森林，这样的场景就像出自法国作家巴尔贝·多尔维利之手。为了给自己打广告的作家创作不出好的艺术作品。所幸的是，这些骗子的好光景为时不久。我曾在另一场合说过，把作者和他的作品混淆起来很危险。当然，对于我们这个时代的作家来说，这种危险尤其严重。在这里可以补充一点，作家招摇过市是十九世纪一种特别普遍的恶习。利奥·亨特夫人为自己做广告，顺便也为她抓来的名人做广告，而出版商为了财务决算屡屡助长这种愚蠢行为。倘若阿波罗和缪斯女神返回地球，他们将被立即邀请到亨特夫人的一个星期六下午五点钟的聚会，而尊贵的客人名单将出现在星期日的报纸上。这就是许多人所理解的文学的激励手段。

当今，不少作家采用了另一种博取公众注意的方法，声称他们的创作具有惊人的原创性。许多作者企图凭借狂热的行为攫取文学王国的荣誉，于是每每强调他们的观点或情感具有完全的新颖性。实际上，真诚的人会坚持他们所言的真实性，而不一定非得表明他们是第一个这样说的人，也许这就绰绰有余了。在有价值的艺术中，追求的终极目标是艺术作品而非作品的创造人。有的人依靠强制推动世人公认而迄今秘而不宣的东西来达到迫使别人关注的目的，或许这是全部自吹自擂的人当中最不道德的一类人。这一诀窍可谓易如反掌，就好像一个壁花美女发现自己在舞会上受人冷落时，只需要扬声恶骂，她马上就可以成为众目睽睽下被注目的中心。

Of books of these various classes Max Nordau has made a dismal list in *Degeneration*, a book itself discouragingly bulky, discouragingly opinionated, discouragingly prejudiced and illogical, and yet not without much rightness both of perception and intention. He says of the books most popular with that portion of society which is most in evidence, that—

> They diffuse a curious perfume, yielding distinguishable odors of incense, eau de Lubin, and refuse, one or the other preponderating alternately.... Books treating of the relations of the sexes, with no matter how little reserve, seem too dully moral. Elegant titillation only begins where normal sexual relations leave off... Ghost-stories are very popular, but they must come on in scientific disguise such as hypnotism, telepathy, or somnambulism. So are marionette plays, in which seemingly naïve but knowing rogues make used-up old ballad dummies babble like babies or idiots. So are esoteric novels in which the author hints that he could say a deal about magic, fakirism, kabbala, astrology, and other white and black arts if he chose. Readers

intoxicate themselves in the hazy word-sequences of symbolic poetry. Ibsen dethrones Goethe; Maeterlinck ranks with Shakespeare; Nietzsche is pronounced by German and even French critics to be the leading German writer of the day; the *Kreutzer Sonata* is the Bible of ladies, who are amateurs in love, but bereft of lovers; dainty gentlemen find the street ballads and gaol-bird songs of Jules Jouy, Bruant, MacNab, and Xanroff very *distingué* on account of "the warm sympathy pulsing in them," as the phrase runs. — *Degeneration*, ii

This is a picture true of only a limited section of modern society, a section, moreover, much smaller in America than abroad. Common sense and a sense of humor save Americans from many of the extravagances to be observed across the ocean. There are too many fools, however, even in this country. To secure immediate success with these readers; a writer needs do nothing more than to produce erotic eccentricities. There are many intellectually restless persons who suppose themselves to be advancing in culture when they are poring over the fantastic imbecilities of Maeterlinck, or the nerve-rasping unreason of Ibsen; when they are sailing aloft on the hot-air balloons of Tolstoi's extravagant theories, or wallowing in the blackest mud of Parisian slums with Zola. Dull and jaded minds find in these things an excitement, as the jaded palate finds stimulation in the sting of fiery sauces. There are others, too, who believe that these books are great because they are so impressive. The unreflective reader measures the value of a book not by its permanent qualities but by its instantaneous effect, and an instantaneous effect is very apt to be simple sensationalism.

在这些不同类别的书籍中，匈牙利作家马克西·诺尔道在《堕落》一书中列出了一份令人沮丧的清单。诺尔道的书内容庞杂、令人沮丧、自以为是、充斥着偏见及混乱，但其观念和意图却并非没有合理性。他谈及那些最受社会上地位显赫的那部分人欢迎的书时认为：

  ……它们散发出一种奇特的香水的奇异味道，鲁宾酒和垃圾混合发出的气味，一种或另一种味道交替占据主导地位……关于两性关系的书籍，无论多么没有保留，似乎在道德上都过于乏味。优雅的挑逗只在正常性关系停止的地方开始……鬼魅的故事倍受欢迎，但必须戴着科学的伪装出现，如催眠术、心灵感应或梦游症。提线木偶戏也是如此，在这些戏中，看似天真但老于世故的无赖借助用过的旧民谣假人发出像婴儿或白痴一样的喋喋不休。神秘小说也是如此，作者暗示如果他愿意的话，他可以谈论很多关于魔术、苦行僧、卡巴拉、占星术和其他黑白艺术的话题。读者陶醉在象征诗歌朦胧的词序中；易卜生夺去了歌德的荣耀；梅特林克与莎士比亚并驾齐驱；德国甚至法国的评论家将尼采称为当时德国的一流作家；《克罗采奏鸣曲》是那些失去情人的恋爱新手女士们的圣经；优雅的绅士们发现朱尔·茹伊、布卢昂、麦克纳布和藏若夫的街头民谣与监狱囚犯的歌非常富有特色，因为正如这句话所说的那样，"温暖的同情心在他们内心深处涌动"。

——《堕落》，第二页

这幅画面只是现代社会中真实场景非常有限的一部分的写照，然而，在美国能看到的场景比在国外所能看见的小得多。美国人的常识和幽默感使他们脱离了在大洋彼岸能观察到的许多奢靡行为。然而，即便如此，在这个国家也有太多的傻瓜。为了与这些愚蠢的读者一道获取立竿见影的成功，作家只需要创造出各种色情怪癖。当仔细阅读梅特林克令人难以置信的愚蠢言行或易卜生的让人神经焦躁的混乱时，当他们乘坐托尔斯泰夸大其词的理论热气球高空飞行时，或与左拉一起在巴黎贫民窟漆黑的泥泞中打滚时，许多理智不安的人还自以为他们在文化上正保持与时俱进。好比迟钝的味觉在火辣的酱汁的刺痛里找到了刺激，沉闷和疲惫的头脑在这些东西中也寻得了一丝刺激。还有一些其他人仍然相信这些书很优秀，因为它们令人印象深刻。不善反思的读者以瞬时的效果而非永恒的品质来衡量一本书的价值，而瞬时的效果极易变成简单的煽情。

It is not difficult to see the fallacy of these amazing books. A blackguard declaiming profanely and obscenely in a drawing-room can produce in five minutes more sensation than a sage discoursing learnedly, delightfully, and profoundly could cause in years. Because a book makes the reader cringe it by no means follows that the author is a genius. In literature any writer of ordinary cleverness may gain notoriety if he is willing to be eccentric enough, extravagant enough, or indecent enough. An ass braying attracts more attention than an oriole singing. The street musician, scraping a foundling fiddle, vilely out of tune, compels notice; but the master, freeing the ecstasy enchanted in the bosom of a violin of royal lineage, touches and transports. All standards are confounded if notoriety means excellence.

There is a sentence in one of the enticing and stimulating essays of James Russell Lowell which is applicable to these writers who gain reputation by setting on edge the reader's teeth.

> There is no work of genius which has not been the delight of mankind. — *Rousseau and the Sentimentalists*.
>
> Notice: the delight of mankind, not the sensation, the pastime, the amazement, the horror, or the scandal of mankind, —but the delight. This is a wise test by which to try a good deal of the best advertised literature of the present day. Do not ask whether the talked-of book startles, amuses, shocks, or even arouses simply; but inquire, if you care to estimate its literary value, whether it delights.

It is necessary, of course, to understand that Mr. Lowell uses the word here in its broad signification. He means more than the simple pleasure of smooth and sugary things. He means the delight of tragedy as well as of comedy; of *King Lear* and *Othello* as well as of *Midsummer Night's Dream*; but he does not mean the nerve-torture of *Ghosts* or the mental nausea of *L'Assommoir*. By delight he means that persuasion which is an essential quality of all genuine art. The writer who makes his readers shrink and quiver may produce a transient sensation. His notoriety is noisily proclaimed by the trumpets of to-day; but the brazen voice of to-morrow will as lustily roar as other fleeting successes, and all alike be forgotten in a night.

I insisted in the first of these talks upon the principle that good art is "human and wholesome and sane." We need to keep these characteristics constantly in mind; and to make them practical tests of the literature upon which we feed our minds and our imaginations. We are greatly in need of some sort of an artistic quarantine. Literature should not be the carrier of mental or emotional contagion. A work which swarms with mental and moral microbes should be as ruthlessly disinfected by fire as if it were a garment contaminated with the germs of fever or cholera. It is manifestly impossible that this shall be done, however, in the present state of society; and it follows that each reader must be his own health-board in the choice of books.

不难看出这些令人惊眩的书籍的荒谬之处。一个无赖在客厅里亵渎和下流的言论可以在五分钟内引来一片哗然之声，这远远胜过一个哲人博学、愉快和深刻的话语多年才能引起的轰动。因为一本书让读者感到畏缩，这绝不意味着作者是天才。在文学中，任何一个智力一般的作家，如果他愿意变得足够古怪、足够奢侈或足够庸俗，他就会变得声名狼藉。驴叫声比黄鹂歌唱更能吸引人们的注意。街头音乐家拨弄一把弃儿的小提琴，荒腔走板，强行招揽路人注目，但大师却能释放出深藏于皇家血统的小提琴中的狂喜，触动心弦，令人心旷神怡。如果臭名昭著就意味卓越，那么所有标准都将令人迷惑。

詹姆斯·罗素·洛厄尔在其中一篇引人入胜且令人振奋的文章中，引用了一句话，非常适合于告诫这些试图通过恶心读者来沽名钓誉的作者。

没有任何天才的作品不曾为人类带来欢乐。

——《卢梭和感伤主义者》

请注意：人类的喜悦不是感觉、消遣、惊奇、恐怖或丑闻，而是喜悦。这是一个明智的检验标准，通过它可以尝试检验当今大量最好的广告文学。不要问所谈论的书是否令人震惊、逗乐、惊悚，甚至只是简单的激励，但是，如果你想评价它的文学价值，请问一问它是否令人喜悦。

当然，有必要理解洛厄尔先生在这里使用喜悦一词的含义很广。他的意思不仅是指光滑和含糖的东西带来的简单快乐，而且包含了从悲剧和喜剧中获得的喜悦，不仅是从阅读《仲夏夜之梦》获取的喜悦，而且也包括从阅读《李尔王》和《奥赛罗》中获得的喜悦。但他并不是指《幽灵》的精神折磨或《小酒馆》的心理恶心。洛厄尔所说的喜悦是信念，这是所有真正艺术的基本品质。令读者感到畏缩和颤抖的作者可以产生一时的轰动效应。当今喧嚣的喇叭声已宣告了这样的作家的恶名，但是明天刺耳之声同样会为其他转瞬即逝的成功起劲喝彩，但所有这一切都将在一夜之间被遗忘。

在第一次谈论中，我坚持这样一条原则，即好的艺术是"人性的、健康的和理智的"。我们需要时刻牢记这些特征，并以此检验思想和想象力所依赖的文学。我们非常需要某种艺术隔离期，文学不应成为精神或情感传染的载体。一部充满精神和道德细菌的作品如同一件被热病或霍乱细菌污染的衣服，应该用烈火无情地消毒。然而，在目前的社会状况下，这显然是不可能的。因此，每个读者在选择书籍时必须充当自己的健康理事。

The practical question which instantly arises is how one is to know good books from bad until one has read them. How to distinguish between what is worthy of attention and what is ephemeral trash has perplexed many a sincere and earnest student. This is a duty which should devolve largely upon trained critics, but unhappily criticism is not to-day in a condition which makes it reliable or practically of very great assistance where recent publications are concerned. The reader is left to his own judgment in choosing among writings hot from the press. Fortunately, the task of discriminating is not impossible. It is even far less difficult than it at first appears. The reader is seldom without a pretty clear idea of the character of notorious books before he touches them. Where the multitude of publications is so great, the very means of advertising which are necessary to bring them into notice show what they are. Even should a man make it a rule to read nothing until he has a definite estimate of its merit, he will find in the end that he has lost little. For any purposes of the cultivation of the mind or the imagination the book which is good to read to-day is good to read to-morrow, so that there is not the haste about reading a real book that there is in getting through the morning paper, which becomes obsolete by noon. When one considers, too, how small a portion of the volumes published it is possible to have time for, and how important it is to make the most of life by having these of the best, one realizes that it is worthwhile to take a good deal of trouble, and if need be to sacrifice the superficial enjoyment of keeping in the front rank of the mad mob of sensation seekers whose only idea of literary merit is noise and novelty. It is a trivial and silly vanity which is unhappy because somebody—or because everybody—has read new books first.

There is, moreover, nothing more stupid than the attempt to deceive ourselves, —especially if the attempt succeeds. Of all forms of lying this is at once the most demoralizing and the most utterly useless. If we read poor books from puerile or unworthy motives, let us at least be frank about it in our own minds. If we have taken up with unwholesome writers from idle curiosity, or, worse, from prurient hankering after uncleanness, what do we gain by assuring ourselves that we did not know what we were doing, or by pretending that we have unwillingly been following out a line of scientific investigation? Fine theories make but flimsy coverings for unhealthy desires.

Of course, this whole matter lies within the domain of individual liberty and individual responsibility. The use or the abuse of reading is determined by each man for himself. To gloat over scorbutic prose and lubricious poetry, to fritter the attention upon the endless repetition of numberless insignificant details, to fix the mind upon phonographic reports of the meaningless conversations of meaningless characters, to lose rational consciousness in the confusion of verbal eccentricities which dazzle by the cunning with which words are prevented from conveying intelligence, —and the writings of to-day afford ample opportunity for doing all of these things! —It is within the choice of every reader. It is to be remembered, however, that no excuse evades the consequence. He who wastes his life finds himself bankrupt, and there is no redress.

这里，马上会冒出一个实际问题，即在阅读完成之前，如何分辨好书和坏书，如何区分什么是值得关注的，什么是短暂的垃圾。这也是一直困扰着很多勤勉学子的问题。这是一项主要应该由训练有素的批评家来承担的职责，但不幸的是，文学批评今天所处状况并不可靠。就最近出版的作品而言，能提供的实际帮助也不大。读者可以自行判断选择出版的热门作品。庆幸的是，鉴别作品的任务并非不可能，它甚至比最初看起来的难度要小得多。读者接触名声不佳的书籍之前，很少非常清楚地去了解它们的特征。在千千万万出版物中，引起读者关注所必需的广告手段往往能说明，它们是什么样的书籍。即便一个读者可以制定一个规定，在他没有明确评估书的价值以前，什么都不读，他最终也会发现这样做，也不会失去什么。为了达到陶冶心灵或培养想象力的任何目的，今天读的好书，明天读照样是好书，这样就不至于像清晨匆匆忙忙浏览的早报一样，到中午就已过时了。当人们考虑到有时间来阅读的出版物仅是沧海一粟，以及通过拥有这些最优秀的书籍来过好每一天生活多么重要时，人们就会意识到不辞劳苦去阅读完全值得。如果需要的话，可以牺牲肤浅的享受，而不必与追求轰动的狂热之徒一道引领潮流，因为他们唯一的文学价值观就是：众声喧哗与标新立异。这是一种令人不悦、琐碎而愚蠢的虚荣心，因有的人或因每一个人已经先睹为快了。

此外，没有什么比欺骗我们自己的企图更愚蠢的了——尤其是当这种企图居然成功了的话。在所有形式的谎言中，自欺欺人是最令人沮丧和最徒然的。如果出于幼稚或卑鄙的动机去阅读劣质书籍，让我们至少在内心中要保持坦然！假如出于无聊和好奇，甚或出于内心追逐淫秽而肮脏的东西，我们开始对一些粗鄙的作家产生兴趣，并且连自己所作所为都不清楚，或者假装违心地坚持一条科学研究的路线，那么我们究竟能从中书中获取什么呢？美好的理论只不过是为那些危险的欲望提供了一层薄薄的遮盖物。

当然，这整个问题都属于个人自由和个人责任的范畴。阅读的使用或滥用应由每个人自己去决断。有的人心满意足地阅读苍白无力的散文和晦涩难懂的诗歌，把注意力浪费在无休止的重复无数无关紧要的细节上，或一门心思用在那些毫无意义的人物毫无意义的对话的录音报告上，他们在令人眼花缭乱的言语怪癖的混乱中失去了理性意识，无法以文字传递智慧。今天的文学作品为去做所有这些事情提供了多么充足的机会！——所有这一切均在每个读者的选择范围内。然而，须记住的是，没有任何借口可以逃避后果。浪费生命的人会发现自己将丧失一切，并且无药可救。

Always it is to be remembered that the classics afford us the means of measuring the worth of what we read. He who pauses to consider a little will see at once something of what is meant by this. He will realize the wide difference there is between familiarity with the permanent literature of the world and acquaintance with the most sensational and widely discussed books of to-day. A man may be a virtuous citizen and a good husband and father, with intelligence in his business and common sense in the affairs of life, and yet be utterly ignorant of how Achilles put the golden tress into the hand of dead Patroclus, or of the stratagem by which Iphigenia saved the life of Orestes at Tauris, or of the love of Palamon and Arcite for Emilie the fair, or of whom Gudrun married and whom she loved, or of how Sancho Panza governed his island, or of the ill-fated loves of Romeo and Juliet, or of the agony of Othello, or of Hamlet, or Lear, or Perdita, or Portia. The knowledge of none of these is necessary to material existence, and it is possible to make a creditable figure in the world without it. Yet we are all conscious that the man who is not aware of these creations which are so much more real than the majority of the personages that stalk puppet-like across the pages of history, has missed something of which the loss makes his life definitely poorer. We cannot but feel the enrichment of mind and feeling which results from our having in classic pages made the acquaintance with these gracious beings and shared their adventures and their emotions. Suppose that the books most noisily lauded to-day were to be tried by the same test. Is a man better for knowing with Zola all the diseased genealogy of the Rougon-Macquart family, morbid, criminal, and foul? It is not that a strong or well-developed man will ignore the crime or the criminals of the world; but it is not necessary to gloat over either. It is not difficult to learn all that it is necessary to know about yellow fever, cholera, or leprosy, without passing days and nights in the pest hospitals.

These unwholesome books, however, are part of the intellectual history of our time. He who would keep abreast of modern thought and of life as it is to-day, we are constantly reminded, must take account of the writers who are most loudly lauded. Goethe said, "It is in her monstrosities that nature reveals herself"; and the same is measurably true in the intellectual world. The madness, the eccentricity, the indecencies of these books, are so many indications by which certain tendencies of the period betray themselves. It seems to me, however, that this is a consideration to which it is extremely easy to give too much weight. To mistake this noisy and morbid class of books, these self-parading and sensational authors, for the most significant signs of the intellectual condition of the time is like mistaking a drum-major for the general, because the drum-major is most conspicuous and always to the fore, —except in action. The mind is nourished and broadened, moreover, by the study of sanity. It is the place of the physician to concern himself with disease; but as medical treatises are dangerous in the hands of laymen, so are works of morbid psychology in the hands of the ordinary reader.

永远切记，经典为我们提供了衡量阅读价值的方法。稍稍停下来想一想，一个人就会立刻明白这句话的含义。他将意识到，熟悉世界上永恒的文学作品与熟悉当今最轰动和讨论最广泛的书籍之间存在巨大差异。一个人可能是有道德的公民、一个好丈夫、一个好父亲，他在生意上很精明，在生活上明白常理，但他却完全不知阿喀琉斯是如何把金色的头发交到死去的帕特洛克罗斯手中的，伊菲革涅亚在陶里斯是如何救了俄瑞斯忒斯一命的，帕拉蒙和阿尔西特对美丽的艾米丽的爱是如何的，古德伦嫁给了谁并且她又爱谁，桑乔·潘萨是如何统治他的岛屿的，或者是关于罗密欧与朱丽叶的命运多舛的爱情，奥赛罗的痛苦，或者是哈姆雷特、李尔、珀蒂塔或波西亚这些人物。对物质生活而言，这些知识都不是所必需的，没有它，也可以成为一个这个世上值得信赖的人。然而，我们都意识到了，这些塑造的人物比大多数历史上像木偶一样高视阔步的人物还要真实得多，但一个人不了解这些人物，他便错过了一些东西，由此他的生活肯定会变得更贫乏。由于在经典书籍的纸页上结识了这些高尚而又仁慈的人物，并分享了他们的冒险经历和情感世界，我们不由自主地感到，我们的思想和情感由此变得丰富多彩了。假设当今最受热捧的书籍要接受同样的检验，一个人与左拉一道了解卢贡·马卡尔家族病态的、犯罪的、下流的所有病态谱系，这样会更好吗？并不是强壮或发达的躯体就可以对世间的罪行或罪犯视若无睹，而是没有必要幸灾乐祸。你要了解有关黄热病、霍乱或麻风病的所有知识并不困难，但没有必要非得在宠物医院度过几日几夜。

然而，一些无益的书籍是我们这个时代思想史的一部分。要跟上现代思想和今天的生活步伐，就要不断提醒自己，必须考虑到那些最受人称道的作家。歌德曾说过："大自然正是在她的可怕之物中揭示了自己"，在知识界此话同样千真万确。这些书中的疯狂、怪癖和猥亵，种种迹象把那个时代的某些癖好暴露无遗。但在我看来，这又是一个非常容易过分看重的考虑因素。把这些嘈杂而病态的书，这些自吹自擂和善于煽情的作者，都误认为是当今思想状况最重要标志，就如同将乐队指挥误认为一般演员，因为乐队指挥是最显眼的，总是处于前面的位置——除了在实际行动中。只有通过思维清醒的学习，心灵才会得到滋养和开阔。医生在其位置上关注的对象是各种疾病，但正如医学论文在外行人手中是不安全的一样，病态心理学的作品在普通读者手中也是如此。

Fortunately, contemporary literature is not confined to books of the unwholesome sort, greatly as these are in evidence. We have a real literature as well as a false one. Time moves so swiftly that we have begun to regard the works of Thackeray and Dickens and Hawthorne, and almost of Browning and Tennyson, as among the classics. They are so, however, by evident merit rather than by age, and have not been in existence long enough to receive the suffrages of generations. The names of these authors remind us how many books have been written in our time which endure triumphantly all tests that have been proposed; books to miss the knowledge of which is to lose the opportunity of making life richer. Certainly, we would be emotionally and spiritually poorer without the story of Hester Prynne and Arthur Dimmesdale, between whom the Scarlet Letter glowed balefully. To have failed to share the Fezziwigs' ball, or the trial of Mr. Pickwick for breach of promise; to have lived without knowing the inimitable Sam Weller and the juicy Micawbers, the amiable Quilp and the elegant Mrs. Skewton, philanthropic Mrs. Jellyby and airy Harold Skimpole, is to have failed of acquaintances that would have brightened existence; to be ignorant of Becky Sharp and Colonel Newcome, of Arthur Pendennis and George Warrington, of Beatrix and Colonel Esmond, is to have neglected one of the blessings, and not of the lesser blessings either. No man is without a permanent and tangible gain who has comprehendingly read Emerson's *Rhodora*, or the *Threnody*, or *Days*, or *The Problem*. Whoever has been sympathetically through the *Idylls of the King* not only experienced a long delight but has gained a fresh ideal; while to have gone to the heart of *The Ring and the Book*, —that most colossal *tour-de-force* in all literature, —to have heard the tender confidence of dying Pompilia, the anguished confession of Caponsacchi, the noble soliloquy of the Pope, is to have lived through a spiritual and an emotional experience of worth incalculable. In the age of Thackeray and Dickens, of Hawthorne and Emerson and Tennyson and Browning, we cannot complain that there is any lack of genuine literature.

Nor are we obliged to keep to what seems to be a high and breathless altitude of reading. There are many readers who are of so little natural imagination, or who have cultivated it so little, that it is a conscious and often a fatiguing effort to keep to the mood of these greater authors. Besides these works to the keen enjoyment of which imagination is necessary, there are others which are genuine without being of so high rank. It is certainly on the whole a misfortune that one should be deprived of a knowledge of Mrs. Proudie and the whole clerical circle in which she moved, and especially of Mr. Harding, the delightful "Warden"; he is surely to be pitied who has not read the story of "*Silas Marner*". No intelligent reader can afford to have passed by in neglect the pleasant sweetness of Longfellow or the wholesome soundness of Whittier, the mystic sensuousness of Rossetti or the voluptuous melodiousness of Swinburne.

　　幸运的是，当代文学并不局限于一些不健康的书籍，这一点是显而易见的。我们拥有真实的文学，也有虚假的文学。岁月如梭，我们已开始将萨克雷、狄更斯和霍桑，甚至勃朗宁及丁尼生的作品视为经典。然而，他们之所以如此，是因为他们作品的特点鲜明而非年代久远。这些作品问世的时间还不长，还未曾经受几代人公认的检验。这些作者的名字提醒我们，在这个时代有多少本书成功地经受住了所有提供的检验。错过对这些书的了解就意味着失去了让生活更丰富的机会。当然，如果没有海丝特·白兰和亚瑟丁梅斯代尔的故事，我们在情感和精神上会更加贫瘠，红字在他们之间闪烁着不详之光；如果未能分享菲茨威格家举行的圣诞舞会，或皮克威克先生因违反承诺而受到的审判；如果不认识狄更斯笔下无人可比的萨姆·维勒和有趣的米考伯夫妇、和蔼可亲的奎尔普、优雅的斯克顿太太、乐善好施的杰莉白夫人和漫不经心的哈罗德·斯基坡尔，那就是不认识能够照亮我们生活的熟人；如果对萨克雷小说中的贝基·夏普和纽康姆上校、亚瑟·潘登尼斯和乔治·沃灵顿、比阿特丽克斯和埃斯蒙德上校一无所知，就是忽略了人生之一的一大幸事，而且还是一件不小的幸事。如果能透彻读懂艾默生的《紫杜鹃》《哀歌》《岁月》《问题》，我们就将受益终生。如果深怀同情之心通读了丁尼生的《国王叙事诗》，我们不仅经历了长久的喜悦，更收获了新的理想；当进入罗伯特·勃朗宁的《指环与书》的核心——所有文学作品中最伟大的杰作——倾听到垂死的庞皮利亚温柔的秘密、卡彭萨基痛苦的忏悔、教皇的高贵独白，我们便经受过了一次价值不可估量的精神和情感体验。在萨克雷和狄更斯、霍桑和艾默生、丁尼生和勃朗宁的时代，我们不能抱怨缺乏真正的文学。

我们无须强迫自己一定要保持一个令人窒息的阅读高度。有许多读者缺乏天生的想象力，或者本身少有培养想象力，要去恪守这些大文豪的情感，是一种费神且常常令人疲倦的努力。除了那些需要具备敏锐想象力才能欣赏的作品外，还有一些真实但并非高不可攀的作品。总体而言，若缺乏了解特罗洛普小说中的普劳迪夫人和她行走出入的整个神职人员圈子，尤其是不了解令人愉快的"监狱长"哈丁先生，这无疑是一件不幸的事；如果没有读过乔治·爱略特的《织工马南》，肯定也会感到遗憾。任何明智的读者都不能忽视朗费罗令人愉快的甜美或惠蒂尔的健康深沉、罗塞蒂神秘的感官愉悦或司文朋令人心旷神怡的旋律。

It is manifestly impossible to enumerate all the authors who illustrate the richness of the latter half of the nineteenth century; but there are those of the living who cannot be passed in silence. To deal with those who are writing today is manifestly difficult, but as I merely claim to cite illustrations no fault can justly be found with omissions. Naturally Meredith and Hardy come first to mind. He who has read that exquisite chapter in *The Ordeal of Richard Feverel* which tells of the meeting of Richard and Lucy in the meadows by the river has in memory a gracious possession for the rest of his days. Who can recall from *The Return of the Native* the noonday visit of Mrs. Yeobright to the house of her son and her journey to death back over Egdon Heath, without a heart-deep thrill? What sympathetic reader fails to recognize that he is mentally and imaginatively richer for the honest little reddle-man, Diggory Venn, for sturdy Gabriel Oak, for the delightful clowns of *Under the Greenwood Tree* and *Far from the Madding Crowd*, or for ill-starred Tess when on that dewy morning she had the misfortune of touching the caddish heart of Angel Clare? To have failed to read and to reread Stevenson, —for one thinks of Stevenson as still of the living, —to have passed Kipling by, is to have neglected one of the blessings of the time.

It may be that I have seemed to imply by the examples I have chosen that the literature of continental Europe is to be shunned. Naturally in addressing English-speaking folk one selects examples when possible from literature in that tongue; and I have alluded to books in other languages only when they brought out more strikingly than do English books at a particular point. It is needless to say that in these cosmopolitan days no one can afford to neglect the riches of other nations in contemporary literature. It is difficult to resist the temptation to make lists, to speak of the men who in France with Guy de Maupassant at their head have developed so great a mastery of style; one would gladly dwell on the genius of Turgenieff, perhaps the one writer who excuses the modern craze for Russian books; or of Sienkiewicz, who has only Dumas*père* to dispute his place as first romancer of the world; and so on for other writers of other lands and tongues. It is unnecessary, however, to multiply examples, and here there is no attempt to speak exhaustively even of English literature.

The thing to be kept in mind is that it is our good fortune to live in the century which in the whole course of English literature is outranked by the brilliant Elizabethan Period only. It is surely worthwhile to attempt to prove ourselves worthy of that which the gods have graciously given us. Men sigh for the good days that are gone, and imagine that had they lived then they would have made their lives correspondingly rich to match the splendors of an age now famous. We live in a time destined to go down to the centuries not unrenowned for literary achievement; it is for us to prove ourselves appreciative and worthy of this time.

——细说十九世纪下半叶如此丰富的作家显然是不可能的。但有些仍然健在的作家却不应被埋没。去讨论那些今天仍在辛勤笔耕的作家显然很困难，但正如我声明过那样，谈论他们只是引以为证而已，如有遗漏也无可厚非。首先自然想到的是梅瑞狄斯和哈代。读过《理查德·法弗尔的苦难》中那篇描写理查德和露西在河边草地上相遇的精美章节的读者，在他余生的日子里便会多了一份值得珍怀的记忆。从《还乡》中回忆起姚伯太太中午去拜访她儿子，却在返回爱墩荒原的途中，命丧黄泉，谁能没有一种发自内心的震颤？富有同情心的读者难道没有意识到，正是因为有了诚实的红土商迪戈里·维恩、坚强的加布里埃尔·奥克、《绿林树下》和《远离喧嚣》中令人愉快的小丑，还有那个在洒满露水的早晨，不幸触动了安吉尔·克莱尔卑鄙的心的运气不佳的苔丝，他的精神和想象才变得更加丰富？没有读过和重读史蒂文森——因为认为史蒂文森仍然是活着的人，或只字不提吉卜林，就是忽视了这个时代的福祉之一。

或许，我选择的例子似乎暗示要避开欧洲大陆的文学。这是自然而然的，在对讲英语的人讲话时，人们会尽可能从该语言的文学作品中选择例子，只有当其他语言书籍比英语书籍在某一特别之处更突出的时候，我才会提到其他语言的书籍。毋庸置疑，在这些国际化的时代，没有人能够忽视当代文学中其他国家的财富。很难抗拒列出一个清单的诱惑，比如在法国以盖伊·德·莫泊桑为首的那些人已经创造了如此精湛的艺术风格；人们也会非常高兴地细说屠格涅夫的天才，或许正是这位作家解释了人们为何如此热衷现代俄罗斯书籍的缘由；或者还有唯有大仲马能与之争夺世界第一传奇小说家地位的捷克作家显克维奇；其他国家和其他语言的作家，如此等等，不一而足。然而，已无必要再增加更多例子了，我在这里甚至没有企望详尽地谈论英国文学。

需要记住的是，我们有幸生活在整个英国文学进程中仅次于辉煌的伊丽莎白时代的世纪。努力证明自己配得上众神赋予我们的才能，这肯定是值得的。人们为逝去的美好时光而叹息，并想象如果他们还活着，他们同样会使生活丰富多彩，以配得上这个辉煌的时代。我们生活在一个注定要延续几个世纪的时代，文学成就将与时代同辉，我们将要证明自己不负这个时代。

XIII
FICTION

Probably the oldest passion of the race which can lay any claim to connection with the intellect is the love of stories. The most ancient examples of literature which have been preserved are largely in the form of narratives. As soon as man has so far conquered the art of speech as to get beyond the simplest statements, he may be supposed to begin instinctively to relate incidents, to tell rudimentary tales, and to put into words the story of events which have happened, or which might have happened.

The interest which every human being takes in the things which may befall his fellows underlies this universal fondness; and the man who does not love a story must be devoid of normal human sympathy with his kind. It is hardly necessary, at this late day, to point out the strong hold upon the sympathies of his fellows which the story-teller has had from the dawn of civilization. The mind easily pictures the gaunt reciters who, in savage tribes, repeat from generation to generation the stories and myths handed orally from father to son; or the professional narrators of the Orient who repeat gorgeously colored legends and fantastic adventures in the gate or the market. Perhaps, too, the mention of the subject of this talk brings from the past the homely, kindly figure of the nurse who made our childish eyes grow large, and our little hearts go trippingly in the days of pinafores and fairy-lore—the blessed days when "once upon a time" was the open sesame to all delights. The responsiveness of human beings to story-telling the world over unites all mankind as in a bond of common sympathy.

What old-fashioned theologians seemed to find an inexhaustible pleasure in calling "the natural man" has always been strongly inclined to turn in his reading to narratives in preference to what our grandparents primly designated as "improving works". In any library the bindings of the novels are sure to be worn, while the sober backs of treatises upon manners, or morals, or philosophy, or even science, remain almost as fresh as when they left the bindery. Each reader in his own grade selects the sort of tale which most appeals to him; and while the range is wide, the principle of selection is not so greatly varied. The shop-girl gloats over "*The Earl's Bride*; *or*, *The Heiress of Plantagenet Park*". The school-miss in the street-car smiles contemptuously as shesees this title, and complacently opens the volume of the "*Duchess*" or of Rhoda Broughton which is the delight of her own soul. The advanced young woman of society has only contempt for such trash, and accompanies her chocolate caramels with the perusal of "*The Yellow Aster*", or the "*Green Carnation*", while her mother, very likely, reads the felicitous foulness of some Frenchman. Those readers who have a sane and wholesome taste, properly cultivated, take their pleasure in really good novels or stories; but the fondness for narrative of some sort is universal.

第十三讲　小说

人类最古老且宣称与智慧相联系的热情可能就是对故事的钟爱，最古老的文学例证主要以叙事的形式得以保存至今。一旦人类征服了语言艺术，超越了最简单的陈述方式，他可能会本能地开始叙述事件，讲述不太成熟的故事，并将已发生的事件或可能发生的事件付诸语言。

人们对可能降临在同伴身上的事情普遍怀有兴趣，这就构成了喜爱故事的基础。而一个不喜欢故事的人必然对其同类缺乏这种正常的同情心。在后来的岁月里，几乎没有必要指出，讲故事的人从文明的曙光开始就对他的同胞们怀有强烈的同情心。脑海中轻易就会浮现出一幅幅画面，原始部落中形容憔悴的朗诵人一代代地重复着那些父子口口相传的故事和神话，同时也会出现那些以讲故事为职业的东方人的身影，他们在门口或市场上反复吟诵着绚丽多彩的传说和冒险故事。或许，一提到本次讨论的主题，就会让人想起那个让孩子们天真的双眼睁得大大的护士朴实而亲切的身影。在围兜和童话故事的岁月里，我们的小心脏轻快地跳动，当"从前"开启了所有快乐的芝麻门，那是多么幸福的时光！人类对全世界讲故事的敏捷反应将全人类联结在一个共同的情感纽带上。

老派的神学家们似乎在称其为"有仁爱之心的人"中，找到了取之不尽的乐趣，因为他们阅读时总是强烈倾向于优先转向叙述故事，而不是我们祖辈最初选定的"改进的作品"。在任何图书馆里，小说的封面肯定都是残缺不全的，而关于礼仪、道德、哲学，甚至科学的论著素净的背影几乎和它们装帧完时一样崭新。不同水平的读者都会选择自己青睐的故事类型，虽然范围很广，但选择的原则并没有多大变化。女店员为阅读《伯爵的新娘或金雀花公园的女继承人》而兴奋不已；街车里的学姐看到这个书名不屑地笑了笑，得意扬扬地翻开了《公爵夫人》或罗达·布劳顿的书卷，这是令她内心最为高兴的东西。一个自由的社会年轻女性通常对这些垃圾作品投以蔑视的眼光，她一边吃着巧克力焦糖，一边细读《黄紫菀》或《绿色康乃馨》，而她的母亲很可能读到的是某个法国人言辞巧妙且污秽不堪的东西。那些有理智和健康品位、经过适当熏陶的读者，会从真正优秀的小说或故事中获得乐趣，但他们普遍偏好于某种叙事故事。

It would be manifestly unfair to imply that there is never a natural inclination for what is known as "solid reading", but such a taste is exceptional rather than general. Certainly, a person who cared only for stories could not be looked upon as having advanced far in intellectual development; but appreciation for other forms of literature is rather the effect of cultivation than the result of natural tendencies. Most of us have had periods in which we have endeavored to persuade ourselves that we were of the intellectual elect, and that however circumstances had been against us, we did in our inmost souls pant for philosophy and yearn for abstract wisdom. We are all apt to assure ourselves that if we might, we should devote our days to the study of science and our nights to mastering the deepest secrets of metaphysics. We declare to ourselves that we have not time; that just now we are woefully overworked, but that in some golden, although unfortunately indeterminate future, for which we assure ourselves most solemnly that we long passionately, we shall pore over tremendous tomes of philosophical thought as the bee grapples itself to a honey-full clover-blossom. It is all humbug; and, what is more, we know that it is humbug. We do not, as a rule, relish the effort of comprehending and assimilating profoundly thoughtful literature, and it is generally more easy to read fiction in a slipshod way than it is to glide with any amusement over intellectual work. The intense strain of the age of course increases this tendency to light reading; but in any age the only books of which practically everybody who reads at all is fond are the story-books.

It has been from time to time the habit of busy idlers to fall into excited and often acrimonious discussion in regard to this general love for stories. Many have held that it is an instinct of a fallen and unregenerate nature, and that it is to be checked at any cost. It is not so long since certain most respectable and influential religious sects set the face steadfastly against novels; and you may remember as an instance that when George Eliot was a young woman she regarded novel-reading as a wicked amusement. There is to-day a more rational state of feeling. It is seen that it is better to accept the instincts of human nature, and endeavor to work through them than to engage in the well-nigh hopeless task of attempting to eradicate them. To-day we are coming to recognize the cunning of the East in inculcating wisdom in fables and the profound lesson of the statement in the *Gospels*, "Without a parable spake He not unto them."

Much of the distrust which has been in the past felt in regard to fiction has arisen from a narrow and uncomprehending idea. Formalists have conceived that the relating of things which never occurred—which indeed it was often impossible should occur—is a violation of truth. The fundamental ground of most of the objections which moralists have made to fiction has been the assumption that fiction is false. Of certain kinds of fiction this is of course true enough, but of fiction which comes within the range of literature it is conspicuously incorrect.

　　如果含蓄地指出，根本不存在所谓的"严肃阅读"的自然倾向显然是不公平的，但这种欣赏能力是特殊的而不是普遍的。当然，一个只喜欢故事的人尚不能被视为智力发展出类拔萃的人，但对其他文学形式的欣赏与其说是自然倾向的结果，倒不如说是后天培养的结果。我们大多数人都有过这样的时期，我们努力说服自己相信，我们是知识精英，无论环境如何对我们不利，内心深处确实渴望哲学，渴望抽象的智慧。我们都倾向于确信，如果可以的话，我们应该把白天花在研究科学上，把晚上花在掌握形而上学最深奥的秘密上。我们声称，没有时间，已过度劳累，但我们生活在某种美好，虽有些不确定的未来，为此，我们郑重保证，我们热切渴望，如蜜蜂奋力扑向沾满花蜜的三叶草花朵，我们将仔细研读哲学思想的巨著。这些都是骗人的谎话，而且更重要的是，我们知道这是欺骗。通常，我们不喜欢付出努力去理解和接受思想深邃的文学作品，并且通常情况下，认为走马观花地阅读小说，比带着娱乐的心态浮光掠影地去阅读思想著作更容易。当然，年龄的巨大压力会增加轻松愉快的阅读意向，但在任何时代，几乎每一个读过书的人唯一喜欢的书籍便是故事书。

　　提到对故事的普遍偏爱，忙里偷闲的人习惯了不时陷入激动且经常是激烈的讨论中。许多人认为这是一种堕落和无可救药的本能，应该不惜一切代价加以遏制。不久之前，某些最受尊敬和最有影响力的宗教派别曾经坚决抵制小说。你可能还记得一个例子，乔治·爱略特还是个年轻女人时，认为阅读小说是一种邪恶的消遣，但今天她却有了一种更理性的情感状态。可以看出，接受人性的本能并努力克服它们，比无望地试图根除它们的任务更好。今天，我们将逐渐认识到东方在寓言中灌输智慧的巧妙，以及《福音》书中的深刻教训："没有寓言，他不会对他们说话。"

　　过去，人们对小说深感不信任，其中大部分原因都源于一种观点，认为小说性质狭隘和无法理解。形式主义者认为，将从未发生过的事情联系起来——实际上通常不可能发生——是对真理的违背。对于某些类型的小说，这当然是正确的，但是对于文学范围内的小说，它显然是不正确的。

Fiction is literature which is false to the letter that it may be true to the spirit. It is unfettered by narrow actualities of form, because it has to express the higher actualities of emotion. It uses incident and character as mere language. It is as unfair to object to the incidents of a great novel that they are untrue, as it would be to say that the letters of a word are untrue. There is no question of truth or untruth beyond the question whether the symbols express that which they are intended to convey. The letters are set down to impart to the intelligence of the reader the idea of a given word; the incidents of a novel are used to embody a truth of human nature and life. Truth is here the verity of the thing conveyed. In a narrow and literal sense Hamlet and Othello and Colonel Newcome and Becky Sharp are untrue. They never existed in the flesh. They have lived, however, in the higher and more vital sense that they have been part of the imagination of a master. They are true in that they express the truth. It is a dull misunderstanding of the value of things to call that book untrue which deals with fictitious characters wisely, yet to hold as verity that which records actual events stolidly and unappreciatively. The history may be false from beginning to end and the fiction true. Fiction which is worthy of consideration under the name of literature is the truest prose in the world; and I believe that it is not without an instinctive recognition of this fact that mankind has so generally taken it to its heart.

The value of at least certain works of fiction has come to be generally recognized by the intellectual world. There are some novels which it is taken for granted that every person of education has read. Whoever makes the smallest pretense of culture must, for instance, be at least tolerably familiar with Scott, Thackeray, Dickens, and Hawthorne; while he will find it difficult to hold the respect of cultivated men unless he is also acquainted with Miss Austen, George Eliot, and Charlotte Brontë, with Dumas *père*,

Balzac, and Victor Hugo, and with the works of leading living writers of romance. "*Don Quixote*" is as truly a necessary part of a liberal education as is the multiplication table; and it would not be difficult to extend the list of novels which it is assumed as a matter of course that persons of cultivation know familiarly.

Nor is it only the works of the greater writers of imaginative narration which have secured a general recognition. If it is not held that it is essential for an educated man to have read Trollope, Charles Reade, Kingsley, or Miss Mulock, for example, it is at least recognized that one had better have gained an acquaintance with these and similar writers. Traill, the English critic, speaks warmly of the books which while falling below the first rank are yet richly worth attention. He says with justice: —

> The world can never estimate the debt that it owes to second-class literature. Yet it is basely afraid to acknowledge the debt, hypocritically desiring to convey the impression that such literature comes to it in spite of protest, calling off its attention from the great productions.

从字面上看，小说是不真实的文学，但其灵魂却可能是真实的。由于小说必须表达情感更为崇高的现实，在形式上，它不受狭隘现实的约束。事件和人物是小说唯一使用的语言。认定一部伟大小说描述的事件是不真实的，就像说一个词的字母是不真实的一样，这是不公平的。除了这些符号是否表达了它们想要传达的内容之外，没有真假问题。字母的排列是为了让读者了解特定单词的概念，小说中的事件主要用于表达人性和生活的真相。真实在这里即指所表达事物的真实性。在狭义和字面意义上，哈姆雷特和奥赛罗以及纽康姆上校和贝基·夏普这些人物都不真实，他们从来没有活生生的存在过。然而，他们却活在更崇高、更重要的意义上，他们是大师想象力的一部分。他们是真实的，因为他们表达了真理。将一本富有才智的描述虚构人物的书称为不真实的书，而把冷冰冰的、毫无欣赏价值的记录真实事件的东西视为真实，这是对事物价值的一种刻板误解。历史可能从头到尾都是虚假的，而小说却是真的。以文学的名义值得考虑的小说是世界上最真实的散文。我相信，人类如此普遍地钟爱小说，并非人类本能地没有认识到这一事实。

至少某些小说作品的价值已被知识界普遍认可。每个受过教育的人理所当然都看过一些小说。例如，任何假冒有文化的人至少勉强熟悉司各特、萨克雷、狄更斯和霍桑，除非他还熟悉奥斯丁小姐、乔治·爱略特和夏洛蒂·勃朗特，或大仲马、巴尔扎克和维克多·雨果，以及在世的主要浪漫主义作家的作品，否则他会发现很难赢得有教养的人的尊重。《堂吉诃德》和乘法表一样，是人文教育的必要组成部分。要扩大这个小说列表并不困难，事实上，这些小说被认为是有文化修养的人理所当然应该熟知的书籍。

并非只有这些富有想象力的更伟大的叙事作家的作品才获得了普遍认可。如果不认为受过教育的人必须读过诸如特罗洛普、查尔斯·里德、金斯利或穆洛克小姐的书，那么至少可以承认，一个人最好了解这些作家和类似的作家。英国批评家特雷尔对那些排名虽然低于一流作品但完全值得关注的书，进行了热烈的讨论。他公正地说道：

> 世界永远无法估计亏欠二流文学的债。然而，它根本害怕承认这笔亏欠，且虚伪地希望传达这样的印象，即尽管有异议，这些文学还是成功了，从而把对伟大作品的关注转移开了。

It is true enough that there is a good deal of foolish pretense in regard to our genuine taste in reading, but in actual practice most persons do in the long run read chiefly what they really enjoy. It is also true that there are more readers who are capable of appreciating the novels of the second grade than there are those who are in sympathy with fiction of the first. The thing for each individual reader is to see to it that he is honest in this matter with himself, and that he gives attention to the best that he can like rather than to the poorest.

Even those who accept the fact that cultivated persons will read novels, and those who go so far as to appreciate that it is a distinct gain to the intellectual life, are, however, very apt to be troubled by the dangers of over-indulgence in this sort of literature. It has been said and repeated innumerable times that the excessive reading of novels is mentally debilitating and even debauching. This is certainly true. So is it true that there is great mental danger in the excessive reading of philosophy or theology, or the excessive eating of bread, or the excessive doing of any other things. The favorite figure in connection with fiction has been to compare it to opium-eating or to dram-drinking; and the moral usually drawn is that the novel-reader is in imminent danger of intellectual dissoluteness or even of what might be called the delirium tremens of the imagination. I should not be honest if I pretended to have a great deal of patience with most that is said in this line. The exclusive use of fiction as mental food is of course unwise, and the fact is so patent that it is hardly worthwhile to waste words in repeating it. When I said a moment ago that there is danger in the eating of bread if it is carried to excess I indicated what seems to me to be the truth in this matter. If one reads good and wholesome fiction, I believe that the natural instincts of the healthy mind may be trusted to settle the question of how much shall be read. If the fiction is unhealthy, morbid, or false, any of it is bad. If it is good, if it calls into play a healthy imagination, there is very little danger that too much of it will be taken. When there is complaint that a girl or a boy is injuring the mind by too exclusive a devotion to novels, I believe that it generally means, if the facts of the case were understood, that the mind of the reader is in an unwholesome condition, and that this excessive devotion to fiction is a symptom rather than a disease. When the girl coughs, it is not the cough that is the trouble; this is only a symptom of the irritation of membranes; and I believe that much the same is the case with extravagant novel-readers.

关于真正的阅读品位，确实存在很多愚蠢的借口，但事实上，从长远来看，大多数人主要阅读的是他们真正喜欢的东西。确也如此，能够欣赏二流小说的读者远比认同一流小说的读者多。对每一个读者来说，要做的是确保在这件事上于己诚实，即关注他自己喜欢的最优秀的小说而不是最差的小说。

即便是那些认可有教养的人会读小说这一事实的人，以及那些甚至赞赏读小说会给知识生活带来明显好处这一事实的人，都很容易为过度沉溺于这种文学所困扰。过度阅读小说会造成精神衰弱甚至道德败坏，这样的看法已经反反复复说过无数次了。这当然也是一个事实。过度阅读哲学或神学，或过度啃食面包，或过分做任何其他事情，都会存在极大的精神风险。小说中最受喜爱的人物常把它比作吸食鸦片或饮酒，其通常的寓意是指，小说读者有陷于无节制的精神放荡的迫在眉睫的危险，甚至有患上被称之为想象性谵妄症的危险。如果我假装对这句话中的大部分内容都表现出极大的耐心，那我就不应该是一个诚实的人。将小说专门用作精神食粮当然是不明智的，而且事实如此明显，浪费笔墨来重复几乎不值得。刚才我说过吃面包过量也会有危险，似乎于我而言，我指出了事情的真相。如果一个人读到好的和有益健康的小说，我相信一个健康的人可以依靠他的自然本能来解决将阅读多少的问题。如果小说不健康的，是病态的或虚假的，那么其中任何一部书都是糟糕的。如果它是好的，如果它能够发挥健康的想象力，那么就不存在多少过度阅读的危险。当有人抱怨女孩或男孩过于专注小说而伤害心灵时，如果了解情况的真相，我认为这通常意味着，读者的心灵处于不健康的状态，并且这种对小说的过度热爱是一种征候而非一种疾病。当女孩咳嗽时，麻烦的不是咳嗽，这只是隔膜受到刺激的症状，我相信沉溺于小说的读者也是如此。

Of course, this view of the matter will not commend itself to everybody. It is hard for us to shake off the impression of all the countless homilies which have been composed against novel-reading; and we are by no means free from the poison of the ascetic idea that anything to which mankind takes naturally and with pleasure cannot really be good in itself. I hope, however, that it will not appear to you unreasonable when I say that it seems to me far better to insist upon proper methods of reading and upon the selection of books which are genuine literature than to wage unavailing war against the natural love of stories which is to be found in every normal and wholesome human being. If I could be assured that a boy or a girl read only good novels and read them appreciatively and sympathetically, I should never trouble myself to inquire how many he or she read. I should be hopefully patient even if there was apparently a neglect of history and philosophy. I should be confident that it is impossible that the proper reading of good fiction should not in the end both prove beneficial in itself and lead the mind to whatever is good in other departments of literature. I am not pleading for the indiscriminating indulgence in doubtful stories. I do not believe that girls are brought to fine and well-developed womanhood by an exclusive devotion to the chocolate-caramel-and-pickled-lime sort of novels. I do not hold that boys come to nobility and manliness through the influence of sensational tales wherein blood-boultered bandits reduce to infinitesimal powder every commandment of the decalogue. I do, however, thoroughly believe that sound and imaginative fiction is as natural and as wholesome for growing minds as is the air of the seashore or the mountains for growing bodies.

　　当然，这种看法并不被所有人接受。我们很难摆脱为了反对小说阅读而创作的数不清的说教作品的印象，并且也绝不可能免于禁欲主义思想的毒害，即人类随心所欲接受的任何事物本身都不会是真正的好东西。然而，我希望坚持正确的阅读方法和选择真正的文学书籍，而不应徒劳地去挞伐每一个正常和健康人身上都能找到的那种对小说的自然而然的钟爱。当我这样说的时候，我希望于你而言，不会显得不合理。如果我能确信，一个男孩或一个女孩只阅读优秀的小说，并且是带着欣赏和同情的态度去阅读它们，我便不会费心去问他或她阅读了多少。即便忽略历史和哲学的现象很明显，我也希望保持足够的耐心。正确阅读好小说不仅最终将被证明本身是有益的，而且还可以引导人们去寻找文学其他方面的有益之处，对此我充满信心。我不是为不加区分地沉迷于令人怀疑的故事而辩护。我不相信，女孩们会因特别钟情于巧克力焦糖和腌酸橙类小说，就变得精致和成熟了。我也不认为，男孩由于受到惊悚故事的影响就变得高贵和有男子气概了。在这些故事中，嗜血成性的土匪还不是照样将十诫的每一条戒条都化为了尘埃。然而，我确实完全相信，健康和富有想象力的小说，对于心智成长就像海边或山上的空气，对于身体的成长一样自然和有益。

The fact is of especial importance as applied to the education of children. A healthy child is instinctively in the position of a learner. He is unconsciously full of deep wonderment concerning this world in which he finds himself, and concerning this mysterious thing called life in which he has a share. His mind is eager to receive, but it is entirely free from any affectation. A child accepts what appeals to him directly, and he is without scruple in neglecting what does not interest him. He learns only by slow degrees that knowledge may have value and interest from its remote bearings; and in dealing with him in the earlier stages of mental development there is no other means so sure and effective as story-telling. It is here that a child finds the specific and the concrete while he is still too immature to be moved by the general and the abstract.

It is "to cater to this universal taste", the circulars of the publishers assure us, that so-called "juvenile literature" was invented. I do not wish to be extravagant, but it does seem to me that modern juvenile literature has blighted the rising generation as rust blights a field of wheat. The holiday counters are piled high with hastily written, superficial, often inaccurate, and, what is most important of all, unimaginative books. The nursery of to-day is littered with worthless volumes, and the child halfway through school has already outlived a dozen varieties of books for the young.

A good many of these works are as full of information as a sugar-coated pill is of drugs. Thirst for practical information is one of the extravagances of the age. Parents to-day make their children to pass through tortures in the service of what they call "practical knowledge" as the unnatural parents of old made their offspring to pass through the fires of Moloch. We are all apt to lose sight of the fact that wisdom is not what a man knows but what he is. The important thing is not what we drill into our children, but what we drill them into. There are times when it is the most profound moral duty of a parent to substitute Grimm's fairy stories for text-books, and to devote the whole stress of educational effort to the developing of the child's imagination. I am not at all sure that it is not of more importance to see to it that a child—and especially a boy—is familiar with "the land east of the sun and west of the moon" than to stuff his brain with the geographical details of the wilds of Asia, Africa, or the isles of the far seas. I am sure that he is better off from knowing about Sindbad and Ali Baba than for being able to extract a cube root. I do not wish to be understood as speaking against the imparting of practical information, although I must say that I think that the distinction between what is really practical and what is not seems to me to be somewhat confused in these days. I simply mean that just now there is need of enforcing the value of the imaginative side of education. No accumulation of facts can compensate for the narrowing of the growing mind; and indeed, facts are not to be really grasped and assimilated without the development of the realizing— the imaginative—faculty.

　　这一事实用于儿童教育尤为重要。从本能上讲，一个健康的孩子处于学习者的位置。他潜意识中对自己所处的世界充满了深深的好奇，对他分享的这个称作生命的神秘事物也充满了惊奇。他的心渴望接受，并且全然没有任何做作之情。一个孩子会欣然接受直接吸引他的东西，但会毫无顾忌地忽视他不感兴趣的东西。他只是渐渐地了解到，知识可能从较远的联系上具有价值和吸引力，因此，在儿童心理发展的早期阶段，与儿童打交道，没有比讲故事更可靠和有效的方法了。正是在这一阶段，一个小孩在其仍然过于幼稚尚不能被一般和抽象事物所打动的时候，却从小说里找到了特殊和具体的东西。

　　出版商的印刷广告证明，正是为了"迎合普遍的口味"，才发明了所谓的"少年文学"。我不想太过度夸张，但在我看来，确实如同麦锈病枯萎了麦田一样，现代青少年文学毁掉下一代。假期长长的台桌上堆满了匆忙写就的、肤浅的、经常不准确的书籍，而更重要的是，这些书籍缺乏想象力。今天的托儿所里杂乱地堆满了毫无价值的书籍，孩子上学到一半的时间就碰到了十几种仅仅适合年轻人阅读的书籍。

　　如同糖衣药丸装满药物一样，很多作品充溢着知识。渴望实用知识是我们这个时代的挥霍浪费之一。就像古时不近人情的父母都要让他们的后代经历摩洛克神之火的考验一样，今天的父母为了他们所谓的"实用知识"，让孩子们备受折磨。我们都容易忽视这样一个事实，即智慧不是一个人知道什么，而是他是什么；重要的不是给孩子们灌输什么，而是灌输他们成为什么。有时，父母最有意义的道德责任是用格林童话替代教科书，并将教育努力的全部重点专注于发展孩子的想象力。我完全相信，让孩子尤其是男孩熟悉太阳以东，月亮以西，比用亚洲、非洲或远海岛屿荒野的地理细节塞满他大脑更重要。我相信，他知道辛巴达与阿里巴巴比能够提取立方根更好。我不希望被理解为反对给孩子们提供实用知识。尽管我必须说，如今真正实用的和不实用的之间的区别在我看来多少有些混乱。我刚刚才说的只是指，需要强化想象力在教育方面的价值。任何事实的积累都无法弥补不断增长的心智的狭窄。实际上，如果没有实现能力即想象能力的发展，就不能真正掌握和吸收事实。

It is even more important for children than for adults that their reading shall be imaginative. The only way to protect them against worthless books is to give them a decided taste for what is good. It is only after children have been debauched by vapid or sensational books that they come to delight in rubbish. It is easier in the first place to interest them in real literature than in shams. The thing is to take the trouble to see to it that what they read is fine. The most common error in this connection is to suppose that children need an especial sort of literature different from that suited to adults. As far, certainly, as serious education is concerned, there is neither adult literature nor juvenile literature; there is simply literature. Speaking broadly, the literature best for grown persons is the literature best for children. The limitations of youth have, and should have, the same effects in literature as in life. They restrict the comprehension and appreciation of the facts of life; and equally they set a bound to the comprehension and appreciation of what is read. The impressions which a child gets from either are not those of his elders. The important thing is that what the growing mind receives shall be vital and wholesome. It is less unfortunate for the child to mistake what is genuine than to receive as true what is really false. We all commit errors in the conclusions which we draw from life; and so will it be with children and books. Books which are wise and sane, however, will in time correct the misconceptions they beget, as life in time makes clear the mistakes which life has produced.

The whole philosophy of reading for children is pretty well summed up by implication in the often quoted passage in which Charles Lamb describes under the disguise of Bridget Elia, the youthful experience of his sister Mary: —

> She was tumbled early, by accident or design, into a spacious closet of good old English reading, without much selection or prohibition, and browsed at will upon that fair and wholesome pasturage. Had I twenty girls, they should be brought up exactly in this fashion. —Mackery End

Fiction—to return to the immediate subject of this talk—is only a part of a child's education, but it is a most essential part; and it is of the greatest importance that the fiction given to a young reader be noble; that it be true to the essentials of life, as it can be true only if it is informed by a keen and sane imagination. Children should be fed on the genuine and sound folk-tales like those collected by the brothers Grimm; the tales of Hans Christian Andersen, of Asbjörnsen, of Laboulaye, and of that delightful old lady, the Countess d'Aulnoy; the fine and robust "*Morte d'Arthur*" of Malory; the more modern classics, "*Robinson Crusoe*" and "*Gulliver*". Then there are Hawthorne's "*Tanglewood Tales*" and the "*Wonder-Book*" "*Treasure Island*" and "*Kidnapped*" "*Uncle Remus*" and the "*Jungle Books*". It may be claimed that these are "juvenile" literature; but I have named nothing of which I, at least, am not as fond now as in my youth, and I have yet to discover that adults find lack of interest in good books even of fairy stories. What has been said against juvenile literature has been intended against the innumerable works mustered under that name which are not literature at all. Wonder lore is as normal food for old as for young, and there is no more propriety in confining it to children than there is in limiting the use of bread and butter to the inhabitants of the nursery.

　　相比成年人，对儿童更重要的是，应该让他们的阅读充满想象力。保护儿童免受毫无价值的书籍侵害的唯一途径就是，给予他们欣赏优秀书籍的能力。只有被乏味或煽情的书籍迷惑之后，孩子们才会开始喜欢垃圾作品。首先，应该让孩子们对真正的文学产生兴趣，这比让他们对虚假的文学产生兴趣更容易做到。要想方设法确保孩子们阅读的内容没有问题。在这方面人们常错误地认为，儿童需要一种不同于只适合成人的特殊文学。当然，就严肃的教育而言，既没有成人文学，也没有青少年文学，有的仅仅是文学。从广义上讲，最适合成年人的文学便是最适合儿童的文学。对年轻人的限制，无论在文学还是在生活中均具有且应该具有相同的影响，它们限制了对生活事实的理解和欣赏，同样，也限制了对所读内容的理解和欣赏。一个孩子从任何一个人那儿获得的印象都不是他的长辈的印象。重要的是，孩子正在发育的心灵应该接受充满活力和有益健康的东西。对儿童而言，误解真实的东西比将真正虚假的东西当作真实的东西更不幸。我们都会在生活得出的结论中犯错误，儿童也少不了从书中得出的结论中犯错。然而，浸润着智慧和理智的书籍会及时纠正他们产生的错误观念，因为时间终会澄清生活产生的错误。

　　查尔斯·兰姆伪装成布里奇特·伊利亚，描述了他妹妹玛丽年轻时候的经历，其中经常被引用的一段话的含义较好地总结了儿童阅读的全部哲理：

　　　　她很早就被有意或无意地摔倒在一个宽敞的壁橱里，里面放着古老的英文读物，没有太多选择或禁止，随意浏览那片美丽而健康的牧场。如果我有二十个女孩，她们就应该完全按照这种方式长大。

——麦凯瑞·恩德

　　回到本次演讲的直接主题，小说只是孩子教育的一部分，但它是极为重要的部分。给年轻读者的小说应该是高尚的，忠实于生活本质的，这一点最为关键，因为只有通过敏锐而理智的想象力告知他的，才能可能是真实的。应该用像格林兄弟收集的那种真实可靠的民间故事去滋养孩子们，这里尚有很多类似儿童文学作品，如汉斯·克里斯蒂安·安徒生、阿斯比·约恩森、拉布拉耶和那位可爱的老太太德奥诺伊伯爵夫人的童话故事；还有马洛精美而雄壮的《亚瑟王》以及比较现代的经典《鲁滨孙漂流记》和《格列佛游记》。最后，还有霍桑的《坦格伍德故事》和《奇迹之书》《金银岛》和《绑架》《雷穆斯叔叔》及《丛林之书》。可以说这些都是"少年"文学，但至少我提到的任何书籍，都是我今天和年轻时代一样喜欢的书籍，我还没有发现成年人对优秀的童话故事书籍缺乏兴趣。我针对青少年文学的言论旨在反对以该名称集结起来的无数作品，因为这些作品根本不是文学。奇异的传说对于老人和年轻人来说都是正常的食物，将它限制在儿童身上，并不比将面包和黄油的使用限制在托儿所住户身上更正当。

XIV
FICTION AND LIFE

The reading of fiction has come to have an important and well recognized place in modern life. However strong may be the expression of disapprobation against certain individual books, no one in these days attempts to deny the value of imaginative literature in the development of mind and the formation of character; yet so strong is the Puritan strain in the blood of the English race that there is still a good deal of lingering ascetic disapproval of novels.

It must be remembered in this connection that there are novels and novels. The objections which have from time to time been heaped upon fiction in general are more than deserved by fiction in particular; and that, too, by the fiction most in evidence. The books least worthy are for the most part precisely those which in their brief day are most likely to excite comment. That the flaming scarlet toadstools which irresistibly attract the eye in the forest are viciously poisonous does not, however, alter the fact that mushrooms are at once delicious and nutritious. It is no more logical to condemn all fiction on account of the worthlessness or hurtfulness of bad books than it would be to denounce all food because things have often been eaten which are dangerously unwholesome.

The great value of fiction as a means of intellectual and of moral training lies in the fact that man is actually and vitally taught nothing of importance save by that which really touches his feelings. Advice appeals to the intellect, and experience to the emotions. What has been didactically told to us is at best a surface treatment, while what we have felt is an inward modification of what we are. We approve of advice, and we act according to experience. Often when we have decided upon one course of life or action, the inner self which is the concrete result of our temperament and our experiences goes quietly forward in a path entirely different. What we have resolved seldom comes to pass unless it is sustained by what we have felt. For centuries has man been defining himself as a being that reasons while he has been living as a being that feels.

第十四讲　小说与生活

在现代生活中，小说阅读占有重要地位，这一点已被世人高度认可。无论对某些个别书籍表达的反对态度多么强烈，当今没有人试图否认想象力文学在思想发展和性格形成方面的价值。然而，清教徒的品质在英语民族血液中极为强大，因此从禁欲主义角度反对小说的意见仍然挥之不去。

在这方面须牢记，小说名目繁多，各式各样。一般而言，针对小说的反对意见时而有之，已堆积如山。就特定的以及那些显而易见的小说而言，这些反对意见是值得的。最没有价值的书大部分恰恰是那些在短时间内最有可能引发热评的书籍。在森林中，最能惹人注目的是火红的猩红色剧毒毒蕈，但这并不能改变蘑菇既美味又营养的事实。差书毫无价值且贻害无穷，但因此就去谴责所有小说，这并不比去谴责所有食物更合乎逻辑，因为人们经常食用的东西可能同样不健康和危险。

小说作为一种智力和道德训练手段的巨大价值在于，除了那些真正触及情感的东西外，人们实际上并没有获取任何重要的教导。忠告诉诸理智，经验诉诸情感。说教告诉我们的充其量是表面处理，而我们所感受到的是，内心对自我的修正。我们赞同忠告，并依据经验行事。通常，当我们决定了一种生活方式或行动时，作为我们气质和经验的具体结果的内在自我，会在一条完全不同的道路上悄然前行。除非得到我们情感的支撑，否则我们心意已决的目标很少会实现。几个世纪以来，人类一直将自己定义为一个理性的存在，但人却一直生活在一个有感觉的存在中。

The sure hold of fiction upon mankind depends upon the fact that it enables the reader to gain experience vicariously. Seriously and sympathetically to read a story which is true to life is to live through an emotional experience. How vivid this emotion is will manifestly depend upon the imaginative sympathy with which one reads. The young man who has appreciatively entered into the life of Arthur Pendennis will hardly find that he is able to go through the world in a spirit of dandified self-complaisance without a restraining consciousness that such an attitude toward life is most absurd folly. A man of confirmed worldliness is perhaps not to be turned from his selfish and ignoble living by studying the history of Major Pendennis, to read about whom is not unlike drinking dry and rare old Madeira. No reader can have felt imaginatively the passionate spiritual struggles of Arthur Dimmesdale without being thereafter more sensitive to good influences and less tolerant of self-deception and concealed sin. These are the more obvious examples. The experiences which one gains from good fiction go much farther and deeper. They extend into those most intangible yet most real regions where even the metaphysician, the psychologist, and the maker of definitions have not yet been able to penetrate; those dim, mysterious tracts of the mind which are still to us hardly better known than the unexplored mid-countries of Asia or Africa.

As a means of accomplishing a desired end didactic literature is probably the most futile of all the unavailing attempts of mankind. In the days when ringlets and pantalets were in fashion, when small boys wore frilled collars and asked only improving questions, when the most delirious literary dissipation of which the youthful fancy could conceive was a Rollo book or a prim tale by Maria Edgeworth, it was generally believed that moral precepts and wise maxims had a prodigious influence upon the young. It was held possible to mould the rising generation by putting one of the sentences of Solomon at the head of a copy-book page, and to make a permanent impression upon the spirit by saws and sermons. If this were ever true, it is certainly not true now. If sermon or saw has touched the imagination of the hearer, it has had some effect which will be lasting; and this the saw does oftener than the sermon, the proverb than the precept. If it has won only an intellectual assent, there is small ground for supposing that it will bring about any alteration which will be permanent and effective.

Taking into account these considerations, one might sum up the whole matter somewhat in this way: To read fiction is certainly a pleasure; it is to be looked upon as no less important a means of intellectual development; while in the cultivation of the moral and spiritual sense the proper use of fiction is one of the most effectual and essential agencies to-day within the reach of men. In other words the proper reading of fiction is, from the standpoint of pleasure, of intellectual development, or of moral growth, neither more nor less than a distinct and imperative duty.

　　小说对人类的可靠支撑取决于它使读者能够间接获得经验这一事实。认真而富有同理心地阅读一个忠实于生活的故事，就是经历一种情感体验。这种情感有多么生动显然取决于阅读时富有想象力的同情心。一个年轻人深怀感激之心走进了亚瑟潘登尼斯的生活将发现，如果不压抑荒诞愚蠢的生活态度的意识，他根本无法以一种高贵的自我满足情绪出入社会。通过研究潘登尼斯少校的历史，也许不会改变一个抱持顽固世俗观念之人自私和卑鄙的生活，这与去了解他和喝干稀有的老马德拉红葡萄酒没有什么不同。没有读者能想象性地感受到亚瑟·丁梅斯代尔充满激情的精神奋争，而此后对良好的影响更加敏感，对自欺欺人和隐瞒的罪恶不再宽容。这些是非常明显的例子。人们从好小说中获得的经验影响深远，可以延伸到那些无形但最真实的领域，甚至可以延伸到形而上学者、心理学家和定义的制定者都无法深入的领域。那些昏暗、神秘的心灵领域，对我们来说，几乎不比亚洲或非洲未经探索的中部国家更为世人所知。

作为实现人们期望的最终目标的一种手段，说教文学可能是人类所有徒劳尝试中最无用的。在卷发和灯笼裤盛行的年代，当小男孩穿着褶边领子，只问一些启发性的问题时，当年轻人能幻想到的最疯狂的文学消遣是罗洛的书或玛丽亚·埃奇沃思的古板故事时，人们普遍认为道德戒律和明智的格言对年轻人具有惊人的影响。可以通过把所罗门的一句话放在字帖开头来塑造下一代，并通过格言和说教给年轻人在精神上留下永久的印记。如果这曾经是真的，那么现在肯定不是真的。如果说教或格言能触动听者的想象力，它就会产生某种持久的效果。格言比说教更常见，谚语比戒律更常见。如果这种方式只赢得了精神上的认可，便没有多少理由认为它会产生恒久而有效的改变。

考虑到这些因素，人们可以这样总结整个事情：阅读小说当然是一种乐趣，被视为智力发展的重要手段，而在道德和精神意识的培养中，合理利用小说是当今人类力所能及范围内，最有效和最重要的媒介之一。换句话说，从愉悦、智力发展或道德成长的角度来看，正确阅读小说恰好是一种独特而必要的责任。

I have been careful to say, "the proper reading of fiction". Whatever strictures may be laid upon careless readers in general may perhaps be quadrupled when applied to bad reading of novels. It is the duty of nobody to read worthless fiction; and it is a species of moral iniquity to read good novels carelessly, flippantly, or superficially. There is small literary or intellectual hope for those whom Henry James describes as "people who read novels as an exercise in skipping". There are two tests by which the novel-reader is to be tried: What sort of fiction does he read, and how does he read it? If the answers to these questions are satisfactory, the whole matter is settled.

Of course, it is of the first importance that the reader think for himself; that he form his own opinions, and have his own appreciations. Small minds are like weak galvanic cells; one alone is not strong enough to generate a sensible current; they must be grouped to produce an appreciable result. One has no opinion; while to accomplish anything approaching a sensation a whole circle is required. It takes an entire community of such intellects to get up a feeling, and of course the feeling when aroused is shared in common. There are plenty of pretentious readers of all the latest notorious novels who have as small an individual share in whatever emotion the book excites as a Turkish wife has in the multifariously directed affections of her husband. It is impossible not to see the shallowness, the pretense, and the intellectual demoralization of these readers; and it is equally idle to deny the worthlessness of the books in which they delight.

What, then, is to be learned from fiction, that so much stress is to be laid upon the necessity of making it a part of our intellectual and moral education? The answer has in part at least been so often given that it seems almost superfluous to repeat it. The more direct lessons of the novel are so evident as scarcely to call for enumeration. Nobody needs at this late day to be told how much may be learned from fiction of the customs of different grades of society, of the ways and habits of all sorts and conditions of men, and of the even more fascinating if not actually more vitally important manners and morals of all sorts and conditions of women. Every reader knows how much may be learned from stories of the facts of human relations and of social existence, —facts which one accumulates but slowly by actual experience, while yet a knowledge of them is of so great importance for the full appreciation and the proper employment and enjoyment of life.

我一直小心翼翼地提道"正确阅读小说"。无论对粗心大意的读者施加什么样的限制，一般而言，阅读不良小说，其限制作用或许可能会增加四倍。没有人有义务去阅读毫无价值的小说，粗枝大叶、马马虎虎、浅尝辄止地阅读优秀小说是一种道德上的恶行。对于那些被亨利·詹姆斯描述为"阅读小说作为跳绳练习的人"来说，他要在文学或知识上的取得进步，可谓希望渺茫。检验小说读者有两个测试办法：即他读什么类型的小说，他怎么读？如果这些问题的答案都令人满意，那么整件事情就解决了。

当然，读者自己能够独立思考是最重要的。他要形成自己的观点，并有自己的欣赏。心胸狭窄的人就像脆弱的原电池，单独一个电池不足以产生让人能察觉的电流，必须将它们聚集在一起方可以产生可观的结果。一个人不可能形成舆论，而要干成任何接近轰动的事情，则需要一个完整的圈子，而要激发一种情感则需要整个的知识群体。当然，这种情感被唤醒时，需要人们共同分享。新近出版的那些名声不佳的小说拥有许多自命不凡的读者，但无论那本书能激发何种情感，每一个读者能占有的份额都很小，这就如同一个土耳其妻子在她丈夫朝三暮四的情感里占有的份额少得可怜。这些读者的浅薄、虚伪和思想道德沦丧，一望而知，但因此就否认这些读者津津乐道的书籍的价值，同样毫无意义。

那么，我们从小说中可以学到什么？如此强调将小说作为智力和道德教育的一部分的必要性又何在？问题的部分答案至少是不争的事实，再三重复似乎显得多余。小说中更直接的经验显而易见，几乎不需要一一罗列。没有人需要在夜深人静的时候，被告知可以从小说中学到多少关于不同阶层社会的习俗、各种人和状况的方式和习惯，以及实际上不是那么重要的更迷人的东西，诸如各种情形下女人的举止和道德。每个读者都知道，从故事描述的人际关系和社会存在的事实中可以学到多少东西——这些事实是一个人通过实际经验日积月累而来的，然而它们对充分确理、正确利用以及享受生活至关重要。

Civilization is essentially an agreement upon conventions. It is the tacit acceptance of conditions and concessions. It is conceded that if human beings are to live together it is necessary that there must be mutual agreement, and as civilization progresses this is extended to all departments and details of life. What is called etiquette, for instance, is one variety of social agreement into which men have entered for convenience and comfort in living together. What is called good breeding is but the manifestation of a generous desire to observe all those human regulations by which the lives of others may be rendered more happy. These concessions and conventions are not natural. A man may be born with the spirit of good breeding, but he must learn its methods. Nature may bestow the inclination to do what is wisest and best in human relations, but the forms and processes of social life and of all human intercourse must be acquired. It is one of the functions of fiction to instruct in all this knowledge; and only he who is unacquainted with life will account such an office trivial.

Intimate familiarity with the inner characteristics of humanity, and knowledge of the experiences and the nature of mankind, are a still more important gain from fiction. Almost unconsciously the intelligent novel-reader grows in the comprehension of what men are and of what they may be. This art makes the reader a sharer in those moments when sensation is at its highest, emotion at its keenest. It brings into the life which is outwardly quiet and uneventful, into the mind which has few actual experiences to stir it to its deeps, the splendid exhilaration of existence at its best. The pulse left dull by a colorless life throbs and tingles over the pages of a vivid romance; the heart denied contact with actualities which would awaken it beats hotly with the fictitious passion made real by the imagination; so that life becomes forever richer and more full of meaning.

In one way it is possible to gain from these imaginative experiences a knowledge of life more accurate than that which comes from life itself. It is possible to judge, to examine, to weigh, to estimate the emotions which are enjoyed asthetically; whereas emotions arising from real events benumb all critical faculties by their stinging personal quality. He who has never shared actual emotional experiences has never lived, it is true; but he who has not shared asthetic emotions has never understood.

What should be the character of fiction is pretty accurately indicated by what has been said of the part which fiction should play in human development. Here, as in all literature, men are less influenced by the appeal to the reason than by the appeal to the feelings. The novelist who has a strong and lasting influence is not he who instructs men directly, but he who moves men. This is instruction in its higher sense. The guidance of life must come from the reason; equally, however, must the impulse of life come from the emotions. The man who is ruled by reason alone is but a curious mechanical toy which mimics the movements of life without being really alive.

　　文明本质上是对约定俗成的赞同，是对各种条件心照不宣的承认和妥协。人们都承认，人类要共同生活，就必须达成共识，而随着文明的进步，这种共识将扩展到生活的各个层面，并将延伸到生活的每一个细节。例如，所谓的礼节就是一种人们为了方便而舒适地生活在一起订立的社会契约。所谓良好的教养不过是遵守所有人类规则的豁达大度的愿望的外在表现。通过这些规则，他人的生活会变得更加幸福。让步和惯例不是自然的，一个人可能天生就有良好教养的气质，但他必须学习它的方式。在人际关系中，人的天性可能会倾向于去做聪明睿智和行善积德的事情，但一个人必须获得社会生活和所有人类交往的方式和过程。教授这些知识是小说的功能之一，只有不熟悉生活的人才会认为小说的这一作用微不足道。

　　深谙人性的内在特征，对人的经历和本性的认识，仍然是来自小说的更重要的获益。明智的小说读者在理解人是什么和他们可能是什么的过程中，几乎不知不觉地成长了。小说艺术使读者在感觉最佳、最敏锐的时刻成为分享者。这种情感体验把看似安静平淡的东西带入生活中，带入到那些未曾有多少实际体验来激励自己的读者的心灵深处，这是一种最美妙的存在感。苍白的生活致人脉搏迟钝，却在生动浪漫的书页上跳动和刺痛。内心拒绝接触现实生活而不再被唤醒，唯有想象使虚幻的激情成为真实，才能使心脏热情跳动，由此才能让生活永远变得更加丰富和充满意义。

　　就某种意义而言，人们有可能从这些富有想象力的体验中获得一种比生活本身更准确的生活知识。审美享受的情感可以判断、考察、衡量、评价，而源于真实事件的情感会因其强烈的个人品质，使人的批判能力变得麻木。事实上，从未分享过实际情感经历的人从未活过，但没有分享审美情感的人永远不会理解。

　　正如前所述，小说在人类发展中应该扮演什么角色已经非常准确地表明了小说的特征。在这里，正如在所有文学作品中一样，人们受诉诸理性的影响要少于诉诸情感的影响。具有强大持久影响力的小说家不会直接说教，而是要去感动人，这是高级意义上的教诲。人生的指引必须来自理性，然而，生命的冲动同样必须来自情感。单凭理性支配的人，不过是一个奇特的机械玩具，它模仿生命的运动，却没有真正地活着。

This prime necessity of touching and moving the reader determines one of the most important points of difference between literature and science. It forces the story-teller to modify, to select, and to change if need be the facts of life, in order to produce an impression of truth. Out of the multifarious details of existence the author must select the significant; out of the real deduce the possibility which shall commend itself to the reader as verity.

Above everything else is an artist who is worthy of the name truthful in his art. He never permits himself to set down anything which is not a verity to his imagination, or which fails to be consistent with the conditions of human existence. He realizes that fiction in which a knowledge of the outward shell and the accidents of life is made the chief object cannot be permanent and cannot be vitally effective. The novelist is not called upon to paint life, but to interpret life. It is his privilege to be an artist; and an artist is one who sees through apparent truth to actual verity. It is his first and most essential duty to arouse the inner being, and to this necessity he must be ready to sacrifice literal fact. Until the imagination is awake, art cannot even begin to do its work. It is true that there may be a good deal of pleasant story-telling which but lightly touches the fancy and does not reach deeper. It is often harmless enough; but it is as idle to expect from this any keen or lasting pleasure, and still more any mental experience of enduring significance, as it would be to expect to warm Nova Zembla with a bonfire. What for the moment tickles the fancy goes with the moment, and leaves little trace; what touches the imagination becomes a fact of life.

Macaulay, in his extraordinarily wrong-headed essay on Milton, has explicitly stated a very wide-spread heresy when he says: —

We cannot unite the incompatible advantages of reality and deception, the clear discernment of truth and the exquisite enjoyment of fiction.

This is the ground generally held by unimaginative men. Macaulay had many good gifts and graces, but his warmest admirers would hardly include among them a greatly endowed or vigorously developed imagination. If one cannot unite the advantages of reality and deception, if he cannot join clear discernment of truth to the exquisite enjoyment of fiction, it is because he fails of all just and adequate comprehension of literature. To call fiction deception is simply to fail to understand that real truth may be independent of apparent truth. It would from the point of view of this sentence of Macaulay's be competent to open the *Gospels* and call the parable of the sower a falsehood because there is no probability that it referred to any particular incident. The stupidity of criticism of fiction which begins with the assumption that it is not true is not unlike that of an endeavor to swallow a chestnut burr and the consequent declaration that the nut is uneatable. If one is not clever enough to get beneath the husk, his opinion is surely not of great value.

这种触动和感动读者的基本需要决定了文学与科学之间最重要的区别之一。如果这种需要是生活事实，它将迫使说书人做出相应的调整、选择和改变，以期产生一种真实的印象。作者必须从繁杂的生活细节中选择有意义的部分，从真实中推断出一种可能性，从而促使读者认可这种真实性。

最重要的是，一位艺术家在他的艺术中，应该成为一个名副其实的艺术家，他从不允许自己写出任何不符合想象，或者不符合人类生存条件的非真实的东西。他会意识到，将存在于外壳表面的知识以及生活中偶然事件作为主要对象的小说，不可能称之为是永恒的，也不会给人以深刻印象。小说家不是被使唤来描述生活的，而他要去诠释生活。成为艺术家是他的荣幸，一个艺术家是一个可以看透表面现象而接近真相的人，他的首要任务是唤醒内心存在，为此他必须准备好牺牲字面意义上的真实。在想象力未觉醒之前，艺术甚至无法开始工作。的确，可能有很多令人愉快的故事叙述，但它们只是轻描淡写而未触发人的幻想，也未触及人的内心深处。诚然，它们通常没有什么害处，但是，期望从中获得任何敏锐或持久的快乐，更重要的是获得任何具有持久意义的精神体验，就如同期望用篝火温暖北极的新地岛一样，都是徒劳无益的。给人一时愉悦的幻想会随时间而消逝，不会留下任何痕迹，触动想象的东西才会成为生活的事实。

麦考利有一篇固执己见的文章，在论述弥尔顿时，他明确指出了一种非常普遍的离经叛道的观点：

> 我们无法将现实与欺骗、对真相的清晰辨别和对虚构的精美享受这些互不相容的优点结合起来。

这是缺乏想象力的人普遍持有的立场。麦考利有许多优秀的天赋和美德，但即便他最热情的崇拜者，也几乎不会把天赋或旺盛的想象力纳入他的才能之中。如果一个人不能将现实和骗局的优势联系起来，如果他不能将清晰的真理辨别与小说的精致享受结合起来，那也是因为他缺乏对文学正确而充分的理解。将虚构称为欺骗只是不了解真实的真相可能独立于表面的真相。从麦考利这句话的角度来看，翻开《福音书》，把播种者的寓言称为虚妄也是正当合法的，因为它不可能涉及任何特定事件。假定小说不是真实的，然后开始指责小说是非常愚蠢的，这与试图吞下栗子毛刺随后声明栗子是不可食用的没有什么不同。如果一个人不够聪明，无法深入到外壳之下，那么他的意见肯定就没有多大价值。

In order to enjoy a novel, it is certainly not necessary to believe it in a literal sense. No sane man supposes that Don Quixote ever did or ever could exist. To the intellect the book is little more than a farrago of impossible absurdities. The imagination perceives that it is true to the fundamental essentials of human nature, and understands that the book is true in a sense higher than that of mere literal verity. It is the cultivated man who has the keenest sense of reality, and yet only to the cultivated man is possible the exquisite enjoyment of "*Esmond*" "*Les Misérables*" "*The Scarlet Letter*" "*The Return of the Native*" or "*The Ordeal of Richard Feverel*". So far from being incompatible, the clear discernment of truth and the exquisite enjoyment of fiction are inseparable.

An artist who is worthy of the name is above all else truthful in his art. He never permits himself to set down anything which he does not feel to be true. It is with a truth higher than a literal accuracy, however, that he is concerned. His perception is the servant of his imagination. He observes and he uses the outward facts of life as a means of conveying its inner meanings. It is this that makes him an artist. The excuse for his claiming the attention of the world is that in virtue of his imagination he is gifted with an insight keener and more penetrating than that of his fellows; and his enduring influence depends upon the extent to which he justifies this claim.

With the novel of trifles it is difficult to have any patience whatever. The so-called Realistic story collects insignificant nothings about a slender thread of plot as a filament of cobweb gathers dust in a barn. The cobweb seems to me on the whole the more valuable, since at least it has the benefit of the old wives' theory that it is good to check bleeding. It is a more noble office to be wrapped about a cut finger than to muffle a benumbed mind.

为了欣赏一部小说，当然没有必要从字面意义上去相信它的真实性。理智的人不会去假设，堂吉诃德曾经存在过或曾经可能存在过。对于才智非凡的人来说，这本书只不过是一堆荒诞不经的大杂烩，但想象力却感知到这种荒诞是忠实于人性的基本要素的，并且理解这本书的真实性远远高于单纯的字面意义上的真实性。有教养的人拥有最敏锐的现实感，而且只有他们才能欣赏《埃斯蒙德》《悲惨世界》《红字》《还乡》或《理查德·法弗尔的苦难》这些小说。对真实的明辨与对小说的细腻欣赏是分不开的，二者并非格格不入。

一位名副其实的艺术家在他的艺术中是最真实的。他从不允许自己写下任何他认为不真实的东西。然而，他所关心的是一个高于字面准确性的真实，感知只是他想象力的仆人。他观察并使用生活的外在事实作为传达其内在意义的手段，正是这一点使他成为一名艺术家。他之所以引人瞩目是凭借了他的想象力，他拥有比其同伴更敏锐、更透彻的洞察力，但他能否具有持久的影响力，将取决于他证明这一主张的合理程度。

对于描写琐碎之事的小说，无论如何人们都难有任何耐心。所谓的现实主义小说就像蜘蛛网的细丝在粮仓中收集灰尘一样，收集了关于细长情节的微不足道的任何内容。蜘蛛网在我看来总体上更有价值，因为它至少具有老生常谈所有的好处，即止血是好的，把被割伤的手指包裹起来，比将麻木的头脑围裹起来能起到更显著的效果。

One question which the great mass of novel-readers who are also students of literature are interested to have answered is, How far is it well to read fiction for simple amusement? With this inquiry, too, goes the kindred one whether it is well or ill to relax the mind over light tales of the sort sometimes spoken of as "summer reading". To this it is impossible to give a categorical reply. It is like the question how often and for how long it is wise to sit down to rest while climbing a hill. It depends upon the traveler, and no one else can determine a point which is to be decided by feelings and conditions known alone to him. It is hardly possible and it is not wise to read always with exalted aims. Whatever you might be advised by me or by any other, you would be foolish not to make of fiction a means of grateful relaxation as well as a help in mental growth. Always it is important to remember, however, that there is a wide difference in the ultimate result, according as a person reads for diversion the best that will entertain him or the worst. It is a matter of the greatest moment that our amusements shall not be allowed to debauch our taste. It is necessary to have some standard even in the choice of the most foamy fiction, served like a sherbet on a hot summer afternoon. One does not read vulgar and empty books, even for simple amusement, without an effect upon his own mind.

Fortunately, we are in this day provided with a great deal of light fiction which is sound and wholesome and genuine as far as it goes. Some of it even goes far in the way of being imaginative and good. As examples—not at all as a list—may be named Blackmore, Crawford, Stanley Weyman, Anthony Hope, or the numerous writers of admirable short stories, Cable, Miss

Jewett, Miss Wilkins, J. M. Barrie, Ian Maclaren, or Thomas Nelson Page. All these and others may be read for simple entertainment, and all are worth reading for some more or less strongly marked quality of permanent worth. There are plenty of writers, too, like William Black and Clark Russell and Conan Doyle, concerning the lasting value of whose stories there might easily be a question, yet who do often contrive to be healthily amusing, and who furnish the means of creating a pleasant and restful vacuity in lives otherwise too full. Every reader must make his own choice, and determine for himself how much picnicking he will do on his way up the hill of life. If he is wise, he will contrive to find his entertainment chiefly in books which besides being amusing have genuine value; and he will at least see to it that his intellectual dissipations shall be with the better of such books as will amuse him and not with the poorer.

　　读者大众，同时也包括学习文学的学生，有兴趣需要回答的一个问题是，为了纯粹娱乐的目的而阅读小说能走多远？带着这一询问，还有一个类似的问题，那就是通过阅读有时被称为"暑期阅读"的轻松故事来放松心灵，是好还是坏呢？对这一问题，不太可能给出一个确信无疑的答案。这就像爬山时间，途中休息几次或休息多久才是明智的？答案显然取决于旅行者本人，没有其他人可以确定一个点，因为这是由登山者自己的感受和条件决定的。总是带着崇高的目标去阅读几乎是不可能的，也是不明智的。无论是我或是其他任何人给你任何建议，如果你不把小说当作一种感恩的放松方式和心理成长的帮助，你就是不明智的。然而，有一点须时刻牢记，最终结果存在很大差异，即使为消遣解闷而阅读，一个人是阅读最优秀的还是最糟糕的作品来娱乐自己？不允许娱乐败坏我们的品位，这是一件关系重大的事情。就像选择炎热夏日午后的果子露一样，即使选择最轻松的泡泡小说，也需要有一定的标准；即使是为了简单的娱乐，一个人不要去读庸俗和空洞的书，这样才不会对自己的思想产生消极影响。
　　幸运的是，如今有大量轻松愉快的小说可供我们阅读，并且就其本身而言，这些小说是健康、有益、真实的。其中一些小说甚至在想象力和优良品质方面非常出色。作为例子——完全不是一个列表——可以列出的作家名字有：布莱克莫尔、克劳福德、史丹利·韦曼、安东尼·霍普；或众多令人钦佩的短篇小说作家，如凯布尔、朱厄特小姐、威金斯小姐或托马斯·纳尔逊·佩奇。所有这些作家和其他内容都可以作为简单的娱乐而阅读，并且都值得一读，因为它们或多或少均具有永久价值的明显品质。也有很多作家，比如威廉·布莱克、克拉克·罗素和柯南·道尔。尽管他们的故事的永恒价值可能很容易成为一个问题，但这些作者时常都在不遗余力地使生活变得健康有趣，并为人们提供了创造一个令人愉快、宁静的真空的方式，要不然生活就太过充实了。每个读者都必须做出自己的选择，并自己决定在人生的山路上他会进行几次野餐。如果他有智慧，他会设法在书籍中找到乐趣。这些书籍除了有趣，还有真正的价值，至少会确保精神消遣能与那些带来乐趣的书籍为伴，而不是与那些低劣的书籍为伍。

The mention of the short story brings to mind the great part which this form of fiction plays to-day. The restlessness of the age and the fostering influence of the magazines have united to develop the short story, and it has become one of the most marked of the literary features of the time. It has the advantage of being easily handled and comprehended as a whole, but it lessens the power of seizing in their entirety works which are greater. It tends rather to increase than to diminish mental restlessness, and the lover of short stories will do well not to let any considerable length of time go by without reading some long and far-reaching novel by way of corrective. Another consequence of the wide popularity of the short story is that we have nowadays so few additions to that delightful company of fictitious yet most admirably real personages whose acquaintance the reader makes in longer tales. The delight of knowing these characters is not only one of the most attractive joys of novel-reading, but it is one which helps greatly to brighten life and enhance friendship. Few things add more to the sympathy of comradeship than a community of friends in the enchanted realms of the imagination. Strangers in the flesh become instantly conscious of an intimacy in spirit when they discover a common love for some character in fiction. Two men may be strangers, with no common acquaintances in the flesh, but if they discover that both admire Elizabeth Bennet, or Lizzie Hexam, or Laura Bell, or Ethel Newcome; that both are familiar friends with Pendennis, or Warrington, or Harry Richmond, or Mulvaney, or Alan Breck, or Mowgli, or Zagloba; or belong to the brave brotherhood of D'Artagnan, Athos, Porthos, and Aramis, they have a community of sympathy which brings them very close together.

It is seldom and indeed almost never that the short story gives to the reader this sense of knowing familiarly its characters. If there be a series, as in Kipling's "*Jungle Book*" or Maclaren's tales, where the same actors appear again and again, of course the effect may be in this respect the same as that of a novel; but cases of this sort are not common. All the aged women of Miss Wilkins' stories, for instance, are apt in the memory either to blend into one composite photograph of the New England old woman, or to stand remotely, not as persons that we know, but rather as types about which we know. The genuine novel-reader will realize that this consideration is really one of no inconsiderable weight; and it is one which becomes more and more pressing with the increase of the influence of the short story.

提到短篇小说，让人想起这种小说形式在今天发挥了重要作用。时代的躁动和杂志孕育的影响共同推动了短篇小说的发展，使之成为这个时代最显著的文学特色之一。短篇小说的优点在于整体上易于处理和理解，在整体上它消减了更宏大的作品的吸引力。长篇小说往往会增加而非减少人们精神上的不安，作为一种矫正，短篇小说爱好者也不妨阅读一些篇幅稍长而影响深远的作品，而不至于让光阴白白流逝。短篇小说盛行的另一个后果是，如今，读者在长篇故事中结识的那些令人愉快的虚构人物和最令人钦佩的真实人物，几乎没有新的增加。认识这些人物的乐趣不仅是阅读小说最吸引人的乐趣之一，而且也是极大助益我们照亮生活和增进友谊的一大乐趣。没有什么比在梦幻般的想象领域中的朋友圈更能增进同伴般的同情之心了。活生生的陌生人发现小说中某个角色是共同喜爱时，便会立即感受到一种精神上的亲密无间。两个男人可能是陌生人，没有彼此共同的熟人，但如果他们发现两者都钦佩伊丽莎白·班纳特、丽兹赫·克萨姆、劳拉·贝尔或埃塞尔·纽科姆，并且他们都是潘登尼斯、沃灵顿、哈里·里士满、马尔瓦尼、艾伦·布雷克、莫格利或扎格巴熟悉的朋友；或者属于达尔大尼央、阿托斯、波尔多斯 和阿拉密斯的勇敢兄弟会，他们组成了一个志同道合的团体，使彼此走得更近。

短篇小说很少，实际上几乎从来没有给读者这种熟悉其中人物的感觉。如果有一个系列小说，比如在吉卜林的《丛林之书》或麦克拉伦的故事中，同样的人物一次又一次地出现，当然在这方面的效果可能和小说一样，但这种情形并不常见。例如，威尔金斯小姐的小说中的所有老年妇女，在记忆中要么融入了新英格兰老妇人的合成照片，要么就是站得远远的，不像是我们所认识的人，而仅是我们知道的各种类型的人。真正的小说读者都会意识到，以上这种考虑确实具有不容忽视的重要性，随着短篇小说影响力的增强，这一考虑会变得越来越紧迫。

This consideration is the more important from the fact that novels in which the reader is able to identify himself with the characters are by far the most effective, because thus is he removed from the realities which surround him, and for the time being freed from whatever would hamper his imagination. That which in real life he would be, but may not, he may in fiction blissfully and expandingly realize. The innate sense of justice—not, perhaps, unseconded by the innate vanity; we are all of us human! — demands that human possibilities shall be realized, and in the story in which the reader merges his personality in that of some actor, all this is accomplished. In actual outward experience life justifies itself but rarely; to most men its justification is reached only by the aid of the imagination, and it is largely by the aid of literature that the imagination works. Even more true is this of the other sex. Much that men learn from life women must learn from books; so that to women fiction is the primer of life as well as the text-book of the imagination. By the novels he reads the man gives evidence of his imaginative development; the woman of her intellectual existence.

Fiction should be delightful, absorbing, and above all inspiring. Genuine art may sadden, but it cannot depress; it may bring a fresh sense of the anguish of humanity, but it must from its very nature join with this the consolation of an ideal. The tragedy of human life is in art held to be the source of new courage, of nobler aspiration, because it gives grander opportunities for human emotion to vindicate its superiority to all disasters, all terrors, all woe. The reader does not leave the great tragedies with a soured mind or a pessimistic disbelief in life. *"Lear" "Othello" "Romeo and Juliet"* tragic as they are, leave him quivering with sympathy but not with bitterness. The inspiration of the thought of love triumphant over death, of moral grandeur unsubdued by the worst that fate can do, lifts the mind above the disaster. One puts down *"The Kreutzer Sonata"* with the very flesh creeping with disgust at human existence; the same sin is treated no less tragically in *"The Scarlet Letter"* yet the reader is left with an inspiration and a nobler feeling toward life. The attitude of art is in its essence hopeful, and the work of the pessimist must therefore fail, even though it be informed with all the cleverness and the witchery of genius.

　　有一点更为重要的考虑是，读者能够认同某些小说中的人物，这样的小说是迄今为止最富感染力的小说，因为这样他就能脱离周围的现实，暂时从所有会妨碍他想象的事务中解脱出来。在真实生活中，他可能会，也可能不会有这样的解脱，但在小说中，他可能会幸福地、越来越广泛地意识到这一点。这是与生俱来的正当理由——也许和天生的虚荣心一样，我们都是人类！都要求实现人的潜能，而在小说故事中，读者将自己的个性与某个演员的个性融为一体，这一切都变得完美了。在实际的外在体验中，生活很少自证其理。对大多数人来说，正当的理由只能通过想象来实现，而想象在很大程度上又是通过文学的帮助来实现的。这一点对其他性别的人尤其如此，男人从生活中学到的很多东西，女人必须从书本中去学习，所以对女性来说，小说是生活的入门书，也是想象力的教科书。通过阅读小说，男人可以证明他想象力的发展，女人则证明了她的智力存在。

小说应该令人愉快，引人入胜，尤其是要鼓舞人心。真正的艺术可能会令人悲伤，但不会令人沮丧，它可能会带来对人类痛苦的全新感受，但从本质上讲，它必须与理想的安慰互相结合起来。人类生活的悲剧在艺术中被认为是新的勇气和更高尚抱负的源泉，因为悲剧为人类情感提供了更大的机会来证明，人类情感可以超越所有灾难、所有恐怖、所有悲痛。读者不会因为悲观的思想或对生活的悲观怀疑而抛弃伟大的悲剧。《李尔王》《奥赛罗》和《罗密欧与朱丽叶》尽管都是悲剧，但这些悲剧留给观众的不是痛苦的战栗，而是同情心的震动。爱情战胜死亡，崇高的道德不为厄运征服，这些思想的启发无不使心灵超越和战胜灾难。一个人放下《克罗采奏鸣曲》，因书中对人类的厌恶而感到毛骨悚然，同样的罪孽在《红字》中也是以悲剧结尾，但这些作品给读者留下了灵感和对生活更高尚的感觉。艺术的态度本质上是令人充满希望，因此悲观主义的作品必然会失败，即使它充满了天才的睿智和邪恶的魔力。

It is, I believe, from something akin to a remote and perhaps half-conscious perception of this principle that readers in general desire that a novel shall end pleasantly. The popular sentiment in favor of a "happy ending" is by no means so entirely wrong or so utterly Philistine as it is the fashion in these super-asthetical days to assume. The trick of a doleful conclusion has masqued and paraded as a sure proof of artistic inspiration when it is nothing of the kind. Unhappy endings may be more common than happy ones in life, although even that proposition is by no means proved; they seem so from the human habit of marking the disagreeables and letting pleasant things go unnoted. Writers of a certain school have assumed from this that they were keeping more close to life if they left the reader at the close of a story in a state of darkest melancholy; and they have made much parade of the claim that this is not only more true to fact, but more artistic. There is no reason for such an assumption. The artistic climax of a tale is that which grows out of the story by compelling necessity. There are many narrations, of course, which would become essentially false if made to end gladly. When the ingenious Frenchman rewrote the last act of "*Hamlet*", marrying off the Prince and dismissing him with Ophelia to live happily ever after, the thing was monstrously absurd. The general public is not wholly blind to these things. No audience educated up to the point of enjoying "*Hamlet*" or "*Othello*" at all would be satisfied with a sugar-candy conclusion to these. The public does ask, however, and asks justly, that there shall be no meaningless agony; and if it prefers tales which inevitably come to a cheerful last chapter, this taste is in the line with the great principle that it is the function of art to uplift and inspire.

It has already been said over and over that it is the office of literature to show the meaning of life, and the meaning of life is not only what it is but what it may be. To paint the actualities of life is only to state a problem, and it is the mission of art to offer a solution. The novel which can go no further than the presentation of the apparent fact is from the higher standpoint futile because it fails to indicate the meaning of that fact; it falls short as art in so far as it fails to justify existence.

Lowell complains: —

> Modern imaginative literature has become so self-conscious, and therefore so melancholy, that Art, which should be "the world's sweet inn," whither we repair for refreshment and repose, has become rather a watering-place, where one's private touch of liver-complaint is exasperated by the affluence of other sufferers whose talk is a narrative of morbid symptoms. —Chaucer

我相信，正是出于对这一准则近乎模糊或许隐约的认识，读者普遍希望小说能够以愉快的方式结尾。支持"大团圆结局"的流行观点绝不是完全错误或全然庸俗的，因为这种观点代表了超审美时代对一种流行风格的假定，悲惨结局的诡计被伪装并炫耀为艺术灵感的必然证明。在生活中，不幸的结局可能比幸福的结局更常见，尽管这个命题并未得到证实。从人类的习惯来看，这样的结局似乎理应如此，即突显不愉快的事情，而让愉快的事情不为人察觉。某一学派的作家由此认为，如果在故事结束时，让读者处于最黑暗的忧郁状态中，小说会更贴近生活。他们大肆宣扬这不仅更符合事实，而且更具艺术性，但做出这一假定并没有什么充足的理由。小说的艺术高潮源于故事的发展，具有令人信服的必要性。当然，如果强行使小说愉快的收尾，那么很多叙述从根本上讲就是虚假的。一位聪明的法国人改写了《哈姆雷特》的最后一幕，奥菲莉亚嫁给了王子，两人一起被遣散，从此过上了幸福生活。这样的结局简直令人啼笑皆非。公众并非完全对这些事情视而不见，任何受过教育能欣赏《哈姆雷特》或《奥赛罗》的观众都不至于对这些甜言蜜语的结局感到满意。但公众确实要求，并且公正地要求，不应有无意义的痛苦。如果观众喜欢最后一章一定要是令人愉快的结局的故事，这种品味也符合一条伟大的准则，即艺术的作用在于提振与鼓舞人心。

已经多次说过，文学的职责是展示生命的意义，而生命的意义不仅是它是什么，而是它可能是什么。描绘生活的现实只是陈述一个问题，提供解决方案是艺术的使命。站在一个更高的立场来看，只能表现明显事实而不能由表及里的小说没有多大作用，因为它没有指出事实的含义。就艺术而言，它没有证明其存在的合理性，因而是有缺陷的。

洛厄尔曾抱怨：

> 现代的想象性文学变得如此不自然，因而变得如此忧郁，以至本应是一个我们可以修身养性的"人间甜蜜客栈"，竟变成了一个海滨浴场，在那里暗自疗伤，却被大谈恐怖征兆的其他患者的炫富所激怒。

——乔叟

We have introduced into fiction that popular and delusive fallacy of emotional socialism which insists not so much that all shall share the best of life, as that none shall escape its worst. The claim that all shall be acquainted with every phase of life is enforced not by an endeavor to make each reader a sharer in the joys and blessings of existence, but by a determined thrusting forward of the pains and shames of humanity. Modern literature has too generally made the profession of treating all facts of life impartially a mere excuse for dealing exclusively with whatever is ugly and degraded, and for dragging to light whatever has been concealed. This is at best as if one used rare cups of Venetian glass for the measuring out of commercial kerosene and vinegar, or precious Grecian urns for the gathering up of the refuse of the streets.

The wise student of literature will never lose sight of the fact that fiction which has not in it an inspiration is to be looked upon as ineffectual, if it is not to be avoided as morbid and unwholesome. Fiction may be sad, it may deal with the darker side of existence; but it should leave the reader with the uplift which comes from the perception that there is in humanity the power to rise by elevation of spirit above the bitterest blight, to triumph over the most cruel circumstances which can befall.

One word must be added in conclusion, and that is the warning that fiction can never take the place of actual life. There is danger in all art that it may win men from interest in real existence. Literature is after all but the interpreter of life, and living is more than all imaginative experience. We need both the book and the deed to round out a full and rich being. It is possible to abuse literature as it is possible to abuse any other gift of the gods. It is not impossible to stultify and benumb the mind by too much novel-reading; but of this there is no need. Fiction properly used and enjoyed is one of the greatest blessings of civilization; and how poor and thin and meagre would life be without it!

我们在小说中引入了流行并带有欺骗性的情感社会主义谬论。这一观点坚持认为没有这么多美好的生活让人人分享，因为没有人能逃避最糟糕的生活。它竭力主张所有人都应该熟悉生活的每一个阶段，小说不应试图使每个读者去分享生活的快乐和幸福，而应坚定地凸显人性的痛苦和耻辱。现代文学过于普遍地宣称，把公正对待生活中的所有事实作为一个借口，去专门应对丑陋和堕落，并使隐藏的东西暴露无遗。这充其量就好像人们使用稀有的威尼斯玻璃杯去量度商业煤油和醋，或者使用珍贵的希腊古瓮收集街道上的垃圾。

明智的学生永远不要漠视这样一个事实，如果小说无法避免病态和不健康的内容，那么，不能鼓舞人心的小说将被视为是徒劳无益的。小说可能是悲伤的，它可能涉及生活的阴暗面，但小说应该让读者感到振奋，因为人们认为，人类有能力通过精神升华来超越令人痛苦的衰败，战胜可能降临的最残酷的环境。

最后，必须加上一个词，那就是告诫：小说永远不能取代现实生活。一切艺术都有可能使人们对真实存在失去兴趣。文学终究不过是生活的诠释者，生活不仅仅是想象的体验。我们需要书籍和行为去完善和丰富人类的生活。正如人可能滥用诸神的任何其他天赋一样，文学也很容易被滥用。小说读得太多，可能使人心智不健全，大脑也会变得麻木不仁，但这本身没有必要。正确使用和欣赏小说是文明最大的福祉之一，离开小说，生活将变得多么不幸，多么浅薄和鄙俗！

XV
POETRY

The lover of literature must approach any discussion of poetry with feelings of mingled delight and dread. The subject is one which can hardly fail to excite him to enthusiasm, but it is one with which it is difficult to deal without a declaration of sentiments so strong that they are not likely to be spoken; and it is one, too, upon which so much has been said crudely and carelessly, or wisely and warmly, that any writer must hesitate to add anything to the abundance of words already spoken.

For there have been few things so voluminously discussed as poetry. It is a theme so high that sages could not leave it unpraised; while there is never a penny-a-liner so poor or so mean that he hesitates to write his essay upon the sublime and beautiful art. It is one of the consequences of human vanity that the more subtle and difficult a matter, the more feeble minds feel called upon to cover it with the dust of their empty phrases. The most crowded places are those where angels fear to tread; and it is with reverence not unmixed with fear that any true admirer ventures to speak even his love for the noble art of poetry. No discussion of the study of literature, however, can leave out of the account that which is literature's crown and glory; and of the much that might be said and must be felt, an effort must be made here to set something down.

There are few characteristics more general in the race of man than that responsiveness to rhythm which is the foundation of the love of verse. The sense of symmetry exists in the rudest savage that tattoos the two sides of his face in the same pattern, or strings his necklace of shells in alternating colors. The same feeling is shown by the unasthetic country matron, the mantel of whose sacredly dark and cold best room is not to her eye properly adorned unless the ugly vase at one end is balanced by another exactly similar

262

ugly vase upon the other. In sound the instinct is yet more strongly marked. The barbaric drum-beat which tells in the quivering sunlight of an African noon that the cannibalistic feast is preparing appeals crudely to the same quality of the human mind which in its refinement responds to the swelling cadences of Mendelssohn's *Wedding March* or the majestic measures of *The Ninth Symphony*. The rhythm of the voice in symmetrically arranged words is equally potent in its ability to give pleasure. Savage tribes make the beginnings of literature in inchoate verse. Indeed, so strongly does poetry appeal to men even in the earlier states of civilization that Macaulay seems to have conceived the idea that poetry belongs to an immature stage of growth, —a deduction not unlike supposing the sun to be of no consequence to civilization because it has been worshiped by savages. In the earlier phases of human development, whether of the individual or of the race, the universal instincts are more apparent; and the hold which song takes upon half-barbaric man is simply a proof of how primal and universal is the taste to which it appeals. The sense and enjoyment of rhythm show themselves in a hundred ways in the life and pleasures of primitive races, the vigorous shoots from which is to spring a splendid growth.

第十五讲　诗歌

　　文学爱好者必定带着喜忧参半的心情来参与讨论诗歌。这个话题不可能不激发出人的热情，但如果没有强烈的情感宣言，就很难讨论这个话题，也可能就此无话可说了。以往人们就此话题已谈论不少了，有的讨论粗糙而马虎，有的睿智而热情，因而，面对已说过的如此丰富的言辞，要说点别的东西，每个作家都必然表现出犹豫不决。

　　因为很少有什么东西像诗歌一样被广泛讨论过。这是一个如此崇高的主题，连圣人都不得不给予赞许。但一个穷困潦倒的文人却不会犹豫写一篇文章来评论崇高而美丽的艺术。这便是虚荣心的后果之一，事情越是棘手和困难，怯弱的灵魂就愈是感到需要空洞无物的言辞的尘灰去掩盖它。最拥挤的地方是天使不敢踏足的地方。任何一个真正的崇拜者都应该怀着一颗未掺杂任何恐惧的崇敬之心，勇于表达对高贵的诗歌艺术的钟爱之情。然而，任何对文学研读的讨论，都不可能忽略文学的皇冠和荣耀，也不可能对有感而发的很多话不予理会，必得努力借此写下一些东西。

　　在人类种族中，没有什么比对韵律的反应更普遍的特征了，这一点是热爱诗歌的基础。最野蛮的原始人身上也存在对称美，他在脸的两侧纹上相同的图案，或者用交替的颜色串起贝壳项链。缺乏美感的乡村女主人也会表现出同样的感觉，她用于祭祀的最好的房间，黑暗阴冷，不过在她眼里，壁炉架装饰得并不恰当，除非壁炉架一端的那支丑陋花瓶要配上另一个完全相似的丑陋花瓶才平衡。在声音中，人的本能会更加凸显。在非洲中午令人眩晕的阳光下，原始部落的人们正在击鼓欢庆，一场食人盛宴正在准备。击鼓之声大然地诉诸人类心灵的相同品质，这种品质在其精致中回应了门德尔松的《婚礼进行曲》喜悦的节奏或贝多芬《第九交响曲》的恢宏旋律。在对称排列的单词中，声音的节奏有力地传递了愉悦之情。原始部落以其不成熟的诗歌开创了文学的先河。事实上，即使在文明的早期阶段，诗歌的吸引力也如此强烈，以至麦考利似乎提出了一个观点，即诗歌属于人类成长的一个不成熟的阶段。这一推论如同假设，因为原始人崇拜太阳，所以太阳对人类文明无关紧要。在人类发展的早期阶段，无论是个体的还是种族的，普遍的本能更为明显，诗歌对未完全开化的人们的吸引力，只是证明了诗歌诉诸的那种品味是多么原始和普遍。节奏感和对节奏的喜爱以多种多样的方式得以在原始民族的生活和乐趣中呈现，由此生机勃勃的嫩芽催生出灿烂的成长。

Not to go so far back as the dawn of civilization, however, it is sufficient here to recall our own days in the nursery, when *Mother Goose*, the only universal Alma Mater, with rhymes foolish but rhythmical, meaningless but musical, delighted ears yet too untrained to distinguish sense from folly, but not too young to enjoy the delight of the beating of the voice in metrically arranged accents.

This pleasure in rhythm is persistent, and it is strongly marked even in untrained minds. In natures unspoiled and healthy, natures not bewildered and sophisticated by a false idea of cultivation, or deceived into unsound notions of the real value of poetry, the taste remains sound and good. In the youth of a race this natural enjoyment of verse is gratified by folk-songs. These early forms are naturally undeveloped and simple, but the lays are genuine and wholesome; they possess lasting quality. Different peoples have in differing degrees the power of appreciating verse, but I do not know that any race has been found to lack it entirely. There is abundant evidence that the Anglo-Saxon and Norman ancestors from whom sprang the English-speaking peoples were in this respect richly endowed, and that they early went far in the development of this power. The old ballads of our language are so rich and so enduringly beautiful that we are proved to come from a stock endowed with a rich susceptibility to poetry. If this taste has not been generally developed it is from some reason other than racial incapacity. Nothing need be looked for in early literatures sweeter and sounder than the fine old ballads of "*Chevy Chace*" "*Tamlane*" "*Sir Patrick Spens*" or "*Clerk Saunders*". Many a later poet of no mean reputation has failed to strike so deep and true a note as rings through these songs made by forgotten minstrels for a ballad-loving people. There are not too many English-speaking poets to-day who could match the cry of the wraith of Clerk Saunders at the window of his love: —

> Oh, cocks are crowing a merry midnight,
> The wild fowls are boding day;
> Give me my faith and troth again,
> Let me fare on my way...
> Cauld mould it is my covering now,
> But and my winding sheet;

The dew it falls nae sooner down
Than my resting-place is weet!

　　然而，无须追溯到文明的曙光那么远，在这里回忆一下我们自己在幼儿园的日子就绰绰有余了。虽说歌谣有点可笑，但富有节奏感，虽然毫无意义，却悦耳动听。尽管未经训练不辨是非，或年幼不懂富有韵律的敲击声带来的欢乐，《鹅妈妈》那首普天之下的校歌却洋洋赢耳。

　　源自节奏的快感经久不衰，即使未加训练，大脑中的这种快感也能留下强烈的印迹。在未遭破坏和健全的大自然中，虚假的教养观念尚未使淳朴的天性迷失或受蒙蔽而相信不可靠的诗歌价值观念，正因如此，人的品位仍然能够保持健全和良好状态。在人类的青春时期，这种对诗歌的自然喜爱是由民歌来满足的。很自然，早期民歌的形式尚未成形且非常简单，然而，它们却真实而健康，拥有持久的品质。不同的民族在不同程度上具有欣赏诗歌的能力，但我不知道是否任何民族身上都可以找到这种能力。有大量证据表明，英语民族起源于盎格鲁-撒克逊人和诺曼人的祖先，他们在这方面具有丰富的天赋，并且他们的这一能力很早就得到了充分发展。我们语言中的古老民谣丰富多产，具有经久不衰的魅力，充分证明我们族群对诗歌具有丰富的敏感性。如果这种鉴赏力没有得到普遍发展，那也是出于其他某种原因，而非我们这个民族的无能。在早期文学作品中，没有什么比《雪佛兰·切斯》《塔姆连精灵王国》《帕特·里克·司本斯爵士》或《克拉克·桑德斯》更精美、更甜美、更动听的老歌谣了。许多后期名不见经传的诗人却未能像曾经唱出响彻云霄歌声的那些被遗忘的吟游诗人那样，为我们这个喜爱民歌的民族留下令人印象深刻而真实的歌谣。今天，已没有太多英语诗人能够媲美卡拉克·桑德斯在他爱人窗前发出的幽灵般的哭泣：

　　　　哦，公鸡在欢乐的午夜鸣叫，
　　　　野鸟是凶兆；
　　　　请再次相信我的忠诚和诚实，

让我顺利上路吧……
冰冷的土堆现在把我盖住，
但那是我的裹尸布；
露水一落下来
我安息的地方就变湿了！

How far popular taste has departed from an appreciation of verse that is simple and genuine is shown by those favorite rhymes which are unwearyingly yearned for in the columns of Notes and Queries, and which reappear with periodic persistence in Answers to Correspondents. In educated persons, it is true, there is still a love of what is really good in verse, but it is far too rare. The general ear and the general taste have become vitiated. There is a melancholy and an amazing number of readers who are pleased only with rhymes of the sort of Will Carleton's "*Farm Ballads*", the sentimentally inane jingles published in the feminine domestic periodicals, and the rest of what might be called, were not the phrase perilously near to the vulgar, the chewing-gum school of verse.

One of the most serious defects in modern systems of education seems to me to be, as has been said in an earlier talk, an insufficient provision for the development of the imagination. This is nowhere more marked than in the failure to recognize the place and importance of poetry in the training of the mind of youth. It might be supposed that an age which prides itself upon being scientific in its methods would be clever enough to perceive that from the early stages of civilization may well be taken hints for the development of the intellect of the young. Primitive peoples have invariably nourished their growing intelligence and enlarged their imagination by fairy-lore and poetry. The childhood of the individual is in its essentials not widely dissimilar from the childhood of the race; and what was the instinctive and wholesome food for one is good for the other. If our common schools could but omit a good deal of the instruction which is falsely called "practical", because it deals with material issues, and devote the time thus gained to training children to enjoy poetry and to use their imagination, the results would be incalculably better.

I say to enjoy poetry. There is much well-meant instruction which is unconsciously conducive to nothing but its detestation. Students who by nature have a fondness for verse are laboriously trained by conscientiously mistaken instructors to regard anything in poetical form as a bore and a torment. The business of a teacher in a preparatory school should be to incite the pupil to love poetry. It is better to make a boy thrill and kindle over a single line than it is to get into his head all the comments made on literature from the beginning of time.

人们在"注释"与"询问"栏目中表现出一中对某些偏爱的韵律孜孜不倦的渴望表明，公众的品位已脱离了对简单而真实的诗歌欣赏，并且这一现象在记者答疑栏目中周期性的反复出现。的确，受过教育的人群中仍然存在对诗歌里真正美好的东西的热爱，但这已十分罕有。一般的音感和品位已经变得每况愈下。悲哀的是，一大群读者只对威尔·卡尔顿忧郁的《农场民谣》之类的押韵感到满意。这些在国内女性期刊上发表的情感空洞的诗句，以及其或可称为口香糖流派的诗，顶多还算不上是近似粗俗的废话。

对我而言，正如在之前的一次演讲中所说的那样，现代教育体系中最严重的缺陷之一乃是，没有做好充分的准备去发展想象力。较为明显的一点便是，未能认识到诗歌在青年思想训练中的地位和重要性。可以假设，一个因其方法科学而引以为豪的时代，应有足够的智慧认识到，从文明早期阶段，就应该发展青年人的智力。原始民族总是通过童话故事和诗歌来滋养他们日益增长的智慧，并扩展他们的想象力。一个人的童年在本质上与人类的童年没有太大的不同。天资和有益健康的东西给一个人带来好处，同样对另一个人也有益处。如果因教学涉及讨论物质问题，普通学校不得不砍掉被误认为是"实用的"教学，转而把获得的时间用于训练孩子们欣赏诗歌和发挥他们的想象力，那么得到的良好结果将无法估量。

我声言喜欢诗歌，但很多并无恶意的教诲在不知不觉中却助长了人们对诗歌的厌恶感。有的学生天生就喜欢诗歌，但在一些观念错误的导师费劲训导下，也会把诗歌形式上的任何东西都视为无聊和折磨。预科学校的教师的职责应该是激发学生热爱诗歌。与其让一个男孩从一开始就把所有文学评论装进他脑子，不如用一句诗去激励他，去点燃他的激情。

The strain and stress of modern life are opposed to the appreciation of any art; and in the case of poetry this difficulty has been increased by a widespread feeling that poetry is after all of little real consequence. It has been held to be an excrescence upon life rather than an essential part of it. It is the tendency of the time to seek for tangible and present results; and men have too generally ceased to appreciate the fact that much which is best is to be reached more surely indirectly than directly. Since of the effects which spring from poetry those most of worth are its remote and intangible results, careless and superficial thinkers have come to look upon song as an unmanly affectation, a thing artificial if not effeminate. This is one of the most absolute and vicious of all intellectual errors. In high and noble truth, poetry is as natural as air; poetry is as virile as war!

It is not easy to discover whence arose the popular feeling of the insignificance of poetry. It is allied to the materialistic undervaluing of all art, and it is probably not unconnected with the ascetic idea that whatever ministers to earthly delight is a hindrance to progress toward the unseen life of another world. Something is to be attributed, no doubt, to the contempt bred by worthless imitations with which facile poetasters have afflicted a long-suffering world; but most of all is the want of an appreciation of the value of poetry to be attributed to the fact that men engrossed in literal and material concerns have not been able to appreciate remote consequences, or to comprehend the utterances of the masters who speak the language of the imagination.

While the world in general, however, has been increasingly unsympathetic toward poetry, the sages have universally concurred in giving to it the highest place in the list of literary achievements. "Poetry," Emerson said, "is the only verity." The same thought is expanded in a passage from Mrs. Browning, in which she speaks of poets as:

> —the only truth-tellers now left to God, —
> The only speakers of essential truth,
> Opposed to relative, comparative,
> And temporal truths; the only holders by
> His sun-skirts, through conventual gray glooms;
> The only teachers who instruct mankind
> From just a shadow on a charnel wall
> To find man's veritable stature out,
> Erect, sublime, —the measure of a man.
> —*Aurora Leigh*

So Wordsworth: —

> Poetry is the breath and finer spirit of all knowledge, it is the impassioned expression which is on the face of all science.

It is needless, however, to multiply quotations. The world has never doubted the high respect which those who appreciate poetry have for the art. It is true also that however general at any time may have been the seeming or real neglect of poetry, the race has not failed to preserve its great poems. The prose of the past, no matter how great its wisdom, has never been able to take with succeeding generations the rank held by the masterpieces of the poets. Mankind has seemed not unlike one who affects to hold his jewels in little esteem, it may be, yet like the jewel owner it has guarded them with constant jealousy. The honor-roll of literature is the world's list of great poets. The student of literature is not long in discovering that his concern is far more largely with verse than with anything else that the wit of mankind has devised to write. However present neglect may at any time appear to show the contrary, the long-abiding regard of the race declares beyond peradventure that it counts poetry as most precious among all its intellectual treasures.

现代生活的紧张和压力与欣赏任何艺术有所相悖。就诗歌而言，这种难题因一种普遍的感觉而增加，即诗歌毕竟没有什么实际意义。诗被认为是生命的赘生物，而非生命的重要组成部分。追求有形和当下的结果乃时代之趋势。人们普遍也不再赞同，很多最美好的东西应该通过间接方式而不是直接方式来获取。由于诗歌产生的最有价值的影响是其间接和无形的结果，故一些考虑问题草率和肤浅的人开始将诗歌视为怯弱的矫揉造作，认为它即使不是柔弱的，也是做作的。这是所有认识错误中最绝对和最恶毒的错误之一。在崇高的真理中，诗歌如空气一般自然，诗歌和战争一样刚强有力！

很难发现，出于什么缘由人们普遍感觉诗歌无足轻重。这种感觉与低估艺术价值的享乐主义紧密相关，而且还可能与禁欲主义的想法不无关联，即为尘世带来快乐的任何东西都是去向另一个世界前所未见的生活的滞碍。毫无疑问，这种感觉还要归咎于无价值的模仿所滋生的蔑视，蹩脚诗人用这种方式令这个苦难的世界饱受煎熬。但最重要的原因还在于，缺乏对诗歌价值的赞赏，这点归因于这样一个事实：一心只关注文字表面及物质层面问题的人，无法意识到间接的结果，也无法理解大师们富有想象力的语言表达。

然而，尽管总体上世人对诗歌越来越冷漠，但智者普遍同意将诗歌置于文学成就的最高位置。艾默生说："诗歌是唯一的真实。"同样的想法在勃朗宁夫人的诗句中得到了延伸，她将诗人称为：

——如今留给神的唯一讲真话的人——
基本事实的唯一言说者，
反对相对的、比较的，
以及现世的真实；唯一举起
他的遮阳的裙边，穿过阴森的黑暗；
教导人类唯一的老师
刚从停尸间墙上来的一个影子
发现了人真正的高度，

挺立、至高——人的标准。

——《奥罗拉·李》

所以华兹华斯说：

> 诗歌是一切知识的气息和优良精神，是一切科学表面充满激情的表达。

但已无须赘述，世人从不怀疑欣赏诗歌的人对艺术的崇高敬意。的确，不管什么时候，尽管对诗歌貌似或真正的忽略比比皆是，人类仍保存了伟大的诗歌。过去的散文，无论其智慧多么伟大，从未随其后代占据诗人杰作的地位。人类似乎和那些故作对自己的珠宝不屑一顾的人没有什么两样，但事实也许是这样，就像珠宝的主人一样，一直用羡妒守护着它们。文学荣誉榜是世界伟大诗人的名录。研读文学者无须多时就会发现，他对诗歌的眷注远远超过对人类智慧创造而写就的任何其他东西的关照。然而，当下对诗歌的轻视在任何时候都可能显示出相反的结果，人类对诗歌历久弥新的敬意无疑表明，在全部知识宝库中，视诗歌最为珍贵。

XVI
THE TEXTURE OF POETRY

In discussing poetry it is once more necessary to begin with something which will serve us as a definition. No man can imprison the essence of an art in words; and it is not to be understood that a formal definition can be framed which shall express all that poetry is and means. Its more obvious characteristics, however, may be phrased, and even an incomplete formula is often useful. There have been almost as many definitions of poetry made already as there have been writers on literature, some of them intelligible and some of them open to the charge of incomprehensibility. Schopenhauer, for instance, defined poetry as the art of exciting by words the power of the imagination; a phrase so broad that it is easily made to cover all genuine literature. It will perhaps be sufficient for our purpose here if we say that poetry is the embodiment in metrical, imaginative language of passionate emotion.

By metrical language is meant that which is systematically rhythmical. Much prose is rhythmical. Indeed, it is difficult to conceive of fine or delicate prose which has not rhythm to some degree, and oratorical prose is usually distinguished by this. The Bible abounds in excellent examples; as, for instance, this passage from Job: —

Hell is naked before Him, and destruction hath no covering; He stretcheth out the north over the empty place, and hangeth the earth upon nothing. He bindeth up the waters in his thick clouds; and the cloud is not rent under them. He holdeth back the face of His throne, and spreadeth His cloud upon it. He hath compassed the waters with bounds until the day and night come to an end. The pillars of heaven tremble, and are astonished at His reproof. He divideth the sea with His power, and by His understanding He smiteth through the proud. —*Job*, xxvi. 6-12.

Here, as in all fine prose, there is a rhythm which is marked, and at times almost regular; but it is not ordered by a system, as it must be in the simplest verse of poetry. Take, by way of contrast, a stanza from the superbchorus to Artemis in "*Atalanta in Calydon*": —

> Come with bows bent and with emptying of quivers,
> Maiden most perfect, lady of light,
> With a noise of winds and many rivers,
> With a clamor of waters and with might;
> Bind on thy sandals, O thou most fleet,
> Over the splendor and speed of thy feet;
> For the faint east quickens, the wan west shivers,
> Round the feet of the day and the feet of the night.

Here the rhythm is systematized according to regular laws, and so becomes metrical. The effect upon the ear in prose is largely due to rhythm, but metrical effects are entirely within the province of poetry.

第十六讲　诗歌的实质

在讨论诗歌时，再次有必要从一些可以作为定义的东西开始。没有人能将艺术的本质禁锢在语言之中，但令人无法理解的是，又可划定一个正式的定义来表达诗歌是什么和意味着什么。然而，诗歌更明显的特征可以用言语来表述，甚至一个不完整的规则时常也能起作用。诗歌的定义已几乎和作家给文学下的定义一样多了，其中一些是可以理解的，而另一些则被指责为难以理解。例如，叔本华将诗歌定义为用文字激发想象力的艺术。一个如此宽泛的说法，很容易覆盖所有真正的文学。如果我们说诗歌是充满激情的韵律，富有想象力的语言的体现，那么对于我们的目的来说，也许就足够了。

韵律语言是指有系统节奏的语言，许多散文也具有节奏。事实上，很难想象没有节奏的优美或细腻的散文，由此演讲散文通常也以此来区分。《圣经》中有很多优秀的例子：

> 地狱在他面前赤身露体，毁灭无影无踪；他将北方铺在空地上，将大地悬在虚无之上。他用浓云包住水，云在他们之下不租。他挡住他宝座的脸，将他的云彩铺在上面。他无边无际地绕水而行，直到昼夜结束。

在这里，就像所有优秀散文一样，存在一种明显的节奏，间或几乎是有规律的节奏，尽管这种节奏还不是依据系统排序的，但最简单的诗歌中也必须按照系统来排序。史文朋的《卡利登的亚特兰大》中对阿尔忒弥斯的精湛合唱中的一节诗可以作为对照：

> 弓上弦，箭袋空
> 最完美的少女，光之女神
> 狂风呼啸，河流纵横
> 借着水的喧嚷和力量
> 系上你的鞋，飞驰而去！
> 越过你的脚步和光彩
> 晨光熹微，夕阳欲坠
> 追随着白天和夜晚的步。

在文中，节奏遵循有规律的法则得以系统化，由此变成韵律。散文中，韵律的影响主要体现在听觉上，但韵律的效果完全属于诗歌的范畴。

This difference between rhythmical and metrical language would seem to be sufficiently obvious, but the difficulty which many students have in appreciating it may make it worthwhile to give another illustration. The following passage from Edmund Burke, that great master of sonorous English, is strongly and finely rhythmical: —

> Because we are so made as to be affected at such spectacles with melancholy sentiments upon the unstable condition of mortal prosperity, and the tremendous uncertainty of human greatness; because in those natural feelings we learn great lessons; because in events like these our passions instruct our reason; because when kings are hurled from their thrones by the Supreme Director of this great drama, and become objects of insult to the base, and of pity to the good, we behold such disasters in the moral, as we should behold a miracle in the physical order of things. —*Reflections on the Revolution in France.*

So markedly rhythmical is this, indeed, that it would take but little to change it into metre: —

> Because we are so made as to be moved by spectacles like these with melancholy sentiments of the unstable case of mortal things, and the uncertainty of human greatness here; because in those our natural feelings we may learn great lessons too; because in such events our passions teach our reason well; because when kings are hurled down from their thrones, etc.

There is no longer any dignity in this. It has become a sort of sing-song, neither prose nor yet poetry. The sentiments are not unlike those of a familiar passage in Shakespeare: —

> This is the state of man; to-day he puts forth
> The tender leaves of hopes; to-morrow blossoms,
> And bears his blushing honors thick upon him;
> The third day comes a frost, a killing frost;
> And, —when he thinks, good easy man, full surely
> His greatness is a ripening, —nips his root,
> And then he falls, as I do.

—Henry VIII. ，iii. 2

In the extract from Burke a sense of weakness and even of flatness is produced by the rearrangement of the accents so that they are made regular; while in the verse of Shakespeare the sensitive **ear** is very likely troubled by the single misplaced accent in the first line. In any mood save the poetic metre seems an artificiality and an affectation, but in that mood it is as natural and as necessary as air to the lungs.

Besides being metrical the language of poetry must be imaginative. By imaginative language is meant that which not only conveys imaginative conceptions, but which is itself full of force and suggestion; language which not only expresses ideas and emotions, but which by its own power evokes them. Imaginative language is marked by the most vivid perception on the part of the writer of the connotive effect of words; it conveys even more by implication than by direct denotation. It may of course be used in poetry or prose. In the passage from *Job* just quoted, the use of such phrases as "empty place" "hangeth the earth upon nothing" convey more by what they suggest to the mind than by their literal assertion. The writer has evidently used them with a vital and vivid understanding of their suggestiveness. He realizes to the full their office to convey impressions so subtle that they cannot be given by direct and literal diction.

　　有节奏的语言和有韵律的语言之间的这种差异似乎非常明显，但是许多学生在理解这一差异时，仍会有困难。就此值得再举出一个例证。爱德蒙·伯克是一位英语大师，其英语铿锵有力，下面一段文字中，节奏感强烈而优美：

　　　　因为我们生来如此，为这样的景象所感染，对人类繁荣的不稳定状况及人之伟大的确定性，深感忧郁。因为在这些自然的情感中，我们学到了很多东西；因为在这样的事件中，我们的激情教会了我们保持理性；因为当国王们被这部伟大戏剧的最高导演从王位上推翻，成为底层人物侮辱的对象以及善良之人怜悯的对象时，我们看到的是一场道德灾难。

——《对法国大革命的反思》

的确，这段引文节奏感显而易见，无须大费周折就能转换成有韵律的散文：

因为我们生来如此，为如此景象所感动，为人类之凡事不稳定状况及人之伟大的极度不确定性，深感忧郁。因为在这些自然的情感中，我们学到了很多教训；因为在这样的事件中，激情教会了我们保持理性；因为当国王们从王位上被推翻，等等。

再也没有尊严可言了，上文变成了一种歌咏，既非散文，亦非诗歌。这些感觉与莎士比亚为人熟知的一段诗句带给人的感觉大同小异：

人世间的事就是这样。一个人今天生出了希望的嫩叶，
第二天开了花，
身上开满了红艳艳的荣誉的花朵，
第三天致命的霜冻来了，
而这位蒙在鼓里的好人还蛮有把握，
以为他的宏伟事业正在成熟呢，
想不到霜冻正在咬噬他的根，
接着他就倒下了，和我一样。

——《亨利八世》，第三幕，第二场

（朱生豪　译）

在伯克的摘录中，产生了一种软弱感甚至是平淡感，但重音的重新排列使文字变得有规律了，而在莎士比亚的诗句中，敏锐的听觉很可能会被第一行中单个错位的重音所困扰。除了诗的韵律显得不自然和矫揉造作外，在那种情绪中，韵律就像空气进入肺部一样自然和必要。

除了韵律之外,诗歌的语言还必须富有想象力,这种语言不仅指传达想象的概念,而且也指语言本身充满力量和暗示。语言不仅表达思想和情感,而且以其自身的力量来唤起思想和情感。想象性语言的特点是作者对文字内涵效果的最鲜明的感知,它当然可以用于诗歌或散文,并通过暗示而非直接运用词汇外延意义来传达更多信息。在刚引用的《约伯记》一节中,使用诸如"天空""将大地悬在虚无"之类的短语,其意义更多的是,通过它们对头脑的暗示而不是字面上的确定意义来传达的。显然,作者在使用暗示性时,已对它有一个必不可少且生动的理解了。作者彻底意识到了在传递印象时,暗示性的作用非常微妙,无法通过直接和字面的措辞表达。

Poetry is made up of words and phrases which glow with this richness of intention. When Shakespeare speaks of skin "smooth as monumental alabaster", how much is added to the idea by the epithet "monumental", the suggestion of the polished and protected stone, enshrined on a tomb; how much is due to association and implication in such phrases as the "reverberate hills" "parting is such sweet sorrow" "the white wonder of dear Juliet's hand" "and sleep in dull, cold marble" —phrases all of which have a literal significance plain enough, yet of which this literal meaning is of small account beside that which they evoke. Poetic diction naturally and inevitably melts into figures, as when we read of "the shade of melancholy boughs" "the spendthrift sun" "the bubble reputation" "the inaudible and noiseless foot of time"; but the point here is that even in its literal words there is constantly the sense and the employment of implied meanings. It is by no means necessarily figures to which language owes the quality of being imaginative. Broadly speaking, a style may be said to be imaginative in proportion as the writer has realized and intended its suggestions.

The language of prose is often imaginative to a high degree, but seldom if ever to that extent or with that deliberate purpose which in verse is nothing less than essential. Genuine poetry differs from prose in the entire texture of its web. From the same threads the loom may weave plain stuff or richest brocade; and thus of much the same words are made prose and poetry. The difference lies chiefly in the fashion of working.

The essentials of the manner of poetry being language metrical and imaginative, the essential of the matter is that it be the expression of passionate emotion. By passionate emotion is meant any feeling, powerful or delicate, which is capable of filling the whole soul; of taking possession for the time being of the entire man. It may be fierce hate, enthralling love, ambition, lust, rage, jealousy, joy, sorrow, any over-mastering mood, or it may be one of those intangible inclinations, those moods of mist, ethereal as hazes in October, those caprices of pleasure or sadness which Tennyson had the art so marvelously to reproduce. Passionate emotion is by no means necessarily intense, but it is engrossing. For the time being, at least, it seems to absorb the whole inner consciousness.

It is the completeness with which such a mood takes possession of the mind, so that for the moment it is to all intents and purposes the man himself, that gives it so great an importance in human life and makes it the fitting and the sole essential theme of the highest art. Behind all serious human effort lies the instinctive sense of the fitness of things. The artist must always convince that his end is worthy of the means which he employs to reach it; and it follows naturally that the writer who uses imaginative diction and the elaborateness of metre must justify this by what he embodies in them. Metrical forms are as much out of place in treating of the material concerns of life as would be court robes or religious rites in the reaping of a field or the selling of a cargo of wool. The poet is justified in his use of all the resources of form and of poetic diction by the fact that the message which he is endeavoring to convey is high and noble; that the meaning which he attempts to impart is so profoundly subtle as to be inexpressible unless the words which he employs are assisted by the language of rhythm and metre.

诗歌由充满丰富含义的字词和短语组成。当莎士比亚说肌肤"像巨大的雪花石膏一样光滑"时，"纪念碑的"一词为表达这一层意思增添了不少色彩，暗示出在坟墓上用作祀奉的光亮而完好的雪花石。诸如"回荡的山丘""离别是如此甜蜜的悲伤""亲爱的朱丽叶的皎洁玉手""安眠在没有感觉、冷冰冰的大理石棺材里"等短语的意义很大程度上是由于联想和暗示带来的，所有这些短语的字面意义一清二楚，但除了所唤起的意义之外，字面意义是微不足道的。诗歌的措辞自然而然不可避免地融入了隐喻，就像当我们读到"忧郁的树枝的阴影""挥霍无度的太阳""虚名""时间的不可听见的无声脚步"，但这里的重点是，即使在其字面意思里，也要不断地利用词语的含义及隐含义。语言具有想象力的品质绝不一定完全归功于隐喻。从广义上讲，一种风格可以说是恰如其分地运用了想象力的结果，因为作者已经意识到并有意识地运用了暗示。

通常在很高程度上，散文的语言是想象性的，只是很少能达到这种程度，也很少有这种深思熟虑的目的，然而想象性对诗歌却是必不可少的。真正的诗歌在其网络的整个结构上不同于散文。同样的纺线，织布机可以编织普普通通的织物，也可以纺出丰富多彩的锦缎，因此，散文和诗歌由大致相同的言辞创造出来，其区别主要体现在操作方式上。

诗歌艺术手法的要素是语言的格律和想象性，本质是强烈的情感表达。强烈的情感是指，任何无论是强大的还是细腻的能够充满整个灵魂，能暂时控制整个人的感觉。情感可能是强烈的仇恨、迷人的爱、野心、欲望、愤怒、嫉妒、喜悦、悲伤、任何征服人的情绪，也可能是那些无形的倾向之一，那些迷雾般的情绪，像十月的阴霾一样缥缈，那些丁尼生用精湛的技艺再现的反复无常的快乐或悲伤。强烈的情感不一定是剧烈的，但它一定是压倒一切的，似乎能令人至少暂时心无旁骛。

正是这种情感的完整性支配着头脑，因此就所有意图和目的而言，人本身在人类生活中赋予情感如此重要的意义，并使其成为最高艺术恰当且唯一的基本主题。在所有人类严肃的努力背后，都隐藏着对事物的适当性的本能感觉。艺术家必须始终能让人相信，他为达到目的而使用的手段是值得的。由此，作家自然会使用富有想象力的措辞和精心设计的格律，并以此通过他在其中体现的内容来证明这一点。利用格律形式来处理生活中的物质问题是不合时宜的，与身着宫廷长袍或宗教仪式在田地收获或出售羊毛货物一样格格不入。诗人有理由利用形式和诗歌文辞，因为他努力要表达的寓意是高尚和崇高的。他试图传达的意义极其深刻微妙，难以言表，除非他使用的词语辅以节奏和格律的语言。

That the reader unconsciously recognizes the fact that the essential difference in the office of prose and poetry makes inevitable a difference also of method, is shown by his dissatisfaction when the writer of prose invades the province of poetry. The arrangement of the words of prose into systematic rhythm produces at once an effect of weakness and of insincerity. Dickens in some of his attempts to reach deep pathos has made his prose metrical with results most disastrous. The mood of poetry is so elevated that metrical conventions seem appropriate and natural; whereas in the mood of even the most emotional prose they appear fantastical and affected. The difference is not unlike that between the speaking and the singing voice. A man who sang in conversation, or even in a highly excited oration, would simply make himself ridiculous. In song this manner of using the voice is not only natural but inevitable and delightful. What would be uncalled for in the most exalted moods of the prose writer is natural and fitting in the case of the poet, because the poet is endeavoring to embody, in language the most deep, the most high, the most delicate experiences of which humanity is capable. The form is with him a part of his normal language. To say in prose, "My love is like a red rose newly sprung in June, or like a melody beautifully played", means not much. Yet the words themselves are not widely varied from those in which Burns conveys the same ideas with so great an added beauty, and so much more emotional force: —

Oh, my luve's like a red, red rose
That's newly sprung in June;
Oh, my luve's like a melodie

That's sweetly played in tune.

The metrical cadences woo the ear like those of a melody sweetly played, and to that which the words may say or suggest they add an effect yet more potent and delightful.

A moment's consideration of these facts enables one to estimate rightly the stricture made by Plato: —

You have often seen what a poor appearance the tales of poets make when stripped of the colors which music puts upon them, and recited in prose. They are like faces which were never really beautiful, but only blooming, and now the bloom of youth has passed away from them.

读者会不自觉地认识到，散文和诗歌的作用有着本质上的差异，必然导致方法上的不同，这体现在散文作家侵入诗歌领域时，诗人会感到不满。将散文的文字安排成系统的节奏，立即便会产生软弱和不真实的效果。狄更斯曾使他的散文具有格律，试图以此达到一种深刻的感伤效果，但其结果却是灾难性的。诗歌的基调高尚，故韵律的规范似乎是恰当和自然的，而即使在最富情感的散文基调中，他们也会显得古怪与不自然。说话的声音和唱歌的声音没有什么不同。一个在谈话中，甚至在非常激昂的演讲中唱歌的人，只会让自己变得滑稽可笑。在歌唱中，这种使用声音的方式不仅是自然的，而且是不可避免的令人愉快。在散文作家最崇高的心境中，他们不需要的东西对诗人来说却是自然而然的，因为诗人一直努力在语言中体现人类能够获得的最深刻、最崇高、最细腻的体验。格律形式是诗人正常语言的一部分，若用散文表达，"我的爱就像六月初绽的红玫瑰，或者像弹奏出美妙的旋律"，其意义不大。然而，这些词本身与彭斯要传达的同样的意思并没有太大的区别，但在诗歌中，这些词具有如此多的美感和更多的情感力量：

呵，我的爱人像朵红红的玫瑰，
六月里迎风初开；

呵，我的爱人象支甜甜的曲子，

奏得合拍又和谐。

（王佐良 译）

韵律节奏像弹奏出甜美的旋律一样吸引着耳朵，而富有旋律的文字可以表达的或暗示的则会增加一种更强大、更令人愉悦的效果。

对这些事实的片刻考虑能够使人们正确评价柏拉图所做的苛责：

你经常看到，当诗人的故事被去掉了音乐赋予的色彩，并以散文形式朗诵时，它们的外表是多么糟糕。就像一张张从来没有真正美丽过，而只是充满活力的面孔，如今焕发的青春芳华已经从它们身上消磨殆尽。

It would be more just and more exact to say that they are like the framework of a palace from which have been stripped the slabs of precious marble which covered it. It is neither more nor less reasonable to object to poetry that its theme told in prose is slight or dull than it would be to scorn St. Peter's because its rafters and ridgepole might not be attractive if they stood out bare against the sky. The form is in poetry as much an integral part as walls and roof and dome, statues and jewel-like marbles, are part of the temple.

Leaving out of consideration those peculiarities such as rhyme and special diction, which although often of much effect are not essential since poetry may be great without them, it is sufficiently exact for a general examination to say that the effects of poetry are produced by the threefold union of ideas, suggestion, and melody. In the use of ideas poetry is on much the same footing as prose, except in so far as it deals with exalted moods which have no connection with thoughts which are mean or commonplace. In the use of suggestion poetry but carries farther the means employed in imaginative prose. Melody may be said practically to be its own prerogative. The smoothest flow of rhythmical prose falls far below the melodious cadences of metrical language; and in this manner of appeal to the senses and the soul of man verse has no rival save music itself.

These three qualities may be examined separately. Verse may be found in which there is almost nothing but melody, divorced from suggestion or ideas. There are good examples in Edward Lear's "*Nonsense Songs*", in which there is an intentional lack of sense; or in the "*Alice Adventures in Wonderland*" books, as, for instance: —

> And as in uffish thought he stood,
> The Jabberwock, with eyes of flame,
> Came whiffling through the tulgy wood,
> And burbled as it came!...
> "And hast thou slain the Jabberwock?
> Come to my arms, my beamish boy!
> O frabjous day! Callooh! Callay!"
> He chortled in his joy.

Or one may take something which will convey no idea and no suggestion beyond that which comes with sound and rhythm. Here is a verse once made in sport to pass as a folk-song in an unknown tongue: —

> Apaulthee kong lay laylarthay;
> Ameeta tinta prown,
> Lay lista, lay larba, lay moona long,
> Toolay échola doundoolay koko elph zong,
> Im lay melplartha bountaina brown.

This is a collection of unmeaning syllables, and yet to the ear it is a pleasure. The examples may seem trivial, but they serve to illustrate the fact that there is magic in the mere sound of words, meaning though they have none.

更公正和准确地说，它们就像一座宫殿的结构，上面覆盖的珍贵大理石板已被揭掉。反对诗歌主题用散文来讲述，是轻蔑或令人生厌的，与蔑视圣彼得教堂一样纯属不合理，因为教堂的椽子和栋梁裸露在天空下，便不会引人注目。在诗歌中形式是构成诗歌整体的一部分，正如墙壁、屋顶和圆顶、雕像和宝石般的大理石一样是寺庙的不可分割的部分。

不考虑韵律和特殊用词的那些独特性，虽说那些特点通常作用很大，但并不是必不可少的，因为没有它们，诗歌可能一样伟大。作为一般考察，大可确切地说，诗歌的效果由思想、暗示和旋律三重结合而生。在思想的使用上，诗歌与散文的基础几乎相同，只是诗歌针对的是与卑鄙或平庸的思想无关的崇高情感。在暗示的使用上，诗歌只是更进一步地运用了想象性散文中所采用的手段。旋律实际上可以说是诗歌自己的显著特性。最流畅的有节奏的散文也远不及韵律语言悠扬的抑扬顿挫，以这种诉诸感官和灵魂的方式，除了音乐本身之外，诗歌没有与之匹敌的对手。

这里可以分别考察这三种品质。可能会发现其中有的诗歌只存在旋律，完全脱离了暗示或思想。爱德华·李尔 的《无意义之歌》中有一个精辟的例子，其中有的属于故意缺乏意义，或在小说《爱丽丝梦游仙境》中，如下例：

> 他的思路正在驰骋纵横，
> 空洞巨龙此时乘风来临，
> 一路飘来依然废话连篇，
> 眼冒凶光俨然咄咄逼人！……
> 空洞巨龙毙命他的寒剑，
> 年轻英雄回到我们身边，
> 欢呼庆贺难言胸中喜悦，
> 欣喜骄傲绽开他的笑颜。

（贾文浩、贾文渊 译）

或者，人们可能会接受一些除了声音和节奏之外，不会传达任何思想和暗示的东西。这里曾有一首在运动中创作的诗，以一种未知的语言作为民歌而流传：

> Apaulthee kong 躺着躺着；
> Ameeta tinta 普朗，
> 躺着利斯塔，躺着拉巴，躺着月亮，
> 图莱 · 乔拉 · 杜杜莱 · 科科 · 埃尔夫宗，
> 我躺在 melplartha bountaina 棕色的。

　　这是一组毫无意义的音节，但在耳朵里却是一种享受。这些例子可能看起来无足轻重，但它们有助于说明这样一个事实，即仅词语的声音中就隐藏着魔力，尽管它们聊无意义。

　　The possibility of pleasing solely by the arrangement and choice of words in verse has been a snare to more than one poet; as a neglect of melody has been the fault of others. In much of the later work of Swinburne it is evident that the poet became intoxicated with the mere beauty of sound, and forgot that poetry demands thought as well as melody; while the reader is reluctantly forced to acknowledge that in some of the verse of Browning there is a failure to recognize that melody is an element as essential as thought.

　　As verse may be found which has little but melody, so is it possible to find verse in which there is practically nothing save melody and suggestion. In "*Ulalume*", Poe has given an instance of the effect possible from the combining of these with but the thinnest thread of idea: —

> The skies they were ashen and sober;
> The leaves they were crispèd and sere, —
> The leaves they were withering and sere;
> It was night in the lonesome October,
> Of my most immemorial year;
> It was hard by the dim lake of Auber,
> In the misty mid-region of Weir—
> It was down by the dark tarn of Auber,

In the ghoul-haunted woodland of Weir.

There is here no definite train of thought. It is an attempt to convey a certain mood by combining mysterious and weird suggestion with melody enticing and sweet.

在诗歌中，单纯依靠安排和选择词语来取悦的可能性已经成为不止一位诗人设下的圈套，因为无视旋律一直是别人的过错。在斯温伯恩后期的大部分作品里，诗人很显然陶醉于声音之美，忘记了诗歌不仅需要旋律也需要思想。尽管读者不情愿地被迫承认，在勃朗宁的某些诗中，诗人未能认识到思想是与旋律同样重要的元素。

正如可以找到只有旋律的诗句，也有可能找到除了旋律和暗示之外几乎没有任何内容的诗句。在《尤娜路姆》中，坡用实例说明了把旋律及暗示与一丝念头结合起来可能产生的效果：

> 天空上一片灰白色而且清淡；
> 树叶是枯干的而且瑟脆，
> 树叶是枯干的而且凋萎；
> 这是我最难追忆的一年，
> 一个荒凉的十月的夜里；
> 紧濒那朦胧的奥伯湖边，
> 在那多雾的维尔的腹地：
> 直下那郁湿的奥伯潭边，
> 在僵尸出没的维尔的林地。

（余光中　译）

这首诗试图通过将神秘而怪异的暗示与诱人而甜美的旋律相结合，来传达某种情绪，但缺乏明确的思路。

A finer example is the closing passage in "*Kubla Khan*". The suggestions are more vivid, and the imagination far more powerful.

A damsel with a dulcimer

In a vision once I saw；

It was an Abyssinian maid，

And on her dulcimer she played，

Singing of Mount Abora.

Could I revive within me

Her symphony and song，

To such deep delight 'twould win me，

That with music loud and long，

I would build that dome in air，

That sunny dome；those caves of ice；

And all who heard should see them there，

And all should cry："Beware! Beware!

His flashing eyes，his floating hair；

Weave a circle round him thrice，

And close your eyes with holy dread，

For he on honey-dew hath fed，

And drunk the milk of Paradise."

　　一个更出色的例子是《忽必烈汗》中的最后一段，暗示更加生动，想象力更加强大。

　　　有一回我在幻象中见到

　　　一个手拿德西马琴的姑娘：

　　　那是个阿比西尼亚少女，

　　　在她的琴上她奏出乐曲，

　　　歌唱着阿伯若山。

　　　如果我心中能再度产生

　　　她的音乐和歌唱，

　　　我将被引入如此深切的欢欣，

　　　以至于我要用音乐高朗而又长久

　　　在空中建造那安乐宫廷，

　　　那阳光照临的宫廷，那雪窟冰窖！

谁都能见到这宫殿，只要听见了乐音。
他们全都会喊叫：当心！当心！
他飘动的头发，他闪光的眼睛！
织一个圆圈，把他三道围住，
闭下你两眼，带着神圣的恐惧，
因为他一直吃着蜜样甘露，
一直饮着天堂的琼浆仙乳。

（屠岸　译）

Here there is a more evident succession of ideas than in "*Ulalume*"; but in both the effect is almost entirely produced by the music and the suggestion, with very little aid from ideas.

How essential to poetry are melody and suggestion is at once evident when one examines verse which contains ideas without these fundamental qualities. Wordsworth, great as he is at his best, affords ready examples here. The following is by no means the least poetical passage in "*The Prelude*", but it is sufficiently far from being poetry in any high sense to serve as an illustration: —

> I was a better judge of thoughts than words,
> Misled in estimating words, not only
> By common inexperience of youth,
> But by the trade of classic niceties,
> The dangerous craft of culling term and phrase
> From languages that want the living voice
> To carry meaning to the natural heart.

Here are ideas, but there is no emotion, and the thing could be said better in prose. It is as fatal to try to express in poetry what is not elevated enough for poetic treatment as it is to endeavor to say in prose those high things which can be embodied by poetry only. Melody alone, or suggestiveness alone, is better than ideas alone if there is to be an attempt to produce the effect of poetry.

Poetry which is complete and adequate adds melody and suggestion to that framework of ideas which is to them as the skeleton to flesh and blood. Any of the great lyrics of the language might be given as examples. The reader has but to open his Shakespeare's "*Sonnets*" at random, as for instance, at this: —

> From you have I been absent in the spring,
> When proud-pied April, dressed in all his trim,
> Hath put a spirit of youth in every thing,
> That heavy Saturn laugh'd and leap'd with him.
> Yet nor the lays of birds, nor the sweet smell
> Of different flowers in odor and in hue,
> Could make me any summer's story tell,
> Or from their proud lap pluck them where they grew:
> Nor did I wonder at the lily's white,
> Nor praise the deep vermilion in the rose;
> They were but sweet, but figures of delight,
> Drawn after you, you pattern of all those.
> Yet seem'd it winter still, and, you away,
> As with your shadow I with these did play.

比起《尤娜路姆》，这首诗歌有更明显的思想连续性，但这两首诗的效果几乎完全由音乐和暗示产生，思想内容的助益却非常少有。

旋律和暗示是诗的基本要素，离开这两个要素来考察诗歌包含的思想时，这一点马上就变得非常明显。华兹华斯在其顶峰时期，已是大名鼎鼎了，他提供了现成的例子。下面这一节诗绝不是《序曲》中最没有诗意的段落，但它远非任何高级意义上的诗，以下足以作为例证：

> 我能更好判断思想，却无法判断言辞
> 判断词的意思会迷失，不仅
> 由于年轻人普遍缺乏经验，

>　　而且通过经典细节的交易，
>　　挑选术语和短语是危险的技艺
>　　来自缺乏活生生的声音的语言
>　　为自然的心赋予意义。

　　诗中有思想，但缺乏情感，这样的情形用散文来表达可能更为合适。试图在诗歌中表达那些尚不足以达到诗意处理高度的东西，与试图在散文中表达那些只有诗歌才能体现的崇高事物一样有着致命的危险。如果要尝试产生诗意的效果，单有旋律或单有暗示比仅有思想更好。

　　完整而充分的诗歌为思想框架增添了旋律和暗示，而思想框架对它们来说就像是血肉之躯的骨架。语言中任何伟大的抒情诗都可以作为例子来印证这一点。读者只需任意翻开莎士比亚的《十四行诗》，就会认识到这一点，例如：

>　　我离开你的时候正好是春天，
>　　当绚烂的四月，披上新的锦袄，
>　　把活泼的春心给万物灌注遍，
>　　连沉重的土星也跟着笑和跳。
>　　可是无论小鸟的歌唱，或万紫
>　　千红、芬芳四溢的一簇簇鲜花，
>　　都不能使我诉说夏天的故事，
>　　或从烂漫的山洼把它们采掐：
>　　我也不羡慕那百合花的洁白，
>　　也不赞美玫瑰花的一片红晕；
>　　它们不过是香，是悦目的雕刻，
>　　你才是它们所要模拟的真身。
>　　因此，于我还是严冬，而你不在，
>　　像逗着你影子，我逗它们开怀。

（梁宗岱　译）

It is not necessary to carry this analysis farther. The object of undertaking it is to impress upon the reader the fact that in poetry form is an essential element in the language of the art. The student must realize that the poet means his rhythm as truly as and in the same measure that he means the thought; and that to attempt to appreciate poetry without sensitiveness to melody is as hopeless as would be a similar attempt to try to appreciate music. When Wordsworth said that poetry is inevitable, he meant the metre no less than the thought; he wished to convey the fact that the impassioned mood breaks into melody of word as the full heart breaks into song. The true poem is the embodiment of what can be expressed in no other way than by that especial combination of idea, suggestion, and sound. The thought, the hint, and the music are united in one unique and individual whole.

　　没有必要进一步进行分析了。诗歌分析的目的是使读者意识到，诗歌形式是艺术语言的基本要素这一事实，因此，学生必须意识到，诗人真正的意欲是他的韵律，同样程度上，诗人的意欲是表达思想。如果缺乏对旋律的敏锐性，试图欣赏诗歌，就如同离开旋律试图欣赏音乐一样，毫无希望。华兹华斯说诗歌是不可避免的，他的意思是指韵律而非思想。他想传达这样一个事实，如同丰富的情感会迸发出诗歌，只有充满激情的情感才会迸发成文字的旋律。真正的诗是思想、暗示和声音特殊组合的具体表现，除此以外，别无其他。思想、暗示和音乐结合在一个独特而独立的整体中。

XVII
POETRY AND LIFE

Vitally to appreciate what poetry is, it is necessary to realize what are its relations to life. Looked at in itself its essentials are emotion which is capable of taking entire possession of the consciousness, and the embodiment of this emotion by the combined effects of imaginative language and melodious form. It is still needful, however, to consider how this art acts upon human beings, and why there has been claimed for it so proud a pre-eminence among the arts.

Why, for instance, should Emerson speak of the embodiment of mere emotion as "the only verity", Wordsworth as "the breath and finer spirit of all knowledge", and why does Mrs. Browning call poets "the only truth-tellers"? Briefly the answer is: Because consciousness is identical with emotion, and consciousness is life. For all practical purposes man exists but in that he feels. The universe concerns him in so far as it touches his feelings, and it concerns him no farther. That is for man most essential which comes most near to the conditions of his existence. Pure and ideal emotion is essential truth in the sense that it approaches most nearly to the consciousness, that is, to the actual being of the race.

I am aware that this sounds dangerously like an attempt to be darkly metaphysical; but it is impossible to talk on high themes without to some extent using high terms. It is useless to hope to put into words all the mysteries of the relations of art to life, yet it is not impossible to approximate somewhat to what must be the truth of the matter, although in doing it one inevitably runs the risk of seeming to attempt to say what cannot be said. What I have been endeavoring to convey will perhaps be plainer if I say that for purposes of our discussion man is practically alive only in so far as he realizes life. This realization of life, this supreme triumph of inner consciousness, comes to him through his feelings, indeed, is perhaps to be considered as identical with his feelings. His sensations affect him only by the emotions which they excite. His emotion, in a word, is the measure of his existence. Now the emotion of man always responds, in a degree marked by appreciation, to certain presentations of the relation of things, to certain considerations of the nature of human life, and above all to certain demonstrations of the possibilities of human existence. If these are made actual and clear to the mind, they cannot fail to arouse that engrossing realization which is the height of consciousness. To enable a man to seize with his imagination the ideal of love or hate, of fear or courage, of shame or honor, is to make him kindle and thrill. It is to make him for the time being thoroughly and richly alive, and it is to increase greatly his power of essential life. These are the things which most deeply touch human creatures; they are the universal in that they appeal to all sane hearts and minds; they are the eternal as measured by mortal existence because they have power to touch the men of all time; hence they are the real truths; they are, for beings under the conditions of earthly existence, the only verities.

第十七讲　诗歌与生活

　　要从根本上理解诗是什么，有必要认识它与生活的关系。就其本身而言，诗歌的本质是能够完全攫取意识的情感，以及通过想象的语言与音乐般的形式共同作用而发出的情感表达。然而，人们仍然需要考虑这种艺术如何作用于人类，以及为什么有人如此自豪地声称，诗歌在艺术中居于卓越地位。

　　例如，为什么艾默生仅仅将情感的体现称作"唯一的真实"，华兹华斯则称其为"一切知识的气息和更纯粹的精神"，勃朗宁夫人称诗人为"唯一讲真话的人"？简而言之，这是因为意识与情感是一致的，意识就是生命。实际上，人的存在就在于他的感觉。宇宙之所以受其关注，乃在于宇宙触动了人的情感，此外无他。情感对人来说最为本质，最接近于他存在的境遇。纯粹而理想的情感是最完美的真实，因为它最接近意识，也就是说最接近人类的真实存在。

我知道这听起来颇为冒险，就像在尝试变得神秘而故弄玄虚。但在某种程度上，如果不使用高深的术语，就不可能谈论深邃的主题。希望把艺术与生活关系的所有奥秘诉诸语言没有益处，但也并非不可能在一定程度上接近事物的真相，尽管这样做不可避免地存在风险，令人觉得所尝试表达之物本就无法诉诸语言。如果我说为了便于讨论的目的，实际上，人只有在他意识到生命的时候才真正活着，那么我一直努力传达的东西也许会更浅显易懂。通过情感，他才会想到，这种对生命的意识，这种内在意识的至高无上的胜利，事实上，也许这种意识可以被认为是与他的感觉相同的。他的感觉只会通过它们激发的情感来影响他。总之，他的情感就是他存在的尺度。人的情感总是回应事物之间关系的某种呈现，回应对人类生活本质的某些考虑，尤其是回应于某种显露出的人类存在前景，这样的情感某种程度上即标志着理解。如果这些对头脑来说是真实的和清晰的，它们就不能不唤起那种令人心驰神往的认识，此即意识的高度。让一个人用他的想象力掳获爱或恨、恐惧或勇气、羞耻或荣誉的典范，就是让他精神焕发和情不自禁，就是让他的生活变得酣畅淋漓、丰富多彩，从而大大提高他完美生活的动力。情感是最能触动人类的东西，人皆有之，理智的心灵无不诉诸情感。以凡人的存在来衡量，它们是永恒的，因为它于们有能力触动所有时代的人，它们是真正的真理。对于尘世生存条件下的芸芸众生，它们是唯一的真理。

The ordinary life of man is not unlike the feeble flame of a miner's lamp, half smothered in some underground gallery until a draught of vital air kindles it into sudden glow and sparkle. Most human beings have but a dull flicker of half-alive consciousness until some outward breath causes it to flash into quick and quivering splendor. Poetry is that divine air, that breeze from unscaled heights of being, the kindling breath by which the spark becomes a flame.

It is but as a means of conveying the essential truth which is the message of poetry, that the poet employs obvious truth. The facts which impress themselves upon the outer senses are to him merely a language by means of which he seeks to impart the higher facts that are apprehended only by the inner self; those facts of emotion which it is his office as a seer to divine and to interpret. The swineherd and the wandering minstrel saw the same wood and sky and lake; but to one they were earth and air and water; while to the other they were the outward and visible embodiment of the spirit of beauty which is eternal though earth and sea and sky vanish. To Peter Bell the primrose by the river's brim was but a primrose and nothing more; to the poet it was the symbol and the embodiment of loveliness, the sign of an eternal truth. To the laborer going afield in the early light the dewdrops are but so much water, wetting unpleasantly his shoes; to Browning it was a symbol of the embodiment in woman of all that is pure and holy when he sang: —

There's a woman like a dew-drop, she's so purer than the purest.

It is evident from what has been said that in reading poetry it is necessary to penetrate through the letter to the spirit. I have already spoken at length in a former lecture upon the need of knowing the language of literature, and of being in sympathy with the mood of the writer. This is especially true in regard to poetry, since poetry becomes great in proportion as it deals with the spirit rather than with the letter. "We are all poets when we read a poem well," Carlyle has said. It is only by entering into the mood and by sharing the exaltation of the poet that we are able to appreciate his message. A poem is like a window of stained glass. From without one may be able to gain some general idea of its design and to guess crudely at its hues; but really to perceive its beauty, its richness of design, its sumptuousness of color, one must stand within the very sanctuary itself.

普通人的生活就像一盏矿灯微弱的火焰，在地下走廊里摇曳将息，直到一股充满活力的空气将它点燃，倏然发出光亮，在黑暗中闪耀。大多数人只是浑浑噩噩，其生命如同微弱的火花，直到一种外部的清风使之迅速闪烁，熠熠生辉。诗歌即是那神圣的空气，那来自存在之巅的微风，是令火花燃烧成火焰的一缕清风。

诗歌仅是传达完美真实的手段，这种真实乃是诗歌的寓意，表明诗人对明显的真实的运用。对诗人来说，那些作用于其外在感觉的事实仅是一种语言，借助这样的语言，他试图参透那些只能被内在自我理解的更崇高的事实，那些基于情感的事实是他作为先知的职责来领悟和解释的。猪倌和流浪的吟游诗人面对着同样的树林、天空和湖泊，但对前者来说，它们是大地、空气和水，而对后者来说，它们是美丽精神的外在和视觉的体现，尽管大地、海洋和天空可以消融，但这种精神永恒不灭。对彼得·贝尔而言，河边的报春花不过是一株报春花而已，但对诗人来说，它是美丽的象征和化身，是永恒真理的标志。对于披着晨曦外出的劳动者来说，露珠不过是凝结的水，弄湿了他的鞋子，令人不快，对勃朗宁来说，它成为一种象征，体现了女人所葆有的所有纯真和圣洁，他这样吟唱道：

> 有女如露珠，洁净无纤尘。

可见，读诗，必须透过文字参透其精神。我在之前的一次演讲中已经详细谈到了解文学语言的必要性，以及与作家共情的必要性。对诗歌来说尤其如此，因为诗歌在处理精神而不是文字时方显其伟大。卡莱尔如是说："当我们参透一首诗时，我们都是诗人。"只有通过进入诗人的情绪，分享诗人的快乐，我们才能理解他的信息。一首诗就像一扇彩色玻璃窗。从外部我们可能大体上了解其设计，粗略揣摩其色调，但要真正领会其美丽、设计的丰富、色彩的华丽，人们就必须站在圣殿本身之内。

It is partly from the lack of sensitiveness of the imagination of the reading public, I believe, that in the latter half of this century the novel has grown into a prominence so marked. The great mass of readers no longer respond readily to poetry, and fiction is in a sense a simplification of the language of imagination so that it may be comprehended by those who cannot rise to the heights of verse. In this sense novels might almost be called the kindergarten of the imagination. In fiction, emotional experiences are translated into the language of ordinary intellectual life; whereas in poetry they are phrased in terms of the imagination, pure and simple. There can be no question of the superiority of the means employed by the poet. Much which is embodied in verse cannot be expressed by prose of any sort, no matter how exalted that prose may be; but for the ordinary intelligence the language of prose is far more easily comprehensible.

What I have been saying, however, may seem to be so general and theoretical that I may be held not yet fairly to have faced that issue at which I hinted in the beginning, the issue which Philistine minds raise bluntly: What is the use of poetry? Philistines are willing to concede that there is a sensuous pleasure to be gained from verse. They are able to perceive how those who care for such things may find an enervating enjoyment in the linked sweetness of cadence melting into cadence, in musical line and honeyed phrase. What they are utterly unable to understand is how thoughtful men, men alive to the practical needs and the real interests of the race, can speak of poetry as if it were a thing of genuine importance in the history and development of mankind. It would not be worthwhile to attempt an answer to this for the benefit of the Philistines. They are a folk who are so completely ignorant of the higher good of life that it is impossible to make them understand. Their conception of value does not reach beyond pecuniary and physical standards; they comprehend nothing which is not expressed in material terms. One who attempted to describe a symphony to a deaf man would not be more at a loss for terms than must be he who attempts to set forth the worth of art to those ignorant of real values. The question may be answered, but to those who most need to be instructed in regard to asthetic values any answer must forever remain unintelligible.

There are, however, many sincere and earnest seekers after truth who are unable to clear up their ideas when they come in contact, as they must every day, with the assumption that poetry is but the plaything of idle men and women, a thing not only unessential but even frivolous. For them it is worthwhile to formulate some sort of a statement; although to do this is like making the attempt to declare why the fragrance of the rose is sweet or why the hue of its petals gives delight.

　　我相信，在十九世纪下半叶，小说所获得的地位如此显赫，部分原因即在于阅读大众的想象力缺乏敏感性。广大的读者不再对诗歌那么易感，在某种意义上小说是想象性语言的简化，它能够便于那些无法达到诗歌高度的人去理解。从这个意义上说，小说几乎可以被称为想象力的幼稚园。在小说中，情感体验被转换成一般知识的生活语言，而在诗歌中，它们是根据想象来表达的，纯粹而简单。毫无疑问，诗人所使用的手段具有优越性。诗歌中所体现的很多东西都无法用任何种类的散文来表达，无论散文有多么崇高，但是对于普通的智力的人来说，理解散文的语言要容易得多。

　　然而，我所讲到的似乎显得如此笼统和理论化，以至我可能被认为，还没有公正地面对我开始时暗示的那个问题，那个非利士人直言不讳提出的问题：诗歌有什么用？非利士人愿意承认从诗歌中可以获得感官上的愉悦。他们能够理解那些喜爱感官愉悦的人，是如何在韵律化为抑扬顿挫的悦耳声中、在富于音乐性的诗行里、在甜美的措辞中找到了一种毫无活力的享受。他们完全无法理解的是，人们既然对自己的现实需要和人类的真正利益有清醒的认识，为何他们在谈论诗歌时显得如此关切，就好像诗歌在人类历史和演进过程中，属于真正重要的东西一样。出于对这些非利士人着想，试图回答这一问题并无多少价值。他们是一群对高尚生活完全无知的人，使他们理解崇高的诗歌是做不到的。他们的价值观念并没有超越金钱和物质的标准，他们不理解任何不是用物质术语表达的东西。试图向聋人描述交响乐会令人感到不知所措，同样，要向对真正价值一无所知的人展示艺术价值也会令人束手无策。这个问题可以回答，但对于那些最需要接受美学价值指导的人来说，任何答案必然总会显得无法理喻。

然而，正如日常生活中必定会看到的那样，在接触到那种认为诗歌不过是闲散男女的消遣，它既非必要，也显琐碎的臆想时，有许多真诚而恳切追求真实的人也无法保持清醒的思路。对他们来说，提出某种论断才是有价值的。尽管这样做类似于试图说明，为什么玫瑰的香味是甜的，或者为什么花瓣的色调给人以愉悦。

First, then, the use of poetry is to nourish the imagination. I have spoken earlier of the impossibility of fulfilling the higher functions of life without this faculty. A common error regards imagination as a quality which has to do with rare and exceptional experiences; as a power of inventing whimsical and impossible thoughts; as a sort of jester to beguile idle moments of the mind. In reality imagination is to the mental being what blood is to the physical man. Upon it the intellect and the emotional consciousness alike depend for nourishment. Without it the mind is powerless to seize or to make really its own anything which lies outside of actual experience. Without it the broker could not so fully realize his cunning schemes as to manipulate the market and control the price of stocks; without it the inventor could devise no new machine, the scientist grasps no fresh secret of laws which govern the universe. It is the divine power in virtue of which man subdues the world to his uses. In a word, imagination is that faculty which distinguishes man from brute.

It is the beginning of wisdom to know; it is the culmination of wisdom to feel. The intellect accumulates; the emotion assimilates. What we learn, we possess; but what we feel, we are. The perception acquires, and the imagination realizes; and thus it is that only through the imagination can man build up and nourish that inner being which is the true and vital self. To cultivate the imagination, therefore, is an essential—nay, more; it is the one essential means of insuring the progression of the race. This is the great office of all art, but perhaps most obviously is it the noble prerogative and province of poetry. " In the imagination," wrote Coleridge, " is the distinguishing characteristic of man as a progressive being." To kindle into flame the dull embers of this god-like attribute is the first office of poetry; and were this all, it would lift the art forever above every cumbering material care and engrossing intellectual interest.

Second, the use of poetry is to give man knowledge of his unrecognized experiences or his unrealized capacities of feeling. The poet speaks what many have felt, but what none save he can say. He accomplishes the hitherto impossible. He makes tangible and subject the vague emotions which disquiet us as if they were elusive ghosts haunting the dwelling of the soul, unsubdued and oppressive in their mystery. The joy of a moment he has fixed for all time; the throb gone almost before it is felt he has made captive; to the evasive emotion he has given immortality. In a word, it is his office to confer upon men dominion over themselves.

那么，第一，诗歌的用途是滋养想象力。我之前说过，如果没有这种能力，就不可能实现生命的更高功能。一个常见的错误是将想象力视为一种与稀有而非凡的经历有关的品质，或者视之为一种能激发奇想异思的力量，或者视之为一种能欺骗闲暇无聊的心灵的弄臣。事实上，想象之于精神存在，就像血液之于肉体。智力和情感意识都依赖于它来获取营养。没有它，心智就无法抓住或真正创造任何超出实际体验的事物。没有它，经纪人就无法完全实现他操纵市场和控制股票价格的巧妙计划。没有它，发明家就无法设计出新机器，科学家也无法掌握支配宇宙规律的新秘密。这是一种神圣的力量，人类凭借它方可征服世界。总之，正是想象力这一才能将人与畜生区分开来。

认知是智慧的开端，感觉是智慧的终端。智力可以日积月累，情感可以同化。我们学过，我们才能拥有，但是我们感受，我们才能存在。我们通过知觉学习，我们通过想象实现，因此，只有通过想象力，人才能建立和滋养内在的存在，即真实而有生命力的自我。因此，培养想象力是必不可少的——不，远甚于此，它是确保人类进步的一种必需手段。这是所有艺术的伟大使命，但或许最明显的是它是诗歌的崇高特权和领域。柯勒律治写道："作为不断发展而存在的人的显著特征，即在想象力之中。"将这种如天神一般的属性的暗淡余烬点燃，是诗歌的第一职分；苟能如此，它将使艺术永远超越一切烦琐的物质关怀和引人入胜的智力追索。

第二，诗歌的用途是让人们了解他未被认识的经历或他未被实现的感知能力。诗人说出了许多人能感受到，但只有他才能表达出的话。他完成了迄今为止不可能完成的任务。他将使我们感到不安的模糊情感变得有形并得以约束，这些情感就像是难以捉摸的鬼魂，萦绕于灵魂的住所，它们以其神秘而不受约束令人苦恼。诗人让瞬间的快乐得以永远定格，俘获了那些几乎还未被感知即已消失的悸动，他赋予那些飘忽不定的情感以永恒。总之，他的职责就是赐予人们主宰自身的能力。

Third, it is poetry which nourishes and preserves the optimism of the race. Poetry is essentially optimistic. It raises and encourages by fixing the mind upon the possibilities of life. Even when it bewails what is gone, when it weeps lost perfection, vanished joy, and crushed love, the reader receives from the poetic form, from the uplift of metrical inspiration, a sense that the possibilities of existence overwhelm individual pain. The fact that such blessings could and may exist is not only consolation when fate has wrenched them away, but the vividness with which they are recalled may almost make them seem to be relived.

That A sorrow's crown of sorrow is remembering happier things.

It is not the whole story. In times of deepest woe it is this very remembrance which makes it possible to live on at all. The unconscious and the inevitable lesson of all true art, moreover, is that the possibility of beauty in life is compensation for the anguish which its existence entails. The poet who weeps for the lost may have no word of comfort to offer, but the fact that life itself is of supreme possibilities is shown inevitably and persuasively by the fact that he is so deeply moved. He could not be thus stricken had he not known very ecstasies of joy; and his message to the race is that such bliss has been and thus may be again. More than this, the fact that he in his anguish instinctively turns to art is the most eloquent proof that however great may be the sorrows of life there is for them an alleviating balm in asthetic enjoyment. He may speak of:

> Beauty that must die,
> And Joy whose hand is ever at his lips,
> Bidding adieu;

But with the very thought of the brevity is coupled an exquisite sense of both beauty and joy in ever fresh renewal, so that the reader knows a subtle thrill of pleasure even at the mention of pain. Poe's proposition that poetry should be restricted to sorrowful themes probably arose from a more or less conscious feeling that the expression of despair is the surest means of conveying vividly a sense of the value of what is gone; and whether Poe went so far as to realize it or not the fact is that the passion of loss most surely expresses the possible bliss of possession. Even when it would, art cannot deny the worth and the glory of existence. The word of denial is chanted to a strain which inspires and affirms. Even when he would be most pessimistic the genuine poet must perforce preach in deathless tones the gospel of optimism.

　　第三，诗歌滋养和保存了人类的乐观主义。诗歌本质上是乐观的，它令人凝神于生命的可能性，从而使人得以提高和鼓励。即使当它哀悼逝去的东西，当它为失去的完美、消失的快乐和破碎的爱而哭泣时，读者从诗的形式、韵律、灵感的升华中，感受到存在的可能性压倒了个人的痛苦。这样的益处可以且能够存在，这一事实不仅让人们在被命运夺走上述美好事物时获得安慰，而且它们被回忆起来的生动性几乎使它们得以重温：

悲伤的冠冕是回忆快乐的时光。

　　故事并没有完全结束。在最深切的悲痛时期，正是这种回忆使人们有可能继续活下去。此外，所有真正的艺术的无意识的、必然的教导是，生活中美的可能性是对其存在所带来的痛苦的补偿。为逝去的东西哭泣的诗人可能没有任何安慰的话，但生活本身是无限可能的，这一事实不可避免地令人信服地表现在他如此深受感动的事实中。如果他不知道狂喜的喜悦，他就不会如此悲痛，他给人类传递的信息是，这种幸福曾经存在，因此可能会再次出现。更重要的是，他在痛苦中本能地转向艺术这一事实是最有说服力的证明，无论生活的悲伤有多大，对他们来说，审美享受都是一种缓解苦痛的香膏。他可能会谈道：

> 美呀，有着必死的劫数，
> 还有欢乐，总是将手指放在唇间，
> 随时准备道别。

　　但是，韶华易逝的感念中伴随着一种强烈的、掺杂着不断更新的美与快乐的感觉，使读者即使在言及痛苦时也能感受到微妙的快感。坡主张诗歌应该限定于悲伤的主题，这可能源于一种或多或少下意识的感觉，即表达绝望对于生动地传达已逝之物的价值来说是最可靠的方式；不管坡是否意识到了这一点，事实上，已逝之物激发的深情最确切地表达了拥有该物可能带来的幸福。即使诗歌有此限定，艺术也不能否认存在的价值和荣耀。表达失去的话语被吟诵成一种鼓舞人心和肯定的语气。即使在他最悲观的时候，真正的诗人也必须用充满生命力的语气宣扬乐观主义的信念。

Fourth, poetry is the original utterance of the ideas of the world. It is easy and not uncommon to regard the art of the poet as having little to do with the practical conduct of life; yet there is no man in civilization who does not hold opinions and theories, thoughts and beliefs, which he owes to the poets. Thought is not devised in the marketplace. What thinkers have divined in secret is there shown openly by its results. Every poet of genius remakes the world. He leaves the stamp of his imagination upon the whole race, and philosophers reason, scientists explore, money-changers scheme, tradesmen haggle, and farmers plough or sow, all under conditions modified by what has been divulged in song. The poet is the great thinker, whose thought, translated, scattered, diluted, spilled upon the ground and gathered up again, is the inspiration and the guide of mankind.

If this seems extravagant, think for a little. Reflect in what civilization differs from savagery; consider not the accidental and outward circumstance, but the fundamental causes upon which these depend. If you endeavor to find adequately expressed the ideals of honor, of truth, of love, and of aspiration which are behind all the development of mankind, it is to the poets that you turn instinctively. It is possible to go farther than this. Knowledge is but a perception of relations. The conception of the universe is too vast to be assimilated all at once, but every perception of the way in which one part is related to another, one fact to another, one thing to the rest, helps toward a realization of the ultimate truth. It is the poet who first discerns and proclaims the relations of those facts which the experience of the race accumulates. From the particular he deduces the general, from the facts he perceives the principles which underlie them. The general, that is, in its relation to that emotional consciousness which is the real life of man; the principles which take hold not upon material things only, but upon the very conditions of human existence. All abstract truth has sprung from poetry as rain comes from the sea. Changed, diffused, carried afar and often altered almost beyond recognition, the thought of the world is but the manifestation of the imagination of the world; and it has found its first tangible expression in poetry.

Fifth, poetry is the instructor in beauty. No small thing is human happiness, and human happiness is nourished on beauty. Poetry opens the eyes of men to loveliness in earth and sky and sea, in flower and weed, in tree and rock and stream, in things common and things afar alike. It is by the interpretation of the poet that mankind in general is aware of natural beauty; and it is hardly less true that the beauty of moral and emotional worlds would be practically unknown were it not for these high interpreters. The race has first become aware of all ethereal and elusive loveliness through the song of the poet, sensitive to see and skillful to tell. For its beauty in and of itself, and for its revelation of the beauty of the universe, both material and intangible, poetry is to the world a boon priceless and peerless.

第四，诗是世界观念的原始表达。认为诗人的艺术与生活的实际行为关联不大，这种观念很容易产生，也很常见，然而，文明中没有人不会持有来源于诗人的意见和理论、思想和信仰。思想不是在市场中设计出来的。思想家们私下领悟的东西借助其成果被公之于众。每一位天才诗人都在重塑世界，给整个人类留下了他的想象力的印记，哲学家的推理、科学家的探索、货币兑换商的计划、商人的讨价还价以及农民的耕种或播种，所有这些活动得以进行的条件都受到歌谣所透露的信息的修正。诗人是伟大的思想家，他的思想经过翻译、散播、淡化、洒在地上、再聚集起来，是人类的启迪与向导。

如果这看起来像是奢谈，我们不妨再斟酌一下。反思文明与野蛮的区别，不要考虑偶然的和外在的情况，而要考虑这些情况所依赖的根本原因。如果你试图找到推动人类所有发展的关于荣誉、真理、爱和抱负之理想的合适表达，那么您会本能地转向诗人。你可能走得更远。知识不过是对关系的感知。宇宙的概念太宽而不能一下子被吸收，但是对于一个部分与另一部分、一个事实与另一个事实、一件事与其他事物之间关联的方式的每一种感知，都有助于实现终极真理。是诗人首先辨别并宣扬了这些人类经验所累积起来的事实之间的联系。他从特殊中推导出一般，从事实中看出构成其基础的原则。这里指的一般就是它与人的真实生活的情感意识的关系；这里的原则不仅适用于物质事物，而且适用于人类生存的境遇。一切抽象的真理都从诗中涌现，就像雨从大海中涌出一样。人们关于世界的思想被改变、扩散、传播到远方，常常被改变得几乎面目全非，这样的思想不过是人们对世界想象的体现；它首先在诗歌中得到了坚实的表达。

a joy not easily to be put into word. Recalling such an experience, you will not find it difficult to understand what is meant by the claim that poetry creates in the mind of man an ideal which in turn it justifies also.

Lastly and above all, the use of poetry is—poetry.

'Tis the deep music of the rolling world
Kindling within the strings of the waved air
Æolian modulations.

It is vain to endeavor to put into word the worth and office of poetry. At the last we are brought face to face with the fact that anything short of itself is inadequate to do it justice. To read a single page of a great singer is more potent than to pore over volumes in his praise. A single lyric puts to shame the most elaborate analysis or the most glowing eulogy; in the end there is no resource but to appeal to the inner self which is the true man; since in virtue of what is most deep and noble in the soul, each may perceive for himself that poetry is its own supreme justification; that there is no need to discuss the relation of poetry to life, since poetry is the expression of life in its best and highest possibilities.

大多数人确实没有受到诗歌这种崇高力量的影响时，他们都奇怪地不愿承认，他们可能会如此感动，因此刚才所说的话在读者看来可能是奢侈和华丽的，这是很平常的想法。然而，令人高兴的是，很少有人没有经历过那种内心通透闪耀的时刻，只要他们愿意，很少有人不会回想起那被想象托起的时刻，那种超脱现实带来的快乐像天启一样，难以言表。回想起这样的经历，你会发现不难理解这样的看法，即诗歌催生了人类心灵的理想，而理想的合理性又反过来被诗歌证明。

最后也是最重要的是，诗歌的功用就在于用诗歌表达：

这是喧嚣世界的深沉音乐
在气浪的和弦中奏响
煦风的变调。

　　努力将诗歌的价值和功能用语言表达出来是徒劳的。最后，我们面对这样一个事实，即任何事物本身之外的东西都不足以公正地对待它。阅读一位伟大歌手的一页歌词就比仔细阅读对他的浩繁赞美更有效。一句歌词就让最详尽的分析或最热烈的颂文蒙羞。最终，只有诉诸内心的自我，也就是真正的人，别无他法。因为凭借灵魂中最深刻和最高贵的东西，每个人都可以自己意识到诗歌才是证明自己最卓越的理由。没有必要讨论诗歌与生活的关系，因为诗歌就是对生活最好和最高可能性的表达。